LEIGH HUNT'S
DRAMATIC CRITICISM

Leigh Hunt
Aged 44
From a drawing by J. Hayter.

LEIGH HUNT'S
Dramatic Criticism

1808-1831

EDITED BY

LAWRENCE HUSTON HOUTCHENS

AND

CAROLYN WASHBURN HOUTCHENS

OCTAGON BOOKS

A DIVISION OF FARRAR, STRAUS AND GIROUX

New York   1977

Reprinted 1977
by special arrangement with Columbia University Press

OCTAGON BOOKS
A DIVISION OF FARRAR, STRAUS & GIROUX, INC.
19 Union Square West
New York, N.Y. 10003

Library of Congress Cataloging in Publication Data

Hunt, Leigh, 1784-1859.
    Leigh Hunt's dramatic criticism, 1808-1831.

    Reprint of the ed. published by Columbia University Press, New
York.
    Most of the essays first appeared in the Examiner and the Tatler.
    Includes bibliographical references and index.
    1. Performing arts—England—London—Reviews. I. Title.
PN2596.L6H84   1977   792'.0942   76-30286
ISBN 0-374-93988-8

Manufactured by Braun-Brumfield, Inc.
Ann Arbor, Michigan
Printed in the United States of America

TO

Charles Godfrey Washburn, Esq.

PREFACE

Much of Leigh Hunt's dramatic criticism has long remained uncollected in fragmentary sets of periodicals scattered throughout England and the United States. Only one edition of his articles on the drama has so far been available, a selection made in 1894 by William Archer and Robert W. Lowe from Hunt's *Critical Essays on the Performers of the London Theatres* (1807) and his contributions to the *Tatler* (1830–1832). Hunt was a prolific journalist, essayist, poet, and editor, keenly interested in the theatre of his day and in drama in general. From 1808 to 1812, and from 1815 to 1821, he published in the *Examiner,* of which he was general editor, a succession of theatrical reviews, few of which have ever been reprinted. Many of these, together with certain of his other articles on the drama, are valuable sources of information to the student of the early nineteenth century. The purpose of the present volume, consequently, has been to select the best of Hunt's uncollected essays on the drama, primarily his theatrical reviews, although his "Theatrical Examiner" and his "Play-Goer" were often extended to include comments on the musical entertainment then being offered to the London public. Here one may find Hunt's appraisal of the performers of his day, the appearance of the playhouses, and the quality of the productions. Nothing seemed to escape his eye or ear: the faulty articulation of a rising young actress, the fitness of her movements and gestures to her part, an actor's artificiality and bombast, an author's wordy, stagnant dullness—all are accurately noted and sharply held up for attention, particularly the attention of the stage manager.

In a day when much dramatic criticism was mere foggy generalization, Hunt was specific. Actors, authors, and stage managers alike found in his criticism something tangibly useful that might be adopted in the next day's rehearsal. If a play were based on ancient tradition, Hunt's knowledge of the classics, usually detailed and thorough, enabled him to express a sound opinion; or, if the play were an adaptation or translation from the French or Italian, again his judgment was based on a firsthand knowledge of the language and a familiarity with the author's other writings, as well as with the historical period in which the plot was laid.

Particular attention may be called to Hunt's numerous discussions of Shakespeare, his essays on the origin and nature of masks and on the art of pantomime, his only separate article on Steele, his only review of a Colley Cibber revival, and his discussions of Handel, Mozart, Rossini, and Paganini. One interesting feature of Hunt's criticism, to which attention is called in the footnotes, is the fact that he gave impetus to the English Romantic Movement by his adoption of romantic criteria in certain reviews for the *Examiner*, an influential London newspaper which disseminated his ideas widely. This contribution, primarily to romantic Shakespeare criticism, has not to our knowledge been pointed out. Hunt's Shakespeare criticism has been said to derive from that of Coleridge; yet the *Examiner* articles reveal little indebtedness to Coleridge, but do show some interesting parallels with Schlegel, whom Hunt admired as the only writer prior to Hazlitt—aside from scattered criticisms by Lamb—"who seemed truly to *understand* as well as feel" Shakespeare. Hazlitt, in Hunt's estimation, was the first English critic to do justice to Shakespeare's characters.

With the exception of the preface "Some Account of the Origin and Nature of Masks," which appeared in both the first and second editions of *The Descent of Liberty* (1815, 1816), none of the selections in the present volume have been previously reprinted. The essay on masks we have felt justified in including because of the rarity of any copy of *The Descent of Liberty*. Throughout the volume, the spelling and punctuation have occasionally been modernized to facilitate reading. The footnotes which are indicated by arabic numbers have been supplied by the editors; those marked by an asterisk or other device are Leigh Hunt's.

We wish to express our appreciation to Professor R. D. Carmichael, Dean-Emeritus of the University of Illinois Graduate

School, and to the University of Illinois Graduate School Committee on Faculty Research for several grants of funds to aid in the preparation not only of this manuscript but of two others, now in the hands of the Columbia University Press. The latter two are editions of Hunt's uncollected essays in literary criticism and his uncollected political and miscellaneous essays. Our research, of course, owes much to the superlatively fine work of Professor Louis Landré in his two-volume *Leigh Hunt (1784–1859): Contribution à l'histoire du romantisme anglais* (Paris: Société d'Édition "Les Belles-Lettres," 1935–1936). We are also indebted to Miss Fanny Dunlap and Miss Alice S. Johnson of the University of Illinois library staff for their untiring aid in locating rare books and identifying little-known persons, and to the late Professor William Abbott Oldfather, head of the Classics Department of the University of Illinois, for help in checking the sources of certain Latin quotations. To the Inter-Relations Committee of Miami University we are grateful for an allotment of funds for additional checking of the manuscript, and to Mrs. Margaret C. Fruehan for assistance in proofreading. We particularly wish to thank Mr. Henry H. Wiggins and Miss Matilda L. Berg of the Columbia University Press for their generous assistance in preparing the manuscript for the printer.

Miami University   L. H. H.
Oxford, Ohio
November, 1948   C. W. H.

CONTENTS

CONTENTS

LEIGH HUNT'S
DRAMATIC CRITICISM

CRITICISM ON SHAKSPEARE'S "MUCH ADO ABOUT NOTHING" AND ITS PERFORMANCE AT COVENT-GARDEN

LEWIS AND ELLISTON COMPARED IN BENEDICK. SINGULAR DRESSES OF THE ACTORS IN THIS PLAY. A QUESTION RESPECTING THE MASKS USED IN PANTOMIME.

January 3, 1808　　　　　　　　　　　　　　　*Covent-Garden*

IT IS MY GOOD FORTUNE to commence my dramatic criticism with Shakspeare.[1] I feel just now like one who ventures out on St. Valentine's morning to draw a good or bad omen for his love from the first woman he meets; he descries a young female; she is very pretty, and seems to smile as she crosses him: he blesses his amorous stars that she is neither ancient nor ugly; thus the first author I meet is Shakspeare, and I bless my critical stars that it is neither Dibo [2]—but, poor fellows, let them rest in the first paper.

The comedy of *Much Ado about Nothing*, which was revived at this theatre on Wednesday night, is one of those happy compounds of wit and humour which can alternately delight the fancy of the polite part of the audience, and call down the jovial roar from the galleries. When this combination is natural, it is always a proof of mastery in the author. The modern sentimental comedies which attempt this double praise always run into extremes to please the two parts of their audience. When they would gain the attention of the boxes, they adopt a stately sentimentality or at best that kind of unwieldy floweriness which like a moving green on May-day is nothing but a splendid concealment of poverty and vulgarity; when they would animate the galleries, a character bursts before you in some fantastic dress, in some quaint reiterated phrase, or in some outrageous combination of trades and feelings that, like a shop in which pastry is exhibited at one window and perukes at the other, invites you at first sight merely to disgust you the more heartily at second.

If the profuse wit of *Much Ado about Nothing* is as natural as it is lively, the humour though it appears as broad as mere farce is rendered equally natural. This is the effect of giving proper characters their proper language.[3] Characters in fact may always be found which may sanction the lowest humour as well as the loftiest wit, and half the secret of the miserable comedies of our modern writers is their want of natural connection between the speakers and the dialogue: their language is not only wretched but unsuitable to their characters, their characters are not only wretched but unsuitable to their language: the beggar's coat in short is not only a system of rags, but it does not even fit him. There is an exquisite harmony throughout the conduct of Shakspeare's play. The piece commences with the return of a number of gay officers from a victorious campaign, and this single posture of affairs gives a lively anticipation to the audience and prepares them for the good humour and gallantry of the whole play. The two principal men and women are excellently contrasted: *Claudio,* instant in his feelings and incapable of concealing them, but altogether rational and resolute, is opposed to the careless, the mirthful, the apparently thoughtless *Benedick;* while the satirical and talkative though good-hearted *Beatrice* presents a fine relief to the retiring sensibility of *Hero.* The merry warfare of raillery between *Benedick* and *Beatrice* is a masterpiece of familiar wit; it is poetry applied to common feelings and common occasions: it has all the art and twice the nature of Congreve, for Shakspeare by confining the wit of the play to these two characters has given the ornament to its proper wearers: Congreve in his prodigality of wit literally dispenses his pearls to swine: his lowest characters are always the greatest geniuses in his plays, for one cannot help wondering at the exquisite polish which they have obtained without the advantages of their superiors. What was said of Congreve's personages by Johnson, in some of the noblest language that pen ever produced, may be applied in all its brilliancy to *Benedick* and *Beatrice;* they are "a kind of intellectual gladiators: their wit is a kind of intellectual gladiators, every sentence is to ward or strike; the contest of smartness is never intermitted; their wit is a meteor playing to and fro with alternate coruscations." [4]

The broad humour in this play would become perfect farce in any other persons but a set of old, ignorant, inefficient watchmen, whose constable of the night is as miserably senseless and conceited as his lowness of life and his shadow of office can make him. Though Fielding, from his legal duties, had sufficient experience for the proper knowledge of such petty despots of justice, yet I dare say he had well studied the humour of these watchmen and the laughable examination of the two courtiers before *Master Dogberry*. It is droll enough to observe the perfect resemblance between Shakspeare's watchmen and those of the present time; they have the same unofficious moderation, the same contempt of bustle, the same patient acquiescence, and the same Epicurean love of ease and retirement that distinguish our own nocturnal guardians, who may be defined to be so many old men in great coats, condemned for a certain small payment to shorten their lives by dozing half the night in boxes exposed to the air.

The play was altogether performed with much animation. Mr. Lewis [5] in *Benedick* naturally provokes a comparison with Elliston, and it is pleasing to see how excellently two actors can support the same character with their own separate originality. Lewis excels in all the lighter parts of the character, Elliston in the more earnest and impassioned: in Elliston you have more of the frank soldier, more of the man of rank, more of the resolute lover; in Lewis you have more of the airy gallant, of the careless hey-day fellow, of the merry soul who turns everything into a jest: when *Benedick's* manner is serious or when his humour acquires an additional dryness from gravity, you are intent upon the forceful style of Elliston, who is the first actor upon the stage in giving what may be called solidity to humour: Lewis, it must be confessed has no seriousness at all:

when he attempts a grave surprise he exhibits a prominence of mouth that any other actor but Fawcett would reckon ludicrous; and the short breathlessness with which he chips his words as they dart forward always hinders him from expressing a natural gravity in his dialogue: but as five parts of *Benedick's* composition are mere wit and carelessness, Mr. Lewis's deficiency in seriousness is perhaps the more natural in a character of such mirthful habits. It is true that those persons who have a strong feeling of the humourous very often display more external gravity than others and perhaps more often feel a real gravity; but it will generally be found that he who is always laughing and always breaking jests is somewhat deficient in serious sensibility, for the soul generally contrives to look out of the features and manner of persons accustomed to society.

Mrs. H. Johnston [6] reappeared after an absence of two years in the part of *Beatrice,* and perhaps it is not paying a great compliment to her performance to prefer her delivery of the harsher feelings of the character to its good-humoured levity. *Beatrice* is a very merry lady with a very good heart, she is the counterpart in short of *Benedick,* and Mrs. H. Johnston mistook the warm satirist when she uttered her wishes of revenge against *Hero's* calumniator with a gloominess and harshness of countenance bordering on malignity. I hope that one may be capable of great severity without distorting one's temper, or manner, or features, with mere rancour. *Beatrice* is sufficiently revengeful, I allow; but there is a proud and there is a mean revenge, there is the revenge of an ancient Spaniard and the revenge of a North-American cannibal: none but bad hearts exhibit in the countenance a mere disgusting malice. In some of the gayer speeches, Mrs. H. Johnston was natural and elegant, but in her general raillery she was a hundred times inferior to Mrs. Jordan [7] and Miss Duncan.[8] The next time she hides herself behind trees and arbours, she would do well to conceal her person as well as face. To hide the countenance and leave a long flowing robe in view, is like the folly of the ostrich, who thinks to escape its pursuers by thrusting its beak behind a tree and shutting its eyes.

I could not discover what was intended by the dresses of the gentlemen in this play. There is an astonishing disregard of chronological propriety at the theatres, and yet they tell us that the acting manager of Covent-Garden is a man of reading. The time of *Much Ado about Nothing* has not been settled, if I recollect rightly, by any of the commentators, but as it introduces a Prince of Arragon, who visits the Governor of Messina with familiar condescension and appears to carry his Court with him into Sicily, it may naturally be supposed that the action is during that period when Sicily was in possession of the House of Arragon. The last Sicilian king of this house reigned at the beginning of the fifteenth century, when the dresses of every polite nation in Europe were totally different from their present mode: the manager of Covent-Garden therefore has dressed his Spanish prince of the 14th or 15th century like a modern English gentleman in a blue coat, white breeches and stockings, and an opera hat; one of his Spanish officers appears in the exact regimentals of our present infantry, and the Italian officers exhibit the same identical coats and breeches which their descendants wear at this day. I do not know how Mr. Kemble [9] reconciles this to his studious soul, to his old affectation of thoughtful propriety.

Drury-Lane and Covent-Garden

THE USUAL Christmas pantomimes [10] are in full activity at both the theatres. That at Drury-Lane was by no means admired the first night, as anybody might have suspected from the string of eulogies in the next morning's play-bill: but then the one at Covent-Garden is universally said to be inferior to no pantomime but *Mother Goose*. This is the opinion of all the little boys of any discrimination. It is evident that Mr. Dibdin means to outshine the whole genius of Sadler's Wells.

I write this article merely because my readers should not think themselves neglected even in the most trifling of trifles, for I do not mean to criticise that indescribable species of drama which consists in mere legerdemain, in a continued bustle of

fiddles and feet, and in giving people huge slaps on the face.
A spectacle in which little is understood and nothing gained
is unworthy serious criticism. The modern pantomime appears
to me to be capable of great improvement without losing any
of its essential qualities. *Harlequin* is a very merry personage;
his many-coloured habit, his fantastic dances, his disjointed
jumps and postures, his conjurations with wooden sword, and
his utter contempt of ease and rest, not to mention that gradual
spin of his pericranium which is so alarmingly facetious, present an inexhaustible fund of merriment to all my little masters.
But why should this good-humoured gentleman be deprived of
his features? Surely if one should meet a pleasant fellow in
company, nobody would wish to cover his sociability of countenance. I allow, that all sensible *Harlequins* endeavour to supply
their deficiency of face by throwing its expression, as much as
possible, into their actions; thus when the party-coloured
humourist is alarmed, he shakes his head and his hands, and
darts away; when he is pleased he wags his sword, just as a dog
wags his tail. All this is very logical and expressive; but cannot
he do quite as much and give us his face too? If custom is in
the way, set it aside: custom is good for nothing but to sanction
what is rational. We do not lie down in cramped postures to
dinner as the Romans did, we do not mask our actors as they
did, why should we mask our pantomimists because the Romans
chose to deprive human expression of its divinest instrument,
or because one Arlequin, some centuries ago, thought proper
to make his face half white-man and half negro? Macrobius re-
lates [11] a very fine anecdote of the celebrated Pylades, who in the
reign of Augustus introduced pantomime on the stage as a distinct species of drama. It is surprising that this pantomimist who
seems to have been capable of the finest conceptions should
never have thought of divesting his face of so unnatural a concealment. He was present one day at a performance, in which
Hylas, his rival, was accompanying by attitude and gesture a
hymn that concluded with speaking of *the great Agamemnon.*
Hylas, to express the greatness of the hero, measured the air
with an elevated gesture, and Pylades immediately cried out,

"You make him tall, not great." The audience requested him to give them an example of the proper action; the hymn was repeated, and when Pylades heard the words, *the great Agamemnon,* he put himself in a posture of profound meditation. Nothing could be more simple or sublime; but only think of the motionless mask all this time!

MR. T. DIBDIN'S MOCK-
MELODRAMA

ITS DAMNATION, ITS MEANS OF EXISTENCE, AND THE GROSS FALSE-
HOODS OF THE PLAY-BILLS. DEFINITIONS OF BURLESQUE AND
MOCK-HEROIC. MR. DIBDIN'S UTTER CONFUSION AND IGNO-
RANCE IN THE MANAGEMENT OF HIS RIDICULE. A QUESTION
RESPECTING PLAYWRIGHTS WHO MAKE VEHICLES FOR MUSIC.
AND AN OLD FABLE EARNESTLY RECOMMENDED TO ALL
WRITERS OF OPERA WHO ENTERTAIN A MODEST OPINION OF
THEMSELVES.

April 10, 1808   *Covent-Garden*

I AM REALLY ALMOST ASHAMED to enter into any serious
criticism upon the new burlesque melodrama,[1] which is the most
stupid piece of impertinence that has disgraced the English
stage for some years past; [2] but when such a writer as Mr. T.
Dibdin commences dramatic satirist, the critics must naturally
be surprised enough to enquire into his pretensions to so unexpected an office. This melodrama, to which Mr. Dibdin has
given the four titles of *Bonifacio and Bridgelina,* or the *Knight
of the Hermitage,* or the *Windmill Turret,* or the *Spectre of the
North-East Gallery,* was so completely damned on its first performance last Tuesday week that the performer who came to
announce its second representation could not obtain a hearing
amidst the universal hisses and groans, and the audience departed under a romantic persuasion that the piece would be
withdrawn. But these petty hints of disapprobation are nothing
to modern dramatists: the managers of the theatres prove their
affection for public opinion by growing bolder from denial, and
the new melodrama was announced, as usual, in the play-bills
of the next day, as an exquisite production which set the audience in *universal and continued peals of laughter.* This was a
miserable artifice as well as a miserable falsehood. Those who

heard the laughter can bear witness with me, that it proceeded
rather from contempt than merriment: the better part of the
audience had never heard anything so grossly ridiculous as the
dialogue, they were amused at the ludicrous presumption of
the author, and they occasionally burst into that kind of laughter
which by its lagging and tremulous depth announces a feeling
very different from that of the loud and sudden shout. Mr.
Kemble, I have understood, is the present Acting Manager of
Covent-Garden, and how that grave actor or any manager
whatever can reconcile the perpetual falsehoods of these play-
bills to the gratitude which is due to the public, or even to the
feelings of honest men and gentlemen, is a problem not to be
solved by the admirers of truth. It is reckoned sufficiently gross
and contemptible in any person to tell a lie to a single man, but
as these bills are intended for the whole town, they of course
tell lies to everybody in the town, and everybody therefore is
insulted. This is the true quackery of theatres: they must im-
pose upon people by the vilest puffs, before their physic can
be swallowed: the new audience on the second night do not
like to condemn a piece which has been so highly applauded
by the critics of a first night; they laugh where they can, say
nothing where they cannot laugh, and with the help of songs,
and scenery, and play-bills, the new piece becomes the standing
opiate of the season. The poets of the modern stage do indeed
live by fiction.

I said in my Paper of last week that "a writer of mock-heroic
should have a correct taste for the true heroic, or he will not
know how to produce the proper contrast between his subject
and its style." I use the term burlesque and mock-heroic indiscriminately, when speaking of Mr. Dibdin's melodrama,
though they are literally very different things; but Mr. Dibdin,
who has no sort of taste for real heroic, has of course been totally
ignorant how to ridicule the violation of it in others. The writers
of mock-poetry have left the different species undefined; but
if the subject be at all considered, it will be found that mock-
heroic consists in the use of serious language upon a familiar
subject, and burlesque in the use of familiar language upon a

serious subject. Thus the *Rape of the Lock* and the *Lutrin* [3] are mock-heroic poems, and the tragedy of *Tom Thumb* [4] a burlesque. The *Splendid Shilling* of Philips,[5] though it wants machinery and is confounded with burlesque, is nevertheless a mock-heroic piece: the author meditates on the possession of a shilling, just as an epic poet might be supposed to meditate on the possession of a good conscience or any other great blessing: he does not, in short, degrade an important subject, but elevates an unimportant one: he renders familiarity great, not greatness familiar. Mr. Dibdin has managed to find out that the language and the subject ought to differ, but his indefinite notions of ridicule have not taught him to separate the mock-heroic from the burlesque: his attempts therefore are perpetually clashing: when he should be pompous he becomes trifling, when he should be trifling he becomes unexpectedly serious. His story is naturally grave and heroic; a Nobleman's estate is usurped by his relation, who is prepared for any villainy that shall secure his ill-gotten elevation: the characters therefore are naturally heroic, because their means and designs are truly substantial, and might appear in a real tragedy or epic; but alas, Mr. Dibdin has confounded the *ridiculous effect*, which these hacknied characters produce in hacknied dramas, with the *real character* they ought to sustain, and imagining them to be ridiculously familiar has endeavoured to *raise* them into heroic by language really lofty; the really serious character therefore of these rich and great personages meets with really serious language, and of course the effect is unexpectedly grave. Mr. Dibdin seems however to have been perplexed with this seriousness as well as ourselves, and therefore has thrust into the middle of grave speeches a few common phrases and vulgar allusions, which merely serve to render the mixture of burlesque and mock-heroic more surprising and to hinder the audience from laughing by keeping them in a state of stupid enquiry: his personages have five serious lines to one comic, and as they talk with common seriousness about a serious business, one is astonished why they should every now and then introduce a ludicrous phrase or allusion in contradiction to their own character. It is necessary both to burlesque and mock-heroic that the characters and dialogue should disagree, and this disagreement should not be partial but continual, otherwise the poem or drama is not a perfect piece of ridicule. In the *Rape of the Lock* the speakers are always serious in the midst of familiar action; in *Tom Thumb* they are always familiar in the midst of serious action. Mr. Dibdin generally gives serious dialogue to serious action, and familiar to familiar action: now where is the ridicule of this? One of his personages, who is a real knight, almost always speaks seriously except in the pronunciation of the word *nephew,* which he invariably calls *nevvy:* now I cannot, with all my exertion, discover the satire of this. His chief humour however consists in making his characters flatly contradict themselves by the most manifest bulls: *Sir Hildebrand* for instance tells us with his own mouth that he was *slain* in battle, and at the same time informs the person with whom he is talking that, as he has told him *all* his story, he will tell him the *rest* another time. All this puts one at a great loss. I rather conjecture that Mr. Dibdin had some vague idea of that burlesque contrast which introduces an extreme familiarity by a preface of important preparation, or in other words, introduces a speech of no meaning by a preparation of some meaning. In *Tom Thumb* for instance, *Lord Grizzle* in answer to some enquiry from the *Queen* tells her that "as far as he could conjecture, &c.&c.&c. he really did not know." This is a touch of ridiculous importance natural enough to a simpleton, and Farquhar has the very same idea in his picture of the ludicrous importance of *Scrub* in the *Beaux Stratagem.* But the most simple of all simpletons would never think of saying that his face was black becaus[e it w]as white; yet Mr. Dibdin's contrasts are evidently of this kind. There are a number of instances similar to those I have already quoted. One of his females begs that the robbers will not deprive her of "all," because she has "nothing to lose." By all this affected pleasantry, the characters themselves become theatrical performers, the performers therefore are but the actors of actors, and the stage is reduced to an imitation of itself. The characters exhibit an intentional burlesque, and the humour entirely loses its zest, just as a man who falls to the ground on purpose loses the ridiculous effect of an unavoidable fall.

I anticipate the common answer to all these objections. The author, it is said, intends his composition for nothing but a vehicle to the music and scenery: he claims little merit for himself, he does not wish to be thought a genius.

In the first place however, as to the vehicle of music and scenery, I really do not see the right which any dramatist possesses to give a bad vehicle to good music. This is not only a dishonour to the music, but it is as much as to say to the audience, "You do not care for poetry: sound is sufficient for your ears." I am very sure that Messrs. Longman and Broderip would never send home one of their pianos on a brewer's sledge; and why should a dramatist be allowed to jolt and destroy good music by any wretched vehicle he chooses? In the second place, I do not suppose that the customary dramatists of opera and pantomime could produce a better vehicle if they wished it: and lastly, when the modern opera writer talks of his little claims and his little wishes, I by no means believe this modesty of claim and this humility of wish: I have very good reasons for supposing that the authors of these wretched pieces regard themselves not only as legitimate dramatists, but as ornaments of the British stage, that they claim the honour of supporting the finest singers, and that with a blind self-importance they refer us to the perpetual performance of their operas as a proof of their consummate genius. I will put them in mind of an old fable. A jackass laden with holy relics and images, happening to pass through a French town, perceived the inhabitants fall down on their knees at his approach and make the customary gestures of adoration: this behaviour tickled him excessively; he pricked up his long ears, and commenced a very awkward kind of stateliness: "Upon my honour," said he to himself, "these fellows have taste: they are doing homage to the beauty of my person."

"KING LEAR" REVIVED

ITS ILL TREATMENT BY TATE AND OTHERS. COMMENTS ON ITS
CATASTROPHE. CHARACTER OF LEAR. SHAKSPEARE'S PATHOS
AND WILD FANCY IN MADNESS. LEAR'S DEATH. MR. KEMBLE'S
BAD, AND MR. C. KEMBLE'S GOOD PERFORMANCE.

May 28, 1808   *Covent-Garden*

THE TRAGEDY of *King Lear* was performed on Wednesday
last[1] as it was altered by Tate, who was altered by Coleman,[2]
who was altered by Garrick. Almost every fine play of Shakspeare
has its genealogy of emendation. Our great bard, whom everybody calls "the divine and the matchless," is indeed so inimitable
that everybody thinks himself capable of mending him; the
different editions are sure to succeed, because the greater part
is still original; the critic grows vain, and thinks he has done
for Shakspeare what Shakspeare evidently does for him. If
Tate had been content to expunge a few anachronisms, to omit
the *Fool* which is now out of date,[3] and to send *Gloster* behind
the scenes whilst he is blinded, he might have been well ex-
cused; but that a mere rhymer, whose dullness has become
proverbial, should create whole scenes of his own and adorn
them with a few extracts from Shakspeare, that he should turn
the current of our poet's feeling into scanty sprinklings over his
own barren fancy and then cry out, "How fertile I am!"—is
really a violation of a man's literary property. Horace tells us
that poets may dare anything, and Tate was resolved perhaps to
shew his poetical talent by his insolence; but he might have been
contented, I think, with claiming the play as his own in one of
his title-pages.

The original *King Lear* is a deep tragedy: it is entirely occupied with the distress arising from violent passions, and with
awful lessons on parental partiality; but Tate (amorous soul)
must divide this interest, and accordingly he has introduced a
love-scene in which the admirable *Cordelia*, the pattern of filial

piety, is made to forget her old, houseless, distracted father, whom she is wildly seeking, and not only to find time for listening to a lover, but to retire with him into a cave in order to dry her clothes before she goes any further. *Cordelia,* in this instance therefore, becomes a lover who sacrifices her filial to her amatory tenderness, and is a different character from the original *Cordelia,* whose whole imagination is filled with one great, pathetic, and disinterested idea. Shakspeare made his play end unhappily, because he knew that real nature required such a catastrophe; [4] but Tate (impassioned soul) must have a marriage between the lovers at the end, and the old father must give them his blessing. Johnson has approved this alteration; but Addison in the *Spectator,* and Richardson, that great master of the passions, in his *Clarissa,* have both protested against it, and Warton in his criticism in the *Adventurer* disdains to give it a notice. Johnson tells us [5] that he was once so shocked by the death of *Cordelia* that he believes he never could read the last scene again till he undertook to edit the tragedy. This confession easily accounts for his approbation of Tate; he was afflicted with a morbid melancholy, and when any great emotion found its way to his feelings, it clung to his irritable fancy and produced that impatient fixture of the mind to one object which is the origin of madness. I have no doubt that he would view the alteration as a sort of revenge for the feelings he had experienced; for we may remember, that when poor Boswell was descanting upon the tearful effects which he sometimes felt from a melancholy movement on the piano, the Doctor told him that, if it had made himself such a fool, he would have broken the instrument to pieces. As to the Doctor's old argument that poetic justice did not allow the innocent to suffer with the guilty, I think it is completely refuted, not so much by the common ill-fortune of virtue, which he seems to consider as the only argument against him, but by the evident maxim that error is never so exemplary in its effects as when they involve the innocent with the guilty; nay, the very death of a virtuous person seems to be a sort of triumph over persecution; the calm repose which we see in the dead body, and the lively enjoyment which we fancy the soul has just fled to partake, form a strong contrast with the anticipated end of the guilty and with their turbulent pleasures on earth. It appears to me, also, that the old age of *Lear* has been too much shattered by his repeated madness to survive a second change of fortune, and that the exhaustion of which he dies in Shakspeare is in every respect natural and unavoidable.

The character of *Lear* has been well defined by Professor Richardson [6] to consist of mere sensibility, he is fond, capricious, and revengeful, and it may be observed that, during his first ill-treatment, we are not so much moved with pity for himself as with horror at his daughters. It is when misfortune has begun to humble him that we pity, because we esteem him more, and our sympathy regularly increases with his humility. There has been a question whether his misery proceeds so much from his disappointed tenderness as from his loss of royalty; but if the latter appeared to be the first cause, it would certainly lessen the natural pathos of the story, and I think the question might have been settled by simple reference to his first interview with *Cordelia*, when he returns to reason and becomes calm and penitent at the sight of his injured daughter without once adverting impatiently to his lost sovereignty: if they tell him that he is in his own kingdom, he merely begs them not to abuse him: he has no pride, no impatience, no revenge, before his forgiving angel. The very first reason he gives for *Edgar's* apparent misery, when he meets him as a wandering maniac, is filial ingratitude; he insists that nothing could have made a human being so wretched but his ungrateful children; and it is wonderful to see the consummate art with which Shakspeare has preserved in these two pictures of madness that single occupation of thought which at once fixes and distracts the mind. *Lear* can think of nothing but his daughters, *Mad Tom* of nothing but the foul fiend. He who can read the shuddering conceits of *Edgar*, who appears thus forsaken of heaven, without peopling the atmosphere about him with visions; or can listen

to the artless reasoning of the abused old father without re-
proaching himself for every little grief he may have occasioned
a fond parent, has neither a head to fancy nor a heart to feel.

Enter Edgar, disguised as a madman
Edg. Away! the foul fiend follows me!
   Through the sharp hawthorn blows the cold wind:
   Humph [7]—go to thy cold bed and warm thee.
Lear. Hast thou given all to thy two daughters,
   And art thou come to this?
Edg. Who gives any thing to poor Tom, whom the foul fiend hath
   led through fire and through flame, through ford and whirlpool,
   over [8] bog and quagmire; that hath laid knives under his pillow
   and halters in his pew, set ratsbane by his porridge, made him
   proud of heart to ride on a bay trotting-horse over four-inch'd
   bridges, to course his own shadow for a traitor? Bless thy five wits!
   Tom's a cold: (*shivering*) O do de, do de, do de. Bless thee from
   whirlwinds, star-blasting, and taking! Do poor Tom some charity,
   whom the foul fiend vexes! There could I have him now—and
   there—and there—and there again—and there.[9]—(*Storm con-
   tinues.*)
Lear. What, have his daughters brought him to this pass?
   Could'st thou save nothing? Did'st thou give them all?
   —Now all the plagues, that in the pendulous air
   Hang fated o'er men's faults, light on thy daughters!
Kent. He hath no daughters, Sir.
Lear. Death, traitor! *nothing could* have subdued nature
   To such a lowness but his unkind daughters.[10]

I can easily conceive that a poet rises from fancies like these,
as Dryden is said to have risen from his celebrated ode, with a
pulse disordered by inspiration. The imagination looks out into
other worlds with an eagerness stretched beyond its natural
tension, and it returns back in languor and irritability. In fact,
one could almost be persuaded, sometimes, that a true poet
in his enthusiasm enjoys nothing but an admirable insanity, and
that more truth is contained than we generally imagine in the
celebrated distich,

> Great wits to madness nearly are allied,
> And thin partitions do their bounds divide.[11]

The same exhaustion that is felt after poetical inspiration is seen
in the effects of less happy transports, and not even Tate's

ignorance can excuse the omission of the concluding scene, in which the spirit of the worn-out old man is broken to its last whisper. He enters with the dead *Cordelia* in his arms, after killing by a desperate effort the soldier who was hanging her. His grief is alternately vehement and patient; it is the last glimmering of his capricious and warm temper. He persuades himself for a moment that he hears her voice, and nothing could be a more delicate tribute to her memory than his praises of its mildness, for such a praise would have been too trivial for departed excellence, did not its very simplicity comprehend all the tender virtues at once:

> Cordelia, Cordelia, stay a little.—Ha!
> What is't thou sayest?——Her voice was ever soft,
> Gentle, and low;—an excellent thing in woman.[12]

His last words seem to recur for an instant to his degraded power, but it is with pity for his follower rather than anger. His spirit is quite subdued, and after a short hysterical feeling, he becomes resigned from despair, fixes his eyes on his daughter's face and expires.

Mr. Warton has noticed that little request in the fifth line of the following extract, which expresses with such perfect nature the swelling of his bosom; but I think he might have remarked also, without any imputation against his feeling, the thanks which are immediately returned by the dying king. So habitual is true politeness that his last misery could not divest him of it: and indeed as beauty adds to the charm of a woman's tears, so does the spirit of a gentleman throw a dignity upon sorrow.

> *Lear.* And my poor fool is hang'd! No—no—no life!
> Why should a dog, a horse, a rat have life,
> And thou no breath at all?—Oh, thou wilt come no more,
> Never, never, never, never, never!
> *Pray you undo this button:* thank you, Sir.—
> Do you see this? Look on her—look—her lips—
> Look there, look there [13]— (*He dies.*)

I must confess I was disappointed in the performance. It is true, passions so minute and so varied are very difficult to represent, but even the scenes were managed badly, and Mr. Kemble seemed to throw a general coldness over the whole that damped the glowing business of the action. He personated the king's majesty perfectly well, but not the king's madness. The insanity of a lively mind is full of sudden looks and attitudes, and though *Lear's* distraction came gradually at first, it suddenly settled upon him with great wildness. The speech beginning "Blow winds and crack your cheeks," was given with a gloomy carelessness, although the sudden change of his fortune, the nocturnal tempest, and everything internal and external conspired to set the king's brain on fire. Even in the intervals of wildness Mr. Kemble was not at all happier in his less agonized mood: we might have at least expected the pauses of a bewildered head trying to be patient and to recollect itself, but the grave actor went through his gentle speeches with the dull calmness of a schoolboy: he is like the man who was so fond of a stick that he would carry a stick everywhere, to balls, to prayers, and to dinner. In short you never see Mr. Kemble on the stage without his stick; he is always stiff, always precise, and he will never, as long as he lives, be able to act anything mad unless it be a melancholy mad statue.[14] Mr. Charles Kemble[15] shone with great lustre by his side. It may be doubted whether his description of the imaginary cliff to the blind *Earl of Gloster* should be given as if he was saying a lesson, though the idea has an air of imposing originality; but it appears to me that the describer, who must evidently be a man of lively fancy, would almost unconsciously try to assist himself by looking downwards and using gestures expressive of his fancied elevation. The madness of poor *Tom* however was assumed with an accuracy and spirit that shew what this actor can do when he is obliged to get rid of his habitual languor. His transitions from a sapient majesty to a stare of idiotism, half smile and half misery, were managed with instantaneous expression; and nothing could be more natural, when he drove away the dogs with his head, than the light run down his voice upon the words *See, see, see, see, see, see,* as he fancied he saw them running away round the scene. Mr. Charles Kemble appears to feel the poetry of his tragedy; his brother nothing but the verses.

MR. YOUNG'S MERITS CONSIDERED

HIS MACBETH COMPARED WITH KEMBLE AND ELLISTON. HIS DAG-
GER-SCENE, SCENE AFTER THE MURDER, AND BANQUET-SCENE.
HIS GAMESTER. HIS ONLY AFFECTATION. FORCIBLE INSTANCE
OF THE DIFFERENCE BETWEEN GREAT AND COMMON ACTORS
IN THE MANAGEMENT OF THE FACE AND ITS MUSCLES.
MODERN FINE ACTORS. GENERAL CHARACTER OF MR. YOUNG.

January 15, 1809   *Covent-Garden Company, Haymarket*

IN MR. KEMBLE's absence the lesser stars are permitted to
shine a little;[1] and Mr. Young [2] has been endeavouring for some
days past to exhibit the lustre of high tragedy. His performance
of *Othello* is no criterion of his genius, for whether the face of
an actor is so obscured, more than half of his powers are indis-
tinguishable; and his *Hamlet,* which I have criticised in another
place, is like all the other *Hamlets* of the day, deficient in various
and powerful equability. The fine union of tragedy and comedy
which renders this character almost unattainable renders it also
no reasonable test of a man's peculiar talent in either department, for the want of one of the two requisites will inevitably
injure the effect of the other. A single bad concord, in a part
so exquisitely harmonious, puts the whole out of tune. I have
selected therefore from Mr. Young's various performances his
Macbeth and his *Gamester,*[3] the one as a criterion of his powers
in loftier tragedy, and the other as their criterion in domestic.

Macbeth has been the touchstone of many an aspiring performer. It has been represented by all the *respectable* as well
as great tragedians since the time of Shakspeare, was acted
with this peculiarity and that peculiarity, with this good trait
and that good trait, but has never been *altogether* attainable
by any but the greatest actors, such as Garrick, Henderson,[4]
and if we are to believe the admiration of the best contemporary writers, by Burbage and Betterton.[5] These names have in
fact become illustrious by the performance of this and other

characters in Shakspeare. But Quin, and Mossop, Booth, Barry, and Mills,[6] men still of some note, failed in the representation, some of them altogether, and all of them in some great requisite. It is the same in our day, because we have no great tragic actor, and I am much inclined to think that the mere assistants of such a man as Garrick would make an alarming rivalry in these times with the best of our modern stage dictators. Mr. Young's *Macbeth* is a specimen, in one sense, of all his tragedy; it is free from every gross fault, but it is not distinguished by any great beauty. Kemble, who is excellent in all that there is of dignity in *Macbeth,* cannot forget, in the more impassioned scenes, those methodistical artifices of dropped eyes, patient shakes of the head, and whining preachments, which always do and ever will injure his attempts at heartfelt nature: and Elliston, who gives us so natural a picture of the noisy despair of the tyrant in the last scenes, wants all the deep thinking of the character in the former ones. Mr. Young therefore, in avoiding the two extremes, is more harmonious in his colouring, more skilful in the dispositions of his lights and shades; but still he wants the occasional touches of both, and is altogether too sombrous. His apostrophe to the imaginary dagger was impressive, but it wanted, what I never saw given to it yet, a variety of countenance approaching to delirium; and he spoke its first lines with his face turned away from *Duncan's* chamber door *directly toward* the side scenes: this appears to me an erroneous position: his face should at least have been a three-quarter one, for to give a most impassioned expression a profile only, except in cases which absolutely require it, is to cheat the audience of the full fancy of the scene. Mr. Young also in that passage,

a false creation
Proceeding from the heat-oppressed brain,[7]

should not have shortened the word into *oppress'd.* The language has suffered enough already from these contractions, and we should at least preserve all the metre we can in our great poet. The wonderful difference of effect between the proper and the

familiar pronunciation of this single word in a line so full of
harsh syllables will be evident to everybody who reads it. The
awful description of night,

> Now o'er the one half world
> Nature seems dead, &c.[8]

particularly in which it raises the figure of murder moving towards his design like a ghost, was perhaps the best delivered passage in the whole performance: it was full of the solemnity for
which the lower tones of Mr. Young are so excellently qualified,
and he managed to give a personal character to the idea of the
ghost, by just rising slowly and shrinkingly as if preparing to
glide, without precisely acting the description, which would
have been unseasonable and unnatural. The scene between
Lady Macbeth and her husband was grand and horrific, for
how could it be otherwise when drawn by Shakspeare and sustained by Mrs. Siddons? [9] But little can be said of Mr. Young
except that he did not absolutely spoil the effect of her performance. An actor in this scene must raise admiration, or he is a poor
substitute for Garrick and Henderson. But only observe, in all
the passages which Mrs. Siddons shares with another, how
singly she bears away the passionate acknowledgment of our
feelings. The same individual prominence was observable in
the banquet-scene, in which Mr. Young was still impressive,
was as good as Mr. Kemble, if he pleases, but evidently had
not the proper powers for a various and preternatural agitation.
The imprecatory action of lifted arms with which he repulsed
the ghost off the stage, according to custom, at that passage—

> Hence horrible shadow!
> Unreal mockery hence! [10]

was too violent and dictatorial: it should have been accompanied with less decision of voice, with more horror and loathing. The concluding scenes were not more correct than the
former ones, in point of powerful expression, except perhaps in
that iron despair of countenance which seems best adapted to
Mr. Young's rigid muscles. At the same time it is no dispraise

to him that his violence is not so good as his thoughtfulness. But we see how little is to be done, in any varying character, with only one or two tragic looks and feelings.

In the *Gamester* Mr. Young was more successful, because the character did not require so much variety; and in domestic tragedy, somewhat of passion is less necessary than in the poetical drama. If Mr. Young's manners are not exactly adapted to heroism, they are always those of the gentleman, and always of an *impressive manliness;* this impressiveness is the general character of his talent in every respect; and as *Beverley,* in his more peaceful moments, is nothing but a serious gentleman, and, in his more passionate ones, is full of a monotonous despair, Mr. Young was enabled to exhibit his manners and his peculiar turn of expression to very great advantage. His prison scene was performed in a style worthy of the company in which he was acting, and upon the whole I think his *Beverley* superior to that of Mr. Kemble for one single reason, because it is less affectedly studious. His only affectation seems to arise from a laborious aim at correct enunciation, which induces him sometimes to use his masticating muscles like a person teaching a child to pronounce O and A, and he drops his mouth sometimes in this toilsome manner, as if, to use the very just expression of a Correspondent in this Paper, he was *champing* his words. This peculiarity, when you see his profile, exhibits a very droll and Quixotic gravity. I have been narrowly observing of late, and it never struck me more forcibly than in Mr. Young's performance of *Beverley* that one very great cause of the common or contradictory expression in the countenances of modern tragedians is the little use, and hardly any at all, which they make of the lower part of the face. They open their mouths with astonishment, bite their lips with vexation, raise them with smiles, drop them with tears, and do all that any common actor can do, or perhaps a little more; but they never chase the expression about with fugitive variety; passion sets them or shakes them, but it does not scatter them; and with all their dreadful scenes and their dying scenes, I never saw a single performer who had the least idea of *convulsed* expression, but Mrs. Siddons.

This single deficiency shews that they do not feel as they ought, and that they are not great performers. Even the beauties which they do occasionally shew, are in general mere copies of former actors: none of them invent like Garrick; the lower ones do not attempt innovation, and what the higher attempt is some miserable piece of pedantry as a substitute for genius. I do not say that a good passage in acting of any kind should not be adopted from former actors; it may descend like an heir-loom for ever and do honour to its users; but why preserve the easy passages only, the mere starts, stamps, and strides? Or why preserve only single expressions? Why not give us the variety, the combination, the ever-shifting genius? They have it not: they have not the power to *re-create*; they can only copy.

In short, Mr. Young's performances are certainly above what is now called mediocrity, that is, they are infinitely superior to what such actors as Henry Siddons [11] or Brunton can do; and approach very near if not closely to Kemble; but when I consider the thousand varieties in which the true genius of acting consists, I form no standard by what is called the excellence of Mr. Kemble; I do not place perfect tragedy in a monotony however dignified, or in a feebleness of muscular expression, however disguised; I think of Garrick; I think of Mrs. Siddons; I think of the lightning which a true actor flashes from *all* corners of his mind and face, and of the thunder that follows such flashes and such only; and it is then that Mr. Kemble becomes an actor of very contracted powers indeed; that Mr. Young, with less of his genius and fewer of his faults, becomes an actor of elegant mediocrity; and Messrs. Brunton and H. Siddons no actors at all. There is but one great tragedian living, and that is Mrs. Siddons.

[COVENT-GARDEN REDECORATED;
O.P. RIOT]

September 24, 1809   *Covent-Garden*

IT WAS ARDENTLY HOPED by all the lovers of the Theatre, that the Managers of Covent-Garden, in shewing their taste for the fine arts would have shewn also a liberality worthy of the taste, and thus increased the respectability and the true interest of the stage: but people, it seems, are destined to be disappointed, who expect from these men anything but the merest feelings of tradesmen. The new theatre opened on Monday night [1] with the increased prices of 4s. to the Pit, and 7s. to the Boxes, and if the town at least expected an increase of comfort on the occasion it was to be disappointed even in that respect.

The *appearance,* indeed, was classical and magnificent throughout. On your entrance through the portico, you turn to the left, and pay your money at the top of a short flight of steps, adorned on each side by a bronze Grecian lamp on a tripod: immediately beyond this is the grand staircase, rising through a landing place adorned on each side with large Ionic pillars in imitation of porphyry, between each of which hangs another lamp of bronze: this brings you directly opposite Mr. Rossi's statue of Shakspeare in the anti-room; it stands in an easy assured attitude, making a sling of its cloak with its left arm, and holding a scroll in the other; its countenance does not much remind you of any of the faces attributed to the Great Poet, nor was it desirable that it should, for of the two commonly received likenesses, the Chandos and the Felton, the former is the head of a coxcomb, and the latter that of a dolt; but Mr. Rossi has very poorly supplied what was deficient in dignity and genius; the poet merely looks as if he good-humouredly enjoyed his elevation, an expression certainly very distant from the noble simplicity of the antique, and in short, the figure altogether exhibits the usual feebleness of this artist, resulting from want of invention. This anti-room leads to the principal lobby, which disappoints one at first sight with regard to size, but it is quite large enough for the proper purposes of ingress and egress, and is very classically adorned with eight casts from the antique, among which are *Minerva, Venus,* and *Bacchus,* the *Apollo de Medicis,* and the *Farnesian Flora,* so justly celebrated for its magnificent breadth of drapery. These entrances are certainly worthy of introducing you to a stage over which Shakspeare presides.

In the audience part of the theatre, *appearances* are still as magnificent, but there is a sad abridgement of comfort. Those who had obtained seats in the *lower boxes* or *pit* might certainly feel themselves comfortable enough to look about and admire the aspect of the place. It is of a chaste and classical elegance. The boxes are of a dove-colour ground in front, the lower circle ornamented with a simple Etruscan border in gold, and the rest with the Grecian honeysuckle alternately upright and inverted. The light pillars that support them remind you of Drury-Lane Theatre; they are of a gold colour, and furnished with superb chandeliers, which, however, do not shew the backs of the boxes to advantage, smeared as they are with glaring red, and abruptly patched with doors of new mahogany that look like common unfinished wood: the slips and galleries are improved in *appearance* by being formed into a row of semicircular arcades, and the arched front of the stage is adorned at top by a short curtain like the Greek peplum, festooned at intervals, and ornamented in each festoon by an Apollo's wreath: the pilasters at the side are in imitation of yellow stained marble, but unaccountably supported upon bases of most evident wood. The drop-scene is worthy the general classicality, and represents a temple dedicated to Shakspeare, who stands in the vista in his usual attitude, while your eye approaches him through two rows of statues, consisting of the various founders of the drama in various nations, Aeschylus, Menander, Plautus, Lope de Vega, Ben Jonson, Molière, &c. They seemed to be looking over the way at each other with surprise to find themselves on a spot so new to a set of wits.

But the Managers, in all this display of taste, seem to have had no eye to the improvement of the public taste, but to have obeyed a certain aristocratic impulse of their pride and consulted little but the accommodation of the higher orders. The people felt this immediately. It is certainly monstrous to pay seven shillings for admission to the garrets at the top of the house, where you can neither see nor hear, and still more monstrous, when you see a whole circle taken from the public by way of private boxes with anti-chambers, to make room for which the places and comforts of the lower orders have been so circumscribed: that old nuisance, the basket, as it is called, has been preserved to give the usual effect to the noise and interruption of the lobbies, and thus, if the accommodations are confined in some respects, the theatre is altogether as large in others as the avarice of the Managers and their contempt for a real taste in the drama could make it. In no such theatre can a true taste be excited, because a true drama, which requires nicety of expression in the voice and countenance, cannot be felt in it: Shakspeare may be played to the pit and side boxes, but he will be little better than dumb and blind shew to the people in the basket, who pay seven shillings to hear nothing but noise, or to those in the upper boxes, who pay seven shillings to see nothing but indecency. Naturally therefore the rise of the old prices entirely disgusted the public, and their disgust was increased by various attempts on the part of the Managers and their friends to plead the excuse of *necessity*. It was stated at one time that the Managers could not reimburse the expences of rebuilding the theatre without raising the prices; at another, that their profits have lately been only six per cent; and the Editor of *Bell's Weekly Messenger* gravely desires us to "look round and point out any one who has been enriched by a patent." "Is *Colman* ² rich?" he asks—"Is *Sheridan* rich? Is *Harris* rich? In the course of nearly one hundred years," he continues, "*Garrick* will be found to be the only man who was enriched by a theatre. But Garrick was at once actor and proprietor," and the writer should have added, an œconomist and no debauchee. The Proprietors he has named would not thank him for obtruding the causes of their poverty on the public recollection. Mr. Harris however, as we see by the papers, keeps his country house, and can entertain Madame Catalani [3] there, and Mr. Kemble, besides his reputation as a bon-vivant, can afford to throw away his fifty and a hundred pounds upon old black-letter books which no man of taste would read. The public therefore neither does nor will believe a syllable respecting any plea of necessity, or rather they will treat it as ridiculous and contemptible, till they are convinced of its truth by inspection of the theatrical accounts.

With these impressions, people went to the new Theatre on Monday night, and though by a stratagem as barbarous as it was mean, numbers had been admitted into the house before the doors were regularly opened, the public feeling most decidedly predominated, and obtained the general voice of the audience.

On Mr. Kemble's appearance in the dress of *Macbeth*, the character he was about to play, he was received with a partial applause, which was instantly drowned in a torrent of execration, and after plaintively bowing, and looking as tenderly disconsolate as he could, for a minute or two, he was compelled to retire. The curtain then drew up, and the noise and outcry that followed were continued with an energy truly terrific the whole evening. It was impossible that more determined resistance could be displayed on any occasion, and as it consisted entirely of noise, it was gratifying to see how much the audience felt themselves in the right by abstaining from every other mode of opposition. Every species of vocal power was exercised on the occasion, and some persons seemed to pride themselves in shewing their invention at making a noise: in one corner of the pit you had a heap of groans, in another a combination of hisses, in a third a choir of yells, in a fourth a doleful undulating moaning, which, mingling with the other sounds, reminded you of infernal regions, when in an instant the whole house seemed about to be rent asunder with a yah! of execration, whenever Mr. Kemble presented himself from the side-scenes. When Mrs. Siddons appeared, and seemed to petition for a little compassion, there was a general groan of disgust; but the death of her brother in the last act was followed by triumphant shouts of exultation, as if the spectators congratulated themselves on this temporary demise. After the farce, some persons, said to be magistrates, appeared on the stage, but soon vanished before the general indignation; and it was not till two o'clock that the audience retired, growling as they went, like Homer's lions, at those who had laid toils for them.

" 'Twas the same the next night, and the next, and the next," as Mr. Colman says in a production much superior to the Prologue which he gave Mr. Kemble to gesticulate on the present occasion. Each succeeding evening increased in noise: to catcalls were added horns and trumpets; and to a placard or two, banners all over the house covered with proverbs, lampoons, and encouragements to unanimity. An attempt on Tuesday night to fasten one of these placards on the stage-curtain at the end of the performances, which closed at half past nine, produced a whole regiment of Bow-street officers, constables, and bruisers on the stage, the trap-doors were opened to guard against approach, and when all this was found to be no intimidation, a noise of pumping was heard by way of inuendo, and one or two engine pipes were insinuated through the stage door, a threat that served no purpose but to make the indignation of the audience ten times hotter. A respectable gentleman of the name of Leigh then addressed them, and exhorted them to a proper perseverance, a lesson which they put in practice the next night, Wednesday, with unabated energy. The actors by this time had become the audience, and the audience the actors, and Mr. Kemble, seeing no probable termination of the tragedy, again presented himself and begged to know in the usual frigid way which he mistakes for dignity, *"of what the House had to complain?"* This ludicrous piece of affectation produced the usual burst of impatience and execration, but after another very temperate and strenuous exhortation from Mr. Leigh, the Manager again made his appearance; he stated that "for the last ten years the Proprietors have not received for their capital more than *six per cent.*," and talked of "the exigencies of dress and scenery," having "doubled, trebled, and quadrupled," besides other expences "too numerous to mention," and "with which he was in fact *unacquainted*." This egregious trifling produced nothing but laughter: the same indignant vociferation was kept up all Thursday evening, and on Friday Mr. Kemble once more presented himself "to submit a proposal." This proposal was to submit the decision of the question to a few great men,[4] such as the "Governor of the Bank of England," the "*Attorney-General of England*," &c., &c., but it said nothing about lowering the prices till the question *should be* decided. Of course, the speaker met with his usual reception. The audience, less molested than before with the interference of the peace officers, were left to amuse their lungs to their hearts' content, and so they were doing last night when this paper went to press. It is evident that the managers cannot proceed in their plan of obstinacy much longer, if such a determined system of opposition be continued, for they must be losing a good deal by it already, in consequence of the temporary retainers they keep about the theatre, and the orders that they scatter by hundreds through the hands of their friends and tradesmen. If it is true, that they have made only six per cent of their property no reasonable person can deny them the advance of price, but when Mr. Kemble talks of *average,* and tells us nothing of the deductions, hazards, crosses, and losses, unconnected with the people's responsibility on these occasions, he must not be surprised that his speeches are treated as so many evasions, and that the people will believe nothing till they can inspect his accounts through an *open and popular medium.* Till then, it is to be hoped that they will repeat and invigorate their efforts, and that, whenever the word necessity is mentioned, they will only answer that they see no necessity why Mr. Harris or Mr. Kemble should grow immensely rich, or why that grave actor should be so pathetic upon his necessities, when he carries hundreds of pounds on his back in *Macbeth,* and has the face to make pitiful bows to the poor fellows cooped up in the galleries.

[THE O.P. RIOTS AND COVENT-GARDEN]

November 19, 1809   *Covent-Garden*

THERE HAS BEEN nothing material for criticism during the past week; [1] and I willingly turn to a subject which demands the attention of every friend of humanity and good morals. The impolite and brutal conduct of the Managers of this Theatre has reached its climax. It is impossible that the public should ever forget the time, when to go to the play was to endanger one's liberty and very life. To seizures and skirmishes has now succeeded an unmixed brutality on the part of the retainers. These men, consisting of the lowest ruffians collected from every pot-house about the place, enter the pit with avowed purposes of malice, some of them with their sticks furnished with spikes; the company are wounded in the face, have their hands run through, and are trodden down beneath the feet of the wretches; and finally, one gentleman of the name of Cowlam, who neither hissed nor wore a placard, but had brought an action against one of the Manager's friends, was assaulted on Wednesday last by a particular gang, and malignantly thrown down and trampled upon in such a manner that he has been confined to an excruciating bed in danger of his life. When people hear of these proceedings, they know not what to think of the apparent apathy of the Lord Chamberlain. With regard to the prices of admission, there are certainly many persons who upon their own calculations, and out of regard for the Theatre, are willing to allow the rise; but nobody who converses on the subject, whether for or against the Manager in this respect, looks upon the theatrical statement as anything but a list of mere *assertions,* which, in stating only a vague expenditure, and not its *causes* or *items,* have no pretence whatever to determine the question. With regard to. the private boxes, I have heard but one opinion even from those who are disposed to allow the new prices; and with respect to the policy and brutality of the Managers, everybody unites in laughing at the one and execrating the other. The private boxes are certainly the most obnoxious part of the whole managerial alterations; the lovers of the Theatre are not, generally speaking, of a temper to begrudge the advance of sixpence or a shilling, abstracted from any imposition; and even in the latter case, time, and good-nature, and indolence, and perhaps the proverbial credulity of Englishmen, might have given the matter up; but a whole circle of the Theatre taken from them to make privacies for the luxurious great is a novelty so offensive to the national habits, both on account of its contemptuous exclusions, and the ideas of accommodation it so naturally excites, that the Managers, granting that they suffer a great loss, deserve to suffer still more for their mercenary and obsequious encouragement of pride and profligacy. In truth, there is not the shadow of a pretence for this foreign piece of indulgence. In Spain, people may want to smoke and drink coffee; and in Italy, they may have such places for a thousand purposes of abandonment; but in an English Theatre, the only object is, or ought to be, to see the play; and plays are seen much better in an open box than behind the best wall in Europe. "Oh," say the Managers, "but the Ladies and Gentlemen can refresh themselves between the acts." Can they indeed? But so they could, as well as the rest, in open boxes; and what kind of refreshment can people want, who dine at five or six, drink their coffee directly, and then go to the Theatre to sit upon easy cushions? "Oh, but they may be ill." Then let them stay at home. "Oh, but they may be *taken* ill." Then let them be taken home. "Oh, but if a new play happen to be dull, they can retire a-while." Really! They can retire a-while, if the play happen to be dull! Delicate and dignified souls! The rest of the boxes must sit still and wait patiently for their seven shillings worth of common-sense, and probably not hear it after all, while these nice-judging and nice-feeling personages are to draw in their horns and retire a-while! And to what purpose are they to retire? *At best*, to lounge, and trifle with a jelly, and drawl a little with Mr. SK—G—A—EFINGTON,[2] and talk nonsense instead of hearing it:—but these are not the innocent amusements of *all* the great persons who lounge at Theatres, and who come there to get rid of the fumes of wine, to idle about after idle acquaintances, and to *intrigue!* These persons will take advantage of every facility offered them; they themselves will enjoy the Private Boxes and introduce of course whom they please. Could there possibly be easier opportunities for the whole progress of seduction and sensuality—for vanquishing the weak, and rioting with the abandoned? Ovid, in the depravity of his heart, takes great pains to teach the art of making love at Theatres; but had he addressed himself to Private Boxes, he would have needed but a word or two. "Oh," cry the Managers, "but really the thing is mistaken: the Private Boxes are to accommodate—they are certainly to accommodate—but they are for none of the vile uses you mention!" Are they not? Then the answer is plain: Do away with them entirely—they have no use at all if they have no such uses; and if they have, they are a thousand times worse than useless.

[THE CONSCIOUS LOVERS]

January 21, 1810   *Covent-Garden*

STEELE's *Conscious Lovers,* the best sentimental comedy
in the language, was performed here on Tuesday,[1] and went off
with as much effect as such comedies can produce in such an
age. The taste of the town must be gradually led round from
the buffoonery in which it has so long been exercised, before
it can relish the delicate character and graceful sentiment of
our purer dramatists. We have been like those unfortunate
youths, who having got among frivolous acquaintances, place
all their enjoyment and idea of social wit in horselaughter and
a certain noisy nonsense, removed from all that is elegant, rational, and respectable. In this condition, if any true enjoyment
or thinking approaches us, it is not only unseasonable to the
taste, but acts upon the conscious feeling like a reproof and
is petulantly resisted. If the town, however, is not yet converted to a proper estimation of the drama, if it yet suffers itself
to be cajoled, for a few evenings at a time, by a broad and bald-
headed Muse, whose whole charm consists in being ridiculous,
it has nevertheless acquired judgment enough to condemn what
it has not yet destroyed; the huge short-lived farces may still
raise laughter among the better part of the audience, but at
least half of the acknowledgment is due to contempt, and at
every stale joke a good-humoured groan goes round among the
wits. Few persons, even among those who consent to be amused
by these productions, are so hardy as to give any serious praise
to the modern farci-comic writers; Messrs. Dibdin, Reynolds,
and Cobb [2] have become what even their plays cannot hope to
be, a standing jest; and what with the late mischances and disputes that have roused the public attention to theatrical matters, the town is just now in that temper which by a few seasonable endeavours may probably do much for the restoration
of the public drama. Of this more in my next.

To witness the *Conscious Lovers,* after being pestered with all the *new* nonsense at the Lyceum, is like going out of a tavern-cellar into an elegant company. Taste and improvement breathe again: you have a respect for yourself and your society; and are prepared once more to venerate the use and beauty of social dialogue. The play is not remarkable either for strong writing or for wit; but its best scenes are in a charming strain of un-affected knowledge, the sentiments as delicate as rational, and the insights into human nature of that nice and feeling discrimi-nation which is the first characteristic of Steele's writings. It is this talent, exemplified throughout the *Tatler* and *Spectator* in so many nice varieties of character and so many touches of pathos exquisitely careless, which certainly gives him the palm of invention in those admirable works, though his genius has been overpowered by the wit and the more dignified wisdom of Addison. The characters of the play are kept up with truth and pleasing contrast to the last—the gentlemanly authority of *Sir John Bevil* and the less prejudiced plain sense of *Mr. Sealand,* who had seen the world—the accomplished sensibility of *Indiana* and the freer though innocent spirit of *Lucinda*—the young coxcomb servant of *Bevil,* and the old staid servant of his father—and lastly, the high gentlemanly rationality and pure manliness of *Bevil* opposed to the intemperate enthusiasm of his friend *Myrtle.* The challenge-scene between these two gentlemen is well known to everybody from childhood, and is one of the best practical arguments that ever were furnished against duelling, since the person challenged has at the same time warmth enough to be worked into momentary provocation, yet philosophy enough to conquer by explanation. It was a delicate point to shew the hero of a play withstanding a chal-lenge and at the same time preserving his character with the audience, and yet this is what Steele has done by the mere force of his hero's solid consistency of character. If we except the coarse character of *Cimberton,* into whose mouth, as satirists are too apt to do, the author put more than was needed, all the scenes are of a piece with this instruction, not omitting the playful follies of *Mr. Tom* and *Mrs. Phillis,* who shew us in what rank of life the coxcomb and flippant coquet ought to be found. The translations of this comedy sufficiently prove its estimation on the Continent, where the imitation of Terence and of nature is still reckoned a mark of taste, and the modern English drama is known only to be despised.

It is not easy to conceive a better *Bevil* than Mr. C. Kemble.[3] His gentlemanly air and elegant composure seem peculiarly fitted for this naturalized *Grandison*. He felt the part to be worthy of his best exertion, and never suffered his manner to degenerate into the languor which he has been too apt to indulge. Mrs. C. Kemble,[4] with her broad coquetry and strong feeling of caricature, was quite at home, to use a newspaper phrase, in the vivacious lady's maid; and Mr. Jones,[5] who in higher characters has too much flippancy to settle himself into the *real* gentleman, was equally *au fait* in *Tom*, whose tripping volubility and affectation could not have found so good a representative on the stage, especially when it is considered that to a face quite as vacant as Mr. De Camp's, Mr. Jones adds a much neater person and a tone more naturally familiar. In that humourous passage in which he describes his first amorous interview with *Mrs. Phillis*, when they were employed to clean the two sides of a window, he would produce perhaps a more humourous effect were he to make a longer and more amiable pause before the last sentence—"when my lips approached— a dirty cloth you rubbed against my face, and hid your beauteous form: when I again drew near, you spit, and rubbed, and—— *smiled at my undoing.*"

[KING JOHN]

IF MR. KEMBLE has not succeeded Garrick in all tragic excellence, as some of his admirers pretend, he has worthily succeeded him in one important respect, that of loving Shakspeare and keeping him before the public.[1] The other Managers of the present day have so little taste, with the exception of Sheridan who cares for no taste but that of port, that were it not for Mr. Kemble's exertions the tragedies of our glorious bard would almost be in danger of dismissal from the stage; and it does him infinite credit to have persevered in his exertions in spite of comparatively thin houses; to have added to the attractions of his poet by a splendour of scene as seasonable as well-deserved; and to have evinced so noble an attachment, and helped to keep up so noble a taste, in an age of mawkishness and buffoonery. It is in this spirit that Mr. Kemble continues to draw from Shakspeare a kind of stock play for the season, which is performed regularly once a week, as he has done with *Macbeth, Hamlet,* and *K. Henry the Eighth,* and is now doing again with *King John.*

"The tragedy of *King John,*" says Johnson, "though not written with the utmost power of Shakspeare, is varied with a very pleasing interchange of incidents and characters. The lady's grief is very affecting; and the character of the *Bastard* contains that mixture of greatness and levity which this author delighted to exhibit."[2] These remarks are sufficiently concise, and in the usual spirit of the Doctor's criticism, consisting of assertions very well founded, but careless of all proof. But even in so compendious a stricture, something might have been said of the pathetic scene between *Arthur* and *Hubert,* and of the fine contrast between the pusillanimous, selfish *John,* and the undaunted, disinterested *Bastard.* The *Bastard,* with his lively spirit breaking out in familiar phrase through the general majesty, is one of those characters in Shakspeare to which the critics object as unworthy of tragic dignity; but familiarity is unworthy of dignity only when it implies meanness of character and habit, not when it implies generosity of feeling. The *Bastard's* familiarity, so far from being little in itself, is the result of a noble disdain of what is little; and corrected as it is by his natural dignity it even adds to that dignity by taking from it all theatrical stiffness, and giving an air of ease and indifference to his noblest actions. The tragedy of *King John* is certainly "not written with the utmost power of Shakspeare," because the utmost power of the poet's wisdom and imagination was not called into play by the nature of the story; [3] but it contains all that is adequate to a just and delicate discrimination of character, and perhaps there is no play of Shakspeare, taken altogether, which exhibits so equable and so elegant a flow of versification.

The *Constance* of Mrs. Siddons is an excellent study for young actresses, to whom it will shew the great though difficult distinction between rant and tragic vehemence. In an inferior performer, the loudness of *Constance's* grief would be mere noise; but tempered and broken as it is by the natural looks and gestures of Mrs. Siddons, by her varieties of tone and pauses full of meaning, it becomes as grand as it is petrifying. Mr. Kemble's *King John*, with its theatrical tone of dignity and its mixture of confidence and whining, is one of his happiest performances: [4] in the scene with *Hubert* he displays much knowledge of effect, and has in particular one excellent expression of the mouth, which, while he is anxiously looking for *Hubert's* reply to his dark hints, is breathlessly opened and gently dropped at the corners; but there is too much pantomimic rolling of the eyes. Charles Kemble, always elegant, with a chivalrous air, and possessing a strong taste for contemptuous irony, is as complete a *Faulconbridge* as one can desire. The effect of this and other tragedies of Shakspeare must give Mr. Kemble great satisfaction. Every person, indeed, who has a regard for the spirit and dignity of his country's literature must be gratified to see that these endeavours, founded on so just an enthusiasm, are properly rising in the public estimation. The audience assembled at *King John* last Monday was as numerous and attentive as it was respectable, and you saw what you ought to see in an English Theatre—an excellent drama properly performed and properly appreciated.

[TWELFTH NIGHT]

March 3, 1811   *Covent-Garden*

OF THE NUMEROUS REVIVALS of late, which do so much credit to Mr. Kemble, the principal have been Shakspeare's *Twelfth Night*, Jonson's *Every Man in His Humour*, Massinger's *New Way to Pay Old Debts*, and Addison's *Cato*.[1] These and other future revivals that present anything new for criticism, either in play or performance, will no longer miss their regular notice from the *Examiner*, in the absence of what is called greater novelty. Why this notice has been interrupted, it is needless to explain, as the cause has been altogether temporary and of a nature foreign to the public and the subject. Such of my readers, however, as have done me the honour of expressing their regret on the occasion, will have the goodness to recollect, at the same time, that the term *revival* is often a catch-word applied by the Managers to pieces that have lain dormant but one or two seasons; and that to criticise every thing that reappears, would be sometimes a spiritless or useless repetition.

Twelfth Night, though it has passages of exquisite delicacy, and two scenes of irresistible humour, is perhaps the last in rank of Shakspeare's more popular dramas. It is inferior to the *Falstaff* pieces in invention, to *Much Ado about Nothing* in wit and interest, and to the *Taming of the Shrew* in effect and completeness of design. Dr. Johnson very justly observes that the character of *Ague-cheek* though "drawn with great propriety" is "in a great measure that of natural fatuity, and therefore not the proper prey of a satirist." [2] Such fatuity however seems to have been a favourite object of ridicule with all the dramatists of that age, owing probably to the abundance of gentlemen with small fortunes, who, not receiving the education common in succeeding times, were uninitiated in the art of concealing ignorance by a well-bred common-place. *Malvolio*, who may have been intended for a contrast to *Ague-cheek*, as opposing a grave and reasoning folly to the grinning idiocy of the other,

is the origin of the sober coxcombs that have since abounded
on the English stage. His anticipation of future dignity, and
of the majestic insults which he intends to deal round him, is
evidently to be traced to that excellent apologue which, from
the Glass-merchant of the Arabian tale to the Milk-maid of our
story-books, has been the delight and instruction of all ages.
The most novel, though by no means the most prepossessing
character in the play, seems to be that of *Sir Toby Belch,* who
is a mere knavish sot; and is only preserved from our contempt
by contrast with his tool *Ague-cheek,* whose excessive stupidity
gives the other an air of sense and even of a taste for irony. The
scene of midnight riot, where *Sir Toby, Sir Andrew,* and the
Clown are in vain interrupted by the entrance and admonitions
of *Malvolio,* whose gravity is at once shocked by their incon-
tinence and mortified by their contempt of him, is one of the
completest pictures ever drawn of the recklessness of a stupid
debauchery; and is sure to convulse the spectators with laughter.
The contrast, presented to these scenes and characters of low
vice by the delicate mind and elegant language of *Viola,* is very
lively and refreshing. It is only a pity that the elegant part of this
drama is inferior to the coarse in point of probability. *Viola's*
patient devotion for the Duke is interesting, particularly as he
is not aware of it; and there is something extremely touching and
gratifying, not only in viewing the disinterestedness with which
she pleads his cause to *Olivia,* but still more so in anticipating
the amends she is to make him for the latter's disdain. But the
disguise of women in male attire, though it continues, and is
likely to continue, welcome in the spectators from causes unconnected with dramatic decorum, always strikes one as a gross
violation of probability, especially if represented as accompanied with delicacy of mind. In Shakspeare's time, when there
were no female performers, the personal absurdity was avoided;
and this circumstance probably gave rise, in other nations as
well as ours, to the fondness for representing women as boys and
pages. It may also have encouraged, and in some measure less-
ened, the still greater absurdity of bringing together two persons perfectly resembling each other, as in the play before us,

and in the *Comedy of Errors*—a trick however, which it is impossible to render complete without resorting to the masks of the ancient stage. In our own times, it could hardly be rendered bearable, even by selecting counterparts of equal size and general appearance; but when the managers of Covent-Garden present us with Mr. Brunton as the facsimile of a delicate little lady, shorter at least by the head and shoulders, they bring the absurdity to its climax: Mr. Brunton, in spite of his effeminate air and voice, becomes by the contrast a rough and sturdy gallant; and nothing can be more ridiculous than to see the persons on the stage affecting an *unaffected* astonishment at the double likeness, and exclaiming,

> An apple, cleft in two, is not more twin
> Than these two creatures! [3]

With the exception of the distaste caused by these aggravated inconsistencies, the Comedy goes off with some spirit, though certainly not well performed upon the whole. Miss Booth's [4] representation of *Viola* is touchingly correct—feminine, feeling, intelligent. The modesty of her dress is suitable to the delicacy of the character; and the breathless timidity she exhibits in her forced duel with *Ague-cheek* is nicely discriminated, on the one hand, from a powerful expression, unsuitable to a delicate female, and on the other, from a comic extravagance, unnatural to such a person actually suffering. Mr. Blanchard's [5] *Ague-cheek* is deservedly applauded for the impotence of its gaiety and the utter weakness of its pretence, in every respect. Perhaps the best touches in his performance are the extravagant and at the same time feeble bursts of laughter with which he acknowledges the clown's bon mots. But the part of a simpleton, having little thought to express and scarcely any variety to put in action, is no great trial of comic power. It is well known that there is scarcely an actor, serious or comic, of any powers of expression, who cannot imitate an idiot. Mrs. C. Kemble [6] in *Olivia*, and Mr. Emery [7] in *Sir Toby*, must, I am afraid, be content on this occasion with the old newspaper praise of being respectable. The clown of Fawcett is not unentertaining, but it wants quaintness, and a greater affectation of humility in the midst of its insolence. *Duke Orsino* is represented by Mr. Barrymore,[8] formerly of Drury-Lane Theatre, who, after some years absence from a company in which he is wanted, has returned to the metropolis and been engaged in one that has no need of him. His parts were already sustained, with at least equal merit, by Mr. Egerton,[9] who, if he has not so tragic an air, can hardly be denied more judgment. Mr. Barrymore has a good and powerful voice, an imposing step, and a face which, though not handsome or dignified, is by no means deficient in intelligence; but his enunciation is snappish in the very midst of its pompousness; his manner at all times theatrical; and in short, he has little or no variety, either in tone, look, or gesture. His delivery of the exquisite lines that open the play,

If music be the food of love, play on, &c. &c.

was like that of a mouthing schoolmaster hastening to finish the passage that he might proceed to lecture upon it—that is to say, upon what he neither feels nor understands. The orchestra were in excellent accompaniment; and when the Duke called for "that strain again," because "it had a dying fall," gave it with as much indifference, and with as little of the *dying* in it, as if they thought his Highness was joking.

[BLUE BEARD]

March 24, 1811   *Covent-Garden*

MR. COLMAN's melodrama of *Blue Beard*,[1] one of those
wretched compounds of pun and parade, which serve to amuse
the great babies of this town and to frighten the less, still forms
the nightly boast of this "classical" theatre.[2] With the jokes
about troopers *trooping* off, and persons unable to keep a secret
because their teeth *chatter,* the reader is no doubt well acquainted, and quite willing, I trust, to have no further acquaintance; and it is needless to point out the gross want of costume
[*sic*] which the author has manifested from beginning to end,
not only in the incidents, but in the language and the habits of
thinking. In one of the songs a Turkish girl is made to talk of her
lover's "ringlets," which said lover, agreeably to truth, is represented on the stage with a turban and no hair at all. But the
stage is not so judiciously inconsistent in other parts of the
story; and it has been well remarked in the *Times* that the introduction of paintings in a room is contrary to the religion as well
as customs of the Mahometans. It may be observed, in fine, that
the story has not even the usual moral of childish tales: there is,
it is true, the "punishment of curiosity," and the curiosity may
be a wrong one; but the excitation of it is at the same time
wanton, the discovery it makes hurtful to the infant spectator,
and the punishment itself unjust. The production indeed is
unworthy of criticism, and would not have been noticed in this
paper but for a singular novelty that has lately been added to
the representation. That actors should make beasts of themselves is no new thing; but the *gravis Esopus* of our Stage, Mr.
Kemble, must turn beasts into actors; and accordingly, after
having had dog actors at Drury-Lane, and jack-ass actors (em-
blematic wags!) at Sadler's Wells, we are now presented with
horse actors at "classical" Covent-Garden. These prepossessing
palfreys [3] appear to be about twenty in number, and come
prancing on the Stage into rank and file with as much orderliness

as their brethren at the Horse Guards, facing directly to the spectators, and treating them with a few preparatory curvettings, indicative of ardour, so that when the riders draw their swords, the appearance is not a little formidable, and seems to threaten a charge into the pit. After this, and a few picturesque gallopings over a bridge, they do not appear till the last scene, when all their powers are put forth, and *Blue Beard* and his myrmidons utterly eclipsed. Firstly, the aforesaid gallopings are repeated over mound and bridge, till every steed has reappeared often enough to represent ten or a dozen others; then one or two of them get interestingly entangled in a crowd; then a drawbridge, breaking down, is scaled by three or four at full gallop, which calls down the thunder of the galleries; then a duel ensues between a couple of the horsemen, of whose desperate blows the reader may have a lively idea if he has ever seen the impassioned images that tap the hour on Saint Dustan's. The excessive politeness, indeed, manifested by these duellists, and the delicate attention they pay to each other's convenience, reminds one of the celebrated battle of Fontenoy, where the officers of the French and English guards, coming together, pulled off their hats to each other and mutually insisted upon giving up the honour of the first fire. The only difference is that the consistency of the thing, the *qualis ab incepto,* was not so well kept up in the latter instance. Lastly, comes the grand display, the dying scene; and here it is difficult to say which is more worthy of admiration, the sensibility or science of these accomplished quadrupeds. When I saw them, there seemed to be but three who performed this part of the ceremony, and it may safely be asserted, that never did horses die with so much resignation. If I knew their names (let us suppose they are *Twitcher, Twirler,* and *Whitenose*), I should say that *Twitcher* and *Twirler,* who were parties in the duel, had most emulation, and *Whitenose* most coolness. The two former seemed to be aware that they were in battle; the latter manifested an indifference to his situation, almost amounting to disdain. *Twitcher* and his antagonist were, if I may so speak, about the pitch of Brunton and Claremont, easy but majestic, and amiably severe; but the presence of mind displayed by *Whitenose* was equal, at least, to that of Laston. Lord Grizzle himself, in his dying moments,[4] could not surpass his philosophic preparation and finished demise. While the other two were occupied with their own rencontre, he entered the stage with as much indifference as if nothing had happened, though it was soon evident that he had received his mortal wound, for after a little meditation he began to die, bending his knees one after the other, like a camel stooping to be loaded, and then turning upon his side and becoming motionless, just as a human actor does upon his back. The other horses, by this time, are disposed also in their respective attitudes; the dismounted warriors are seen fighting across their bodies; drums, trumpets, smoke, and confusion complete the effect; and the close of the scene lets loose a thousand exclamations in praise of the new performers.

Joking apart, it is no doubt interesting to see of what so noble an animal as the horse is capable; and it is still more agreeable to be relieved from those miserable imitations of him, which come beating time on the Stage with human feet, and with their hind knees the wrong way. If it were possible to present the public with such exhibitions and at the same time to cherish a proper taste for the Drama, they might even be hailed as a genuine improvement in representation; for if men, and not puppets, act men, there seems to be no dramatic reason why horses should not act horses. But there are always two very strong objections, staring this kind of novelty in the face—one respecting the public taste, and the other the poor beasts themselves. The success of such exhibitions is not only allowed to be a mark of corrupted taste with regard to better things, but it materially helps to produce that corruption. They are too powerful a stimulus to the senses of the common order of spectators, and take away from their eyes and ears all relish for more delicate entertainment. The managers and the public thus corrupt each other; but it is the former who begin the infection by build-

ing these enormous theatres in which a great part of the spectators must have noise and shew before they can hear or see what
is going forwards. In time these spectators learn to like nothing
else; and then the managers must administer to their depraved
appetite, or they cannot get rich. Are these the persons to cry
out against the erection of a new and smaller theatre?

But the animals themselves are to be considered, with regard to *their* comfort. A sprightly horse has a profusion of graceful and active movements; and it is his nature perhaps to be
fond of a certain kind of exertion. He delights, when in health
and vigour, in scouring the fields; and feels, we are told, an
emulous ardour in the race; but then the fields and the race-
ground are proper places for him; the turf incites him to activity,
and the open air breathes health and pleasure into his veins.
On the other hand, it will take a great deal to persuade a rational
spectator at the theatre that the closeness of a stage, the running
round and round, the bending of knees, the driving up steep
boards, and above all, the mimicry of absolute death, do not
give the animal considerable pain, and have not cost a hundred
times as much in the training. It is a common observation respecting these horses at Covent-Garden, that in galloping about
the stage, they exhibit a manifest constraint and timidity; and
when they pretend to come in at full speed, have a jumping
and feeble motion resembling that of rabbits. We all know by
what merciless practices bears and camels are taught to dance;
and anybody who has been at a country fair and seen the
wretched mode in which dogs and birds are worried through
their feats will be slow to believe that the docility necessary for
such purposes is obtained by good usage. The Arabs, it is true,
and other nations, whose uncivilized state brings the animal
and his master into familiarity from their birth, can teach their
horses to perform a thousand surprising feats with no other
means than habit and kind treatment; but this is a very different case; the sphere of action is different, and the animal is
put upon no other action than it is natural and pleasant to him
to perform. The Managers of Covent-Garden should know that
what is said by many, and thought by most people, of the train-

ing of these horses, is not favourable to the humanity of their masters; and till there is some explicit statement on the subject it will be as difficult to think otherwise as it is impossible to applaud their introduction at all.

[QUADRUPEDS]

July 21, 1811   *English Opera, Lyceum*

THE PROPRIETORS of Covent-Garden Theatre have learnt by this time how completely they overshot their mark in building that overgrown edifice [1]—overgrown, not because it is too large to be externally an ornament to the metropolis, for nobody will deny its claims in that point of view, but because it is fully ascertained that such large theatres are not fit for a delicate and just representation of the drama, and that they inevitably lead to the substitution of shew for sense.[2] It is in vain therefore that they effect, as I understand, to throw the blame of their spectacles and hippodramas upon the vitiated state of the public taste. It was the vitiated state of their own wants that induced them to grasp at profit in this manner; and, if the taste of the town was bad enough not to relish even Shakspeare where Shakspeare was not to be seen or heard, they begin to find, nevertheless, that it is still good enough not to be fond of the extreme to which they have lately run; and that it does not follow people must like to see bad things, because they cannot see good ones. Mr. Kemble, therefore, in violating his promises so grossly respecting the "classical" stage of which he told us, has justly subjected both himself and his splendid theatre to ridicule; and it must be not one of his least mortifications to see the lesser theatres joining in the general scorn, and perfectly warranted in so doing by their own more respectable exertions.

A piece, engrafted on this subject, called *Quadrupeds*, or *The Manager's Last Kick*, was brought forward at the Lyceum on Thursday night; and the Haymarket has another in preparation, which is to appear to-morrow. The former is a revival of the burlesque tragedy of the *Tailors*,[3] introduced by a scene between the manager and his creditors, to whom he announces his intention of bringing quadrupeds on his stage by way of forlorn hope, in order to be enabled to bear up against the increasing losses occasioned him by similar exhibitions on the part of a rival theatre. This piece, which was written, I believe, not by Foote, as the prelude tells us, but by an anonymous correspondent of his, is a burlesque account of a dispute between the master tailors and their journeymen, which terminates in a general battle; and this battle is made a good vehicle for the introduction of mules, zebras, and asses, on which the respective champions are mounted. Taken altogether, the original is not a happy production: the language will run with real seriousness for lines together, humourous only by reference to the look and dress of the actors; and when the humour does come, it is abrupt and at long intervals: in short, it is not the coat that is humourous, but the patches; and this is very different from true and entire burlesque; so that there is internal evidence that the piece was not written by so excellent a master of drollery as Foote.

It is not much to say of the performers in general, that they act up to the faults of their original, and mistake a flat abruptness for quaintness. Mr. Raymond, who performs the journeyman hero, seems to have no notion of burlesque, and is only noisy; the only actor in the piece, who seems properly to understand the contrast of vulgarity with affected dignity, is Mr. Lovegrove,[4] whose portrait of the master hero has considerable finish of touch. The songs introduced are better written than might be expected, and well adapted to jovial or vulgar tunes; but the crown of all is unquestionably the battle scene, which affords a good and palpable ridicule of the Kemble horses, and with its kickings, chatterings, and ragged warriors, pommelling each other in all directions, looks like Hogarth's picture of the battle of *Hudibras*, brought into life.

[M.P.; OR, THE BLUE STOCKING]

September 15, 1811   English Opera, Lyceum

THE DEGRADED CONDITION of the modern drama has long been a matter of ridicule, regret, or contempt, as the passing feeling predominated; [1] the Shadwells and Durfeys [2] were really dishonoured by a comparison with writers of no acquirements whatsoever, their mother-tongue not excepted; and what seemed to render the thing hopeless was that, as soon as any of the elder brethren gave symptoms of retreat, their places were supplied by a set of undaunted younglings, of the true family vulgarity, who began displaying the same nonentities. The only consolation that could be drawn from such appearances was to indulge a patient hope that, as the whole race were quite a class of themselves, and were to be considered rather as the vermin of untenanted houses than as the natural and human occupiers, the first writer of a different description who should present himself would put them to the rout by the admission of a little light, and take quiet and honourable possession of the premises. When it was understood, therefore, that an Opera was forthcoming from the pen of Mr. Moore, a general anticipation was excited, as natural as it was lively. People did not stop to inquire whether his general style of writing rendered his dramatic success probable; it was enough that he was a man of genius, a being to whom the dramà had been a stranger for years,[3] and the town was delighted at once. It is true, an Afterpiece of his is said to have failed at the Haymarket formerly, but the fact was little known, and less heeded: it happened a long time back; and the public had since known the author as one of the most accomplished men of his time, one too who had lately shewn that he could get rid of more dangerous habits [4] than bad joking, so that they expected everything that was refreshing and reputable. Accustomed so long indeed to language without grammar, sentiment without common sense, and song without even rhyme, what was it that they had not *a right* to expect from a scholar, a man of wit, and a poet? Nothing less certainly than a solid, if not successful, contrast to the flimsy manufacturers of the stage. This then was what they did expect, and most confidently; the frequenters of the theatre were all impatience, and the critics prepared to be all gratitude. The promised Monday arrives; the house is filled; expectant congratulation runs from bench to bench; the most rigid and critical faces thaw in the general smile; the overture begins—why is it not over?—the curtain rises, the actors come forward, and lo, instead of an opera worthy of its poet, a farce in three acts of the old complexion! A string of common-places, the more unsightly from the few pearls mingled with them! An unambitious, undignified, and most unworthy compilation of pun, equivoque, and clap-trap!

The scene of *M. P., or The Blue Stocking,* is laid at a watering-place and the principal incidents of the story are such as may be found in most places of the kind that possess a library. *Sir Charles Canvas* (Oxberry),[5] a Baronet and M. P. not content with having usurped his title from an elder brother (Horn) [6] who was born before their mother's marriage was publicly acknowledged, is endeavouring to deprive him of the affections of a rich heiress of the name of *Selwyn* (Mrs. Mountain),[7] and takes advantage of his absence at sea to pay her his addresses for that purpose. His foppery, senatorial egotism, and pride of his title induce him to believe that he is succeeding, when unfortunately he happens to encounter an emigrant family consisting of a *Madame de Rosier* (Mrs. Hamilton) and her son *Henry* (Philipps),[8] who from the rank of a nobleman is reduced by the Revolution to become assistant at a circulating library. The lady, though not aware of his being a second son, had been acquainted with his mother in France, and is in possession, he finds, of a disagreeable secret affecting his right to the Baronetcy. He frightens her therefore with a threat of sending *De Rosier* out of the kingdom as an alien, and only relinquishes what he represents as an act of duty, by exacting from her a promise of secrecy respecting his mother's marriage on the Continent. All then appears safe for the present, but in the meantime his brother, *Captain Canvas,* returns from sea, and he thinks himself under the necessity of securing the French lady by bribes as well as threats, and of inducing her to get entirely out of the way. In procuring an agent for the execution of this design, he fixes unluckily upon an old man (Raymond), who by his ragged appearance seems a fit person for temptation, and who, in order to stimulate his exertions in getting rid of the lady, is just made acquainted with enough of the Baronet's feelings to discover that the latter is in his power. Accordingly, the old gentleman, who in spite of appearing like a common beggar is in reality (sly rogue!) a wealthy philanthropist in disguise, and who takes advantage of his ragged elbows and sordid hat to relieve distressed worthies who give him luncheons, hastens to make the best use of his secret; *Sir Charles* finally loses his title as well as his mistress; and *De Rosier* is blessed with the hand of the old gentleman's daughter, *Miss Hartington* (Miss Kelly) [9] who had been faithful to him in all his misfortunes. There is evidently nothing in this story which surpasses the invention of one of our common dramatists, and the characters do not put it to the blush. Those above-mentioned are of an ancient order of personages; and so are two others, who have not a jot to do with the story, the library-keeper (Lovegrove) and a chemical pedant in petticoats (Mrs. Sparks). Of the humour it is quite lamentable to think, after the touches of real pleasantry and wit that are to be found in the author's works. One of the main buttresses of the piece is a scene between the two personages just mentioned, in which they keep up a long equivoque founded on the meanings which they respectively attach to the words *Sal Ammonia,* the lady talking of the heroine of a chemical poem on the Darwinian plan, which she wishes the librarian to publish, and the librarian, in consequence of mistaking a letter of hers, flattering himself that she is offering him the hand of her niece in marriage. There is also a great deal of a well-established sort of wit, something between equivoque and pun, which is founded on the application of the titles of books to particular characters or circumstances. Puns also are abundant, in all their naked dignity, the chief language of the M.P. consisting in

applying technical parliamentary phrases to the common oc-
currences before him; and as to clap-traps, if there are not
many, the few are not calculated to make us regret the deficiency.
One of them deserves particular mention, an account of a charge
to which it has subjected the author, certainly, I think, without foundation. In one part of the piece, a horse-race is supposed
to take place behind the scenes, and a spectator rushing forward, announces that the noble horse Regent is about to start,
and "promises a *glorious race.*" For this clap-trap, he has been
accused of a courtly servility; but from the free tone of his
political writings, and even of the other political allusions in
the Opera itself, there is not the least reason to consider it in
any other light than as an adoption of a common stage trick,
quite unworthy indeed of Mr. Moore, both as a politician and
a writer, but not affecting, I am persuaded, the general and
practical independence of his spirit. With regard to the language,
considered in its composition and sentiment, it is certainly not
what the Dibdins and the Cherrys [10] could write; and it has
two or three real touches of wit, which rank it at once high above
the reach of their vulgar hands: but wherever it is serious, it is
too florid; it is not good, unaffected, characteristic language, and
seems to be decisive against the author's turn for the drama.
The only part in which the hand of Mr. Moore can be said to be
truly visible is in the songs—not in many of them indeed, for
a general disease of common-place seems to have seized him in
approaching the Theatre, and several of the serious ones, as
well as *all* the humourous, are not above the pitch of Mr. Colman; but still there is enough of elegance and of poetry to
awaken all our regret at the company in which they are found;
and for the very first time, I believe, since the appearance of this
paper, our readers may be gratified by seeing one or two songs
extracted in it from a modern opera. The idea of the following is
a favorite with Mr. Moore, and is touched with his usual good
keeping:

Miss Hartington (Miss Kelly)
> When Leila touch'd the lute,
> Not then alone 'twas felt,

But, when the sounds were mute,
    In memory still they dwelt.
Sweet Lute! in nightly slumbers
Still we heard thy morning numbers.

Ah! how could she, who stole
    Such breath from simple wire,
Be led, in pride of soul,
    To string with gold her lyre?
Sweet Lute! thy chords she breaketh!
Golden now the strings she waketh!

But where are all the tales
    Her lute so sweetly told?
In lofty themes she fails,
And soft ones suit not gold.
Rich Lute! we see thee glisten,
But, alas! no more we listen!

The next is a pretty allegorical amplification of the common proverb—When Poverty comes in at the door, Love flies out at the window. I have ventured to point out the lines that most please me in these extracts by putting them in italics.

Susan (Mrs. Bland)

Young Love liv'd once in an humble shed,
    Where roses breathing,
    And woodbines wreathing
Around the lattice their tendrils spread,
As wild and sweet as the life he led.
    His garden flourish'd,
    For young Hope nourished
The infant buds with beams and showers;
But lips, tho' blooming, must still be fed,
    And not even Love can live on flowers.

Alas! that Poverty's evil eye
    Should e'er come hither,
    Such sweets to wither!
The flowers laid down their heads to die,
And Hope fell sick, as the witch drew nigh.
    She came one morning,
    Ere Love had warning,

And rais'd the latch, where the young god lay;
"Oh ho!" said Love—"is it you? good bye";
So he oped the window, and flew away!

The lines beginning, "Dear Aunt, in the olden time of love,"
have a touch of wit in each stanza; those with the burthen "Oh,
Woman," are fluent, and finish well; and "Oh think, when a
hero is sighing," has the sweetness and the swell of the trumpet
which it describes. All these, and the last in particular, should
be quoted, if the paper had room; but I must content myself
and conclude with the following, which notwithstanding the
quaintness of *entwineth* and *shineth*, and the confusion of metaphor in the third line, is highly spirited, and has naturally been
admired from its subject.

De Rosier (Mr. Phillips)
            Tho' sacred the tie that our country entwineth,
                And dear to the heart her remembrance remains,
            Yet dark are the ties where no liberty shineth,
                And sad the remembrance that slavery stains,
            O thou! who wert born in the cot of the peasant,
                But diest of languor in Luxury's dome,
            Our vision, when absent—our glory, when present,—
                Where thou art, O Liberty! there is my home.

            Farewell to the land where in childhood I wander'd!
                In vain is she mighty, in vain is she brave!
            Unblest is the blood that for tyrants is squander'd,
                And Fame has no wreaths for the brow of the slave.
            But hail to thee, Albion! who meet'st the commotion
                Of Europe, as calm as thy cliffs meet the foam;
            With no bonds but the law, and no slave but the ocean,
                Hail, Temple of Liberty! thou art my home.

Such are the beauties and the defects of a piece which so
raised and has so disappointed expectation—the beauties much
superior indeed to those of common operas, but far from being
among the happiest efforts of the author, the defects precisely
of the poor quality of those operas and utterly unworthy of
him. That Mr. Moore himself thinks well of it, nobody who is
acquainted with his real powers could suppose for an instant;

and that nobody else may suppose otherwise, he has not scrupled to say so in the following letter, which appeared in the *Sun* the other evening:—

To the Editor of the *Sun*

Sir,—In the account which you have given in your last paper, of the Musical Trifle at present acting at the Lyceum, you have stated that the story is evidently meant to allude to "a certain recent event of a memorable nature," and that in one of the scenes there is a manifest reference to another occurrence that has lately attracted the attention of the public.

Though it is with considerable reluctance I thus avow myself the author of a bagatelle, which has been received much more indulgently than it deserves, I cannot allow this statement to pass without declaring, that, however hastily the frivolous *dialogue* of this piece may have been written, I had thought of the *story* long before those events occurred, by which you, and perhaps many others, suppose it to have been suggested.

I have the honour to be, Sir, yours, &c.

Sept. 11　　　　　　　　　　　　　　　Thomas Moore

Mr. Arnold, the Manager of the Lyceum, thinks it necessary to differ with the author on this occasion, flattering himself undoubtedly that the dissent of so exalted and practical a judge will induce Mr. Moore to think better of it; whereas it is evident that a good writer could meet with no greater humiliation than after writing such a piece to have such a defender. The passage about his sense of "what is due to the public" is too gross, unless he means to put Mr. Moore on a level with himself and Mr. Pocock; [11] and in mentioning the applause which the piece obtained, he forgot to mention the disapprobation which accompanied it.

To the Editor of the *Morning Chronicle*

Sir,—Observing in your paper of yesterday a letter from Mr. Moore, on the subject of his new Opera of *M. P.; or, The Blue Stocking,* I feel myself called upon to dissent from that Gentleman's opinion of his own performance, and to state, that had I conceived it to be merely a "*musical trifle,*" I am too sensible of what is due to the public, to have ventured to offer it to their notice.

The event of its brilliant and unqualified success has justified my opinion of the merits of Mr. Moore's Drama; and I am confident that

if the Author had witnessed the splendid reception of its first representation (which he did *not*), he would not have suffered an excess
of modesty to pay so bad a compliment to public taste as to term that
dialogue *"frivolous"* which was interrupted in almost every scene by
as gratifying applause as ever repaid the most anxious labours of a
dramatist.

I am, Sir, yours, &c., &c.

Theatre Royal Lyceum   SAMUEL JAMES ARNOLD
Sept. 12, 1811

Well as we may agree, however, with Mr. Moore on this subject, and admire the spirit with which he can condemn his own
faults, still his sense of the frivolity of the dialogue does not
excuse him for having written it: on the contrary, seated as he
is immeasurably above the dramatists of the day, and qualified
to enlighten the sphere below him with his brilliant powers,
it is rather an aggravation of his offence that he has condescended to mingle with those imitative cattle, and thus furnished
them with a most afflicting excuse for their awkward frisks and
vagaries. More indeed might have been said and lamented
on this head, had he not expressed himself as he has done in the
letter just quoted, which, it is to be earnestly hoped, in spite of
Mr. Arnold's appeal to their self-love, will have its proper effect
on all those who had prepared to secure their own ignorant
productions by the example of a poet who had forgotten himself.

The new opera must have its run, for, considered without
a reference to what was expected from its author, it is really
more amusing than our farces in general; but may it be hoped
that there will be no appearance in *print?* This hope was suggested in an excellent criticism in the *Times,* and it is fervently
repeated here. The true admirers of Mr. Moore—those who
wish to see him put his great talents to proper and large account—would be sorry that his present literary disgrace should
be anything but momentary. Possessed of a native and flowing
fancy, enriched with the stores of ancient learning, and master
of a versification singularly sweet and emphatic at once, so that
he may easily be discerned as possessing the true lyric character

of old, and uniting the poet and musician, everything is to be expected of him which so felicitous a combination may be able to effect for the cause both of poetical and moral taste. He has been hitherto chiefly known as a writer of voluptuous songs, the Chaulieu or the Anacreon of his day: but his best readers are greatly mistaken if there is not in his later poetry, particularly in his Epistles from abroad, a much higher and more honourable character of genius: his last production but one, the songs for the Irish Melodies, in departing from that voluptuousness lost nothing of their elegance and acquired a great deal of spirit; and in his last little effusion, the Melologue, though evidently and avowedly written in haste, there are one or two passages of the highest character, in composition, in feeling, and in fancy. There seems to me to be an original path open to him in the union of fancy with ethics, or rather perhaps, I should say, of poetical ornament with observation of men and manners. Our moral didactic writers have never given us both together: Pope is in general either entirely solemn or entirely familiar; Young pours forth nothing but epigrams; and Cowper, with much power of description, does not appear to have had an abundant imagination, not to mention the vein of bitter prejudice that runs through all his moralizing. Be this as it may, it is of importance, in every point of view, that a poet of such talents as Mr. Moore should be found not only in his happiest but in his most useful sphere; and there, I trust, he will soon be again, with a wing strengthened by just ambition, and sparkling and purifying himself in his own sunshine.

> Scarce vanish'd out of sight,
> He buoys up instant and returns to light:
> He bears no token of the sabler streams,
> But mounts far off among the swans of Thames.[12]

[ORATORIO]

No INSTITUTIONS have so much declined from their original purposes, or are so likely in their nature to decline, as those of feasts, fasts, and other church ordinances, which depend on times and feelings that cannot possibly last.[1] Thus we have Saints'-days in our calendar, of which nobody ever dreams but those who get a holiday by them: the celebration of some of them is even confined to particular schools and foundations; and then the holy personage is only regarded as a sort of annual procurer of a play-day, as one Bishop Hugh [2] for instance, whose name is attached to the 17th of November, and to whom my schoolfellows used to reckon themselves under particular though mysterious obligations on that account. In like manner, not even the political feelings connected with the sanctification of the 30th of January,[3] a day of fasting and mortification, could prevent it from degenerating into uses ludicrously foreign to its design; and all that it now does of any consequence is to enable the young clerks in office to go visiting and feasting with their sweethearts, and two worthy persons of the name of Ashley [4] to put some money in their pockets by playing the fiddle.

The Oratorio conducted by these gentlemen was commenced accordingly on Thursday last, and consisted of a Selection made on the usual principle, from the works of Handel, Haydn, and others, with the addition of this innovation—that Italian singing was introduced, and Catalani and Tramezzani made their appearance as the principal performers. The audience did not entirely relish this novelty; and though the disapprobation was as one to fifty, and was ultimately silenced by the charm of Catalani's inspired voice, yet it seems to have arisen from a proper feeling, for Italian singing already enjoys a large and superior sphere of its own in this country, and, if suffered to extend it in encroachments like these, will leave no room for the growth and habitation of our native art. Neither does it appear to be the real interest of these two singers—of one of them, most certainly not—to exhibit themselves on such an occasion; for Tramezzani, whose vocal powers are so much inferior to his taste, and who wants every assistance that a theatre can furnish him, loses five parts of himself when he is not acting; and Madame Catalani, who excels in giving what may be called a flow of spirits to a voice, does not appear to advantage in those simple and devout songs of Handel, with which, it seems, she is occasionally to treat us in the English words. On the present occasion, for instance, she sung "Angels ever bright and fair"; but it was plain, by her shakes and ornaments, either that the meaning and general character of the words had not been properly explained to her, or that she had not a taste sufficiently primitive and unsophisticated for that exquisitely abstracted melody, the singer of which is supposed to be anticipating the stroke of death, and to be wrapped up in a few grand and unearthly anticipations of the society of the blest. Setting aside these material objections, it is impossible not to be pleased with the taste of Signor Tramezzani, and not to be enchanted with the wonders of Catalani; but it is unfortunate for him to stand by her side; the difference between their powers is too great and surprising. The heaving gentleness of his voice is full of sensibility, and he plays very agreeably with a turn or little wandering of notes before conclusion; but compared with Madame Catalani's warmth of feeling and vividness of execution, it is mere feebleness and timidity, and a stealing about in the dark. She occasionally throws out a note which reaches us at a distance like vocal lightning, and makes us wonder what her voice would be if she exerted it through a whole song; but this vehemence and swell she can contrast with the utmost delicacy and tenuity of warbling; her shake on the upper tones is pure, crystal quivering, like water in sunshine, and seems as if it would be as perpetual; and when she suddenly springs aloft from a low note to one of inconceivable height and fineness, dropping down from thence a few still, small utterances, you might shut your eyes, and fancy a fairy being, who has shot up to the music of the spheres, and with one finger after another touches them to our distant ears.

It will easily be supposed that the other singers were quite eclipsed; but to shew the power of unaffected simplicity, it is observable, that after Madame Catalani had been heard, Mrs. Bland's [5] singing was much more agreeable than that of Mrs. Dickons,[6] whose voice and manner, coming into a sort of rivalry with those of the enchantress, became almost obnoxious. Nor did she vindicate the best English style of singing, by a proper attention to the composer's expression. The character, for instance, of Haydn's beautiful song, "With verdure clad," is a gradual and as it were plastic benevolence, expressive of the growth of the herbs and plants and their genial effect upon the senses; but Mrs. Dickons took every opportunity of interspersing it with ornament, and frisked and fluttered about like a romp in a hay-field, instead of expressing the fine, intellectual enjoyment of a soul contemplating creation.

Upon the whole, an Oratorio is a very laudable and elevating entertainment, and with the help of a little of that theoretical knowledge which a good ear may always pick up, and which is as necessary to a true relish of music as a certain connoisseur-ship is to that of painting, would be found thoroughly delightful to a multitude of persons who now think it tedious. The sweetness of the solos, the intermingling richness of the trios and quartettes, and the world of grandeur in the choruses, present us with all the variety of which the human song is capable; and if ever there should be added to such an enjoyment as this, that of fine poetry for the whole of the words, and of fine painting for the walls of the music-room, as may be reasonably hoped in a country like ours, we shall have witnessed the height and perfection of intellectual luxury. I cannot deny myself, at the close of this article, the pleasure of transcribing that noble, Platonic effusion of Milton, which he wrote upon some such occasion as the present, and which has been very finely set to music, I understand, by Mr. Stafford Smith.[7] Why do we not hear it at the Oratorios? It is, of all other pieces, suited to their object, and is calculated to make us, as the Poet himself must have been when it was meditated, all unclouded ear and glorious abstraction.

At a Solemn Musick

Blest pair of Syrens, pledges of Heaven's joy,
Sphere-born harmonious sisters, Voice and Verse,
Wed your divine sounds, and mix'd power employ,
Dead things with inbreath'd sense able to pierce;
And to our high-rais'd phantasy present
That undisturbed song of pure concent,
Aye sung before the sapphire-colour'd throne
To HIM that sits thereon,
With saintly shout and solemn jubilee;
Where the bright Seraphim, in burning row,
Their loud, uplifted angel-trumpets blow;
And the cherubick host, in thousand quires,
Touch their immortal harps of golden wires,
With those just Spirits that wear victorious palms,
Hymns devout and holy psalms
Singing everlastingly:
That we on earth; with undiscording voice,
May rightly answer that melodious noise,
As once we did, till disproportion'd sin
Jarr'd against nature's chime, and with harsh din
Broke the fair music that all creatures made
To their great LORD, whose love their motions [8] sway'd
In perfect diapason, whilst they stood
In first obedience, and their state of good.
O, may we soon again renew that song
And keep in tune with Heav'n, till GOD ere long
To his celestial consort us unite
To live with him and sing in endless morn of light!

[JULIUS CAESAR]

IT IS HIGHLY CREDITABLE to the taste of the public, that in
spite of the largeness of this theatre, which at certain distances
sets the ear and almost the eye itself at nought, the revival of
Julius Caesar continues to fill the house twice every week.[1] The
play is indeed, to use a theatrical phrase, excellently *got up;* and
on the part of two of the principal actors, most excellently performed; so that what with the propriety of the costume, the
splendour of the decorations, and the intellectual treat always
to be found in Shakspeare, the piece goes off in a very satisfac-
tory manner; and an impression is left upon us of Roman manners and greatness, of the appearance as well as intellect of
Romans, which to a young mind in particular must furnish an
indelible picture for the assistance of his studies, resembling
perhaps the clearness of local conception which is afforded us
by a panorama.

"Of this tragedy," says Dr. Johnson, "many particular passages
deserve regard, and the contention and reconcilement of *Brutus*
and *Cassius* is universally celebrated; but I have never been
strongly agitated in perusing it, and think it somewhat cold and
unaffecting,[2] compared with some other of Shakspeare's plays:
his adherence to the real story, and to Roman manners, seems to
have impeded the natural vigour of his genius." [3] With all due respect to the powers of Dr. Johnson, this is a sorry piece of criticism: it is, at best, like most of his criticisms, only so much gratuitous opinion without analysis, without argument; but at bottom, I
am afraid, it is an additional betrayal of his absolute unfitness
for poetical criticism, at least with regard to works of a higher
order. A writer, who by his own confession was insensible to
Painting and Music, has at least very suspicious claims to become a critic; but when we see his taste so ready on all occasions
to pollute itself with political prejudices, when we find him
really insensible to the infinite and glorious variety of Milton's

numbers, and when he acknowledges, in the instance before us, that he feels no strength of emotion in witnessing the workings of great minds in awful situations, in beholding the sudden downfall of guilty greatness, and in sitting with the patriot in his tent, during the silence of night, in the wakefulness of a noble affliction, and on the eve of the last struggle for liberty, then he signs his own condemnation, and leaves us still in want, as we certainly are to this day, of a true critical authority with respect to our great poets.[4] *Julius Caesar*, with the exception of *Coriolanus*, has perhaps less of the poetical in it than any other tragedy of Shakspeare; but fancy and imagination did not suit the business of the scene; and what is wanting in colour and ornament, is recompensed by the finest contrasts of character. It is of itself a whole school of human nature. The variable impotence of the mob, the imperial obstinacy of *Caesar*, the courtly and calculating worldliness of *Anthony*, the vulgar jealousy of *Casca*, the loftier jealousy and impatient temper of *Cassius*, the disinterestedness and self-centered philosophy of *Brutus*, seem to bring at once before us the result of a thousand different educations, and of a thousand habits, induced by situation, passion, or reflection. *Brutus*, however, is clearly the hero of the story, and as Gildon [5] observes, should have given his name to the piece; for *Caesar* appears but in two short scenes and is dispatched at the beginning of the third act; whereas *Brutus*, after his first interview with *Cassius* in the commencement of the play, is the arbiter of all that succeeds, and the predominant spirit to the last.

Of the Performance, next week.

April 5, 1812

THE MOST PROMINENT ATTRACTION in the performance of *Julius Caesar* is the *Cassius* of Mr. Young.[6] It is full of fire, and yet marked with the nicest discrimination—a rare combination, in which this actor promises to excel all his contemporaries, and of which the passage in his conference with *Brutus*, beginning "I know that virtue to be in you," would alone be a finished specimen. This speech is a string of varieties, from the commonest colloquial familiarity to the loftiest burst of passion; and Mr. Young passes from one to another with the happiest instantaneousness of impression—from an air of indifference to one of resentment, from anecdote to indignant comment, from the subdued tone of sarcastic mimicry to the loud and impatient climax of a jealousy wrought up into rage. The transition in particular from the repetition of *Caesar's* sick words to the contemptuous simile they occasion, and from that again to the concluding burst of astonishment, accompanied with a start forward and a vehement clasp of the hands, is exceedingly striking. As there is no single passage in Shakspeare more various in expressing the shades of passion and discourse, so I do not remember a speech delivered on the stage by which the actor more nearly approaches to the ideal picture of the person he represents. There is none therefore that deserves better to be recorded as one of the uniques of its day; and if Mr. Young proceed in this manner to study his part *ambitiously,* and to read his part with that searching and patient eye which will alone enable us to catch all the pith and scope of his eloquence, I repeat with still greater confidence than before that he will soon oust Mr. Kemble from the throne which his grave cant has usurped, and place in it a proper being of flesh and blood, who feels and speaks like a susceptible creature.

The next performance in merit is certainly that of *Anthony* by Mr. Charles Kemble, who in pronouncing the celebrated speech over the dead body of *Caesar* manages with great nicety the difficult point of insinuating the sarcasms against the conspirators without coming broadly to them at once. He also looks the character to perfection, as Shakspeare has represented it; and so do Messrs. Young and Kemble theirs, with the exception of their respective ages, which ought to look the reverse of what they appear, for *Cassius* was an old man compared with *Brutus.* With respect to Mr. Kemble's performance, it is excellent as far as philosophic appearance and manner can make it so, and his general conception of the character is just and impressive; but *Brutus,* who affected pithiness of speech, never thought of

recommending it by a drawling preachment; and really this
artificial actor does so dole out his words, and so drop his syllables
one by one upon the ear, as if he were measuring out laudanum
for us, that a reasonable auditor, who is not to be imposed upon
with the multitude in general, has no alternative between laughing or being disgusted.

But in the name of all that is serious and fitting, let us have
a more endurable *Caesar* by next year, if the play keep possession so long. Shakspeare has distorted and tumified *Caesar's*
character enough, as it is; but what little remained of familiarity
and of gentlemanly bearing in it, Mr. Egerton [7] is determined
to make all of a piece with the rest. Every action is lofty, every
look tragic, every turn of step and of feature imperial and bluff.
When *Caesar,* upon a representation of *Anthony's,* that *Cassius*
was not a dangerous man, pleasantly wishes that "he were fatter," Mr. Egerton takes it in the light of a serious and impassioned desire, and mouths out the words like a stage-tyrant who
wishes a man in his grave; and when *Anthony* is familiarly requested to step on the other side of him, because the ear at
which he is standing is deaf, he delivers the request with as much
dignity, and motions him round with as much mysterious solemnity, as if he were asking him to defend his other side from an
assassin.

[MRS. SIDDONS' FAREWELL
PERFORMANCE]

July 5, 1812   *Haymarket*

Mr. TERRY's performance of *Sir Anthony Absolute*,[1] which
is a character of decided comedy, and may therefore be considered as a criterion of his comic powers, at least in one cast of
characters, has not much tended to raise his abilities in our estimation, though he still remains an excellent and original actor.[2]
The violent part of it is good, and as he always appears to have
a complete possession of himself, as well as a good knowledge of
his author, no part of it can be absolutely said to be bad; but it
provokes an unlucky comparison with Dowton,[3] whose performance of it is perfection itself: and in all the niceties and
shadows of its feeling, in the benevolence that lurks at the bottom of its anger, in the wish to be pacified that appears in spite of
itself, in the tremulous turn of voice when pacified, the little
fatherly yearnings, and all indeed which constitute more particularly the paternal part of the character, it leaves that great
actor in unapproachable possession of its beauties.

Covent-Garden

Mrs. Siddons, after a theatrical life of forty years, took her
leave of the Public on Monday last. We were not among the
spectators, though we have in general taken some pains to be
present on such occasions; but as we had seen the Play times
out of mind, and as little sensibility was expected to be manifested at parting, we thought it allowable for once to escape
the felicities of a crowd. According to all accounts, we lost nothing by our absence. At the close of the sleep-walking scene, it
appears that some persons wished it to be repeated, and that
others, in making their objections, gave rise to a noise and confusion which disturbed the requisite solemnity of the evening.
Whether it was owing to this circumstance, or to a delicate com-

pliment on the part of the audience, we know not; but the Play
[*Macbeth*] closed with this scene, and Mrs. Siddons pronounced
the following Farewell, in verse, written by Mr. Horace Twiss [4]
—a young barrister, we believe, and a relation of hers:

> Who has not felt, how growing use endears
> The fond remembrance of our former years?
> Who has not sigh'd, when doom'd to leave at last
> The hopes of youth, the habits of the past,
> The thousand ties and interests, that impart
> A second nature to the human heart,
> And, wreathing round it close, like tendrils, climb,
> Blooming in age and sanctified by time?
> Yes! at this moment crowd upon my mind
> Scenes of bright days for ever left behind,
> Bewildering visions of enraptured youth,
> When hope and fancy wore the hues of truth,
> And long-forgotten years, that almost seem
> The faded traces of a morning dream!
> Sweet are those mournful thoughts: for they renew
> The pleasing sense of all I owe to you,
> For each inspiring smile, and soothing tear—
> For those full honours of my long career,
> That cheer'd my earliest hope, and chased my latest fear!
> And though, for me, those tears shall flow no more,
> And the warm sunshine of your smile is o'er,—
> Though the bright beams are fading fast away,
> That shone unclouded through my summer day,—
> Yet grateful Memory shall reflect their light
> O'er the dim shadows of the coming night,
> And lend to later life a softer tone,
> A moonlight tint, a lustre of her own.
> Judges and Friends! to whom the tragic strain
> Of nature's feeling never spoke in vain,
> Perhaps your hearts, when years have glided by,
> And past emotions wake a fleeting sigh,
> May think on her, whose lips have pour'd so long
> The charmed sorrows of your SHAKESPEARE's song:—
> On her, who, parting to return no more,
> *Is* now the mourner she but *seem'd* before,—
> Herself subdued, resigns the melting spell,
> And breathes, with swelling heart, her long, her last
>   farewell!

It is a pity that performers should ever make use of verses on this occasion, inasmuch as the previous air of design is calculated to throw a damp on our sympathy, and make us resist the appeal as something cold and unseasonable; two or three sentences of plain, warm-hearted prose, like those spoken by Mr. Lewis the comedian, when he thanked the public with a faltering voice for their attachment, and made the honest boast that ne had never displeased them for thirty years, are a thousand times better than all which Campbell himself might write: but if verse is to be spoken at all, it should at least be of the simplest and most unaffected description, produced as it were at a heat, and making no such regular assault upon us with its metaphor and its mawkishness, as the lines before us. They are very respectable common-place, and as smooth as the custom of a century can make them; but "moonlight tints" and "sanctified tendrils" are not the phrases which we should naturally use in taking leave of an assembly of honest people. Mr. Twiss, we believe, is the same pleasant and posthumous gentleman who, in the preface to a late publication called *Scottish Melodies,* gives out that he was born in the time of the Stuarts; for so, of course, we must construe his modest insinuation that he is the first person in the language who has written songs with a natural and idiomatic simplicity, he being thus to all intents and purposes the precursor of *Prior,* of Dorset, of Rochester, and a hundred other obscure writers, not to mention all the other songsters in Ritson's and Aikin's Collections, down to Thomas Moore, whom he imitates. Mr. Twiss is not destitute of talent, and had better mind his profession, instead of making food for the critical waggery of his Learned Brothers.

Mrs. Siddons began her career, we believe, with comedy, or even with opera; but having no comic or vocal powers, she soon found her footing upon what was destined to become her exclusive ground as a female performer—that of lofty tragedy. It is out of our power to compare her with former celebrated and rival actresses whom we have never seen; but if any of them excelled her in certain characters, the public must form to itself a nobler idea of a stage than any which it is accustomed to entertain. Her *Queen Katharine, Constance,*[5] and *Lady Macbeth* were almost perfect pieces of acting—the first perhaps completely perfect, though of a less striking nature than the others. The sleep-walking scene in the last has been much and deservedly admired; the deathlike stare of her countenance, while the body was in motion, was sublime; and the anxious whispering with which she made her exit, as if beckoning her husband to bed, took the audience along with her into the silent and dreaming horror of her retirement; but we know not whether in attempting a natural monotony of gesture she did not throw too great an air of indolence over the scene in general, and whether in particular the dribbling and domestic familiarity with which she poured the water on her hands and slid them over each other, was not even unnatural in a person so situated: we are aware that in every species of passion a sublime effect is producible by the occasional mixture of every-day action with strong feeling; but in the instance before us the character is one of violence; and after a general wash of the hands, the poet seems to have marked out the single and decided action with which *Lady Macbeth* aims continually at the "damned *spot.*" Her finest passages in this character appear to have been those of the scene before the murder and the dismissal of the guests, the latter of which she performed with a finished royalty. The performance of *Constance* was unexceptionable; and here her lofty indignation came into play with all its nobleness in the scene with the Cardinal; her performance of this part also, the violence of which is such a provocation to the noise of inferior actresses, set a fine example of majestic excess, and was even clamorous without losing its dignity. But it was in *Queen Katharine* that this dignity was seen in all its perfection; never was lofty grief so equally kept up, never a good conscience so nobly prepared, never a dying hour so royal and so considerate to the last. That was a beautiful touch with which she used to have her chair and cushions changed, during the wearisome pain of her resting body! And her cheek too against the pillow! We could almost as soon forget the grand and melancholy composure of its parting despair as the gentler meekness of that of *Clarissa Harlowe* with the dying tinge in it—that dying cheek, virgin in spite of the despoiler. In considering these performances of her loftier tragedy, it will be found, we think, that, although there was no passion in the range of that loftiness which Mrs. Siddons could not finely portray, the predominant feature of her excellence, and that which gave a cast to its whole aspect, was a certain regality and conscious dignity, which exalted her powers in proportion to the rank and supposed consequence of her characters. What she failed in particularly was the meekness or humility opposed to this general feature, including every species of gentler tenderness, especially that of love. Her *Belvidera*,[6] for instance, was excellent where she had to complain of wrong or to resent injustice, but little less than distasteful in the amatory part of it. This deficiency she partook with her brother John: but while she resembled him in this respect, as well as in the singular advantages of his person and the dignity of his aspect, she was in everything else as much his superior as nature is to art, or as a fine, unaffected, and deep-toned picture is to one full of hard outlines, stiff attitudes, and coldness of colour. After all, it is more difficult to make an exact estimate of what does or does not belong to a performer's talents than of the merits of any other profession; and it is difficult to say whether it is lucky for the performer or not that it is so; for if, on the one hand, there is the advantage of getting rid of comparison with *celebrated predecessors*, there is the disadvantage on the other of having beauties referred to them which may be original. From what may be discovered, however, in theatrical memoirs and other works relating to the stage, the advantage appears to be the greater. The worst thing an ambitious actor has to contemplate is the want of something to leave behind him, that shall carry down an idea of his talents to posterity; and, if he makes use of the beauties of those that have preceded him, he is rewarded with the mortifying consciousness that all which survives of him will in like manner become the portion and the display of others. What was original, for instance, with Garrick, is confounded with what has descended from him to living actors; and what may be original with them, will be lost in the imitation of their successors. The painter and writer are their only resource against absolute oblivion; and like Garrick, Mrs. Siddons has fortunately wanted neither. Her portrait, as the *Tragic Muse,* by Sir Joshua Reynolds,[7] will perpetuate the lofty character of her powers, and her possession of the theatrical throne; and among the small number of happy compliments, will never be forgotten the one paid her by Dr. Johnson, when he could not find her a chair in his room—"Where-ever you appear, Madam, you see there are no seats to be had."

[THE BEGGAR'S OPERA]

September 13, 1812   *Covent-Garden*

COVENT-GARDEN Theatre has opened for the season.[1] Its first novelty was the appearance of a Mrs. Sterling, on Thursday last, as *Polly*, in the *Beggar's Opera*.[2] This lady, with a good stage figure, an unobtrusive demeanour, a clear voice, and a correct ear, promises to be what is called a respectable singer, but is not calculated, we think, to take any leading part. She seemed to have a proper and sensible idea of the simplicity with which the ballads of this Opera should be sung, though she unaccountably deviated from it in the song of "Cease your Funning"—a deviation, by the bye, which proved that her better taste was her most politic one, for her graces were of a very prim and deliberate description, and she ran down her notes with full as much caution as correctness. But even her simplicity wants the proper amount of feeling. Her mode of giving "Oh ponder well" was extremely dry; and the want of a liquid facility in her voice, that is to say, of a proper flow where flowing is requisite, made her halt occasionally upon a note before she could make it speak, though when it came at last it was perfectly true. A painter would say that her style had a hard outline. Her best performances were her answer to "Pretty Polly, say," and her part in the duet of "The Miser thus."

Incledon,[3] after a lapse of two years, returned in this opera to his old character of *Macheath*, and was heartily welcomed. In one respect, he appears to more advantage in it than he used; in another, not to so much—he plays it better, most probably from having seen Elliston in it, but his voice is not so stout as it was, and his notes begin to grow indistinct in particular passages, a deficiency, which his propensity to gabbling renders the more observable. He still, however, possesses considerable power, when he chooses to put it forth; and there is always an English something about his voice, which in spite of his vulgar volubility and splay-mouthed pronunciation it is pleasant and invigorating to hear. His *Macheath* altogether is very far from being the true one. He is too doleful in some parts of it, and has too little of the metropolitan about his general appearance: he looks in short like a jolly young farmer sporting a new pair of boots and buckskins on a market day; whereas *Macheath*, who affects a knowledge of the town and of the cant of fashion, should at least have a certain slang of good breeding about him—something between the pertness of the footman and the bravado of the town buck. If Elliston had Incledon's voice, with a little leaven of De Camp to tower his gentility, he would do it to perfection.

It is easy to see that the *Beggar's Opera* would long ago have lost its attractions had it not been for the never-dying charm of simplicity in its songs and music, and for one or two gross scenes which the audience are glad enough to enjoy in an old piece, though they would never tolerate them in a new one. Gay was a man of no great positive talent. His taste for a humourous simplicity was the best part of him, and even that was of a negative cast, and rather told him what to avoid than to do. The merits of the *Beggar's Opera* are of this description, possessing no strong feature of talent either in the language, manner, or satire, but always true to good sense, with a pleasant feeling for burlesque, and a vein of ridicule against the vices of high life, which is perfectly intelligible to everybody, and particularly welcome to the majority of a promiscuous assembly. It was this feature of general intelligibility to which the great success of the piece was most probably owing on its first appearance. The upper orders, who were not as refined as they are at present, were pleased with so plain a picture of the lower; and the lower were delighted to find themselves so much at their ease with a satirist of the upper. The habit of appealing, however, to common life, though it assisted the temporary views of the school in which Gay was formed, was a most serious injury to it upon the whole. If it abounded, as it certainly did to exuberance, in wit, the exuberance was of a most rank description; and there grew up a vulgarity about their habits of mind, originating perhaps with

Swift, the contamination of which even the purity of Arbuthnot could not escape, and which not only polluted the language of Pope, but appears to have materially kept down and depraved his imagination.

NOTE UPON DESDEMONA

NOTE UPON NOTE, OR A WORD OR TWO ON THE PASSION OF LOVE,
IN ANSWER TO SOME OBSERVATIONS IN OUR LAST WEEK'S
"EXAMINER"

August 14, 1814

WE ARE about to say a few words on a delicate subject; [1] and though neither our words nor our thoughts will be of a nature calculated to alarm the nicest mind, that is really and unaffectedly so, yet we think it necessary to advise some persons that such is the case. Among those, for instance, whose feelings we would spare are all such ladies as have a very quick and strong habit of blushing, often to the wonder and admiration of those about them; all such as are eager to express their abhorrence of the smallest appearance of indelicacy, particularly when the persons present may not be aware of the danger; and all such, as with pretty pursed-up mouths, and in a tone between hasty resentment and good-humoured forgiveness, are swift to cry out "For shame!" or "Fye!" or "How can you talk so?"— sometimes accompanying their exclamations with a fidgety jerk of the elbow, or an airy slap with the back of the fingers.

Having premised this much, we shall proceed safely, as well as with a good conscience. There was a note in last week's *Examiner* to some observations on the character of *Iago*, which has not a little startled some of our readers. We certainly did not agree with it ourselves, though perhaps we may have occasionally startled our readers as much upon other subjects; but difference of opinion is not, of necessity, a reason why we should omit the remarks of others; they are as open to criticism as our own; and an author might have reason to regret that he ventured his ideas at all in this way, if they were to be hacked and chipped to the standard of every editorial Procrustes. It may be observed also, that all plain-speaking enquiries into the nature of ourselves and our passions are apt to be startling, at least in the first instance. Our self-love feels as if it were to undergo a living dissection.

We shall first repeat the observations in question, and then assign our reasons for holding a different opinion.

If *Desdemona* really "saw her husband's visage in his mind," or fell in love with the abstract idea of "his virtues and his valiant parts," she was the only woman on record, either before or since, who ever did so. SHAKSPEARE's want of penetration in supposing that those are the sort of things that gain the affections, might perhaps have drawn a smile from the ladies, if honest *Iago* had not checked it by suggesting a different explanation. It should seem by this, as if the rankness and gross impropriety of the personal connection, the difference in age, features, colour, constitution, instead of being the obstacle, had been the motive of the refinement of her choice, and had, by beginning at the wrong end, subdued her to the amiable qualities of her lord. *Iago* is indeed a most learned and irrefragable doctor on the subject of love, which he defines to be "merely a lust of blood, and a permission of the will." The idea that love has its source in moral or intellectual excellence, in good nature or good sense, or has any connection with sentiment or refinement of any kind, is one of those preposterous and wilful errors, which ought to be extirpated for the sake of those few persons who alone are likely to suffer by it, whose romantic generosity and delicacy ought not to be sacrificed to the baseness of their nature, but who treading secure the flowery path, marked out for them by poets and moralists, the licensed artificers of fraud and lies, are dashed to pieces down the precipice, and perish without help.

It is with the general and sweeping assertion contained in the concluding part of this note that we have to do at present; for we shall perhaps give an additional startle to our readers by declaring that, with regard to *Desdemona* herself, our opinion has always been much the same as that of the writer. Not that we go quite to his extreme, or believe that the intellectual qualities of *Othello* had *nothing* to do with her choice; [2] but *Iago's* observations, as far as a connexion like hers is concerned, have had their weight with us; and there always appeared to us, we confess, a more than usual superabundance of temperament in her composition. The reverse, we are aware, has been a favourite persuasion, especially with minds, from whom we should be most loth to differ in matters of sentiment. The great-

est poet of the present time, in mentioning the "personal themes"
of which he is fond, instances two as being

> dearer than the rest;
> The gentle lady married to the Moor,
> And heavenly Una with her milk-white lamb.*

Of *Una* we have the same idea, and nothing can disturb it. It
comes upon us, whenever we turn our thoughts to it, as the
moon comes upon our faces, with the same quiet abstraction
and uniform loveliness; but if we were to join with her a female
character from Shakspeare, we should prefer *Miranda, Ophelia,*
or *Cordelia. Desdemona* undoubtedly possesses amiable and
generous qualities, and her behaviour under affliction has in it
something very wifely and feminine; but in the predominant
part of her nature she appears to us as little qualified to go by
the side of *Una* as a wanton Italian by the side of one of the
most perfect of our countrywomen.

When our writer, however, in objecting to the notion that
Desdemona fell in love with *Othello* out of pure admiration of
his fine qualities, runs out from particular instances of extremes
into an assertion that all women are, as it were, *Desdemonas,*
and that love has no connexion with sentiment or refinement
of *any* kind, we take our leave of him, and think that in opposition to one extreme of opinion he is only getting into another.
We do not mean to deny that there is a great deal of the animal
passion in the most refined love; perhaps indeed that passion
becomes the more intense in proportion to the admixture of
intellectual qualities, and to the taste for enjoyment of every
kind, which one partly may suppose the other to bring with it.
But if he would give us to understand that in everyone's love
there is literally nothing but animal passion, and that there is no
difference between the love of the most refined and intelligent
for the particular objects of their choice and the love of the
Turk for the Circassian, how is he to account for that particu-
larity and choice, when the object of it, *compared* with others,
is often deficient in what is most calculated to excite the animal

---

* Wordsworth's Poems, Vol. II, p. 191. [See "Personal Talk," ll. 40–42.]

feeling! We are not intimate with the language of metaphysics, and are aware that we have to deal with one who is a master in that science; but our turn of thinking has perhaps been of a more metaphysical cast than we could have wished it; and he will understand us when we say that he appears to us to confound the first natural movements of love, as a general law, with its direction and modification, as a particular passion. If he should answer that he does not mean to deny the accompaniment of esteem, friendship, &c. with the love of such persons as we allude to, but that such feelings are only accompaniments, and do not interfere with the particular nature of the passion, then, we conceive, the dispute becomes only a matter of words, and that while he applies the term *love* to that animal passion which nobody denies to exist in the most refined attachments, we apply it to the mixture of animal passion with mental or moral regard—that he is talking of a simple note, and we of a concord—that he is describing the ground of a picture, and we the drawing and the colouring, and all that gives it its finished beauty.

How persons of generosity and delicacy are to be benefited by adopting a reverse opinion, we cannot conceive. Seduction may come to the unguarded under the guise of a moral or intellectual attachment; but it will be conceded, we presume, that there are a much greater number of generous and delicate persons who are not seduced than the contrary; and the loss of a belief in these redeeming qualities of love would be to them a disquietude and humiliation, certainly not to be compensated by having their eyes opened to what is here called, not very philosophically we think, "the baseness of their nature." Granting even for the sake of argument, and to use the ordinary language of such suppositions, that they deceived themselves, still the distinction between reality and deception, between what is and what seems to be, or between what we are intended to think by nature and what some persons would have us think, remains to be argued. When Swift wanted to disgust us with our very skins, he made us, as it were, look through a microscope; but he forgot that nature had given us eyes of a different vision, and that, after all, even the microscope may deceive them.

That the poets and moralists, therefore, wish us to have a better idea of our nature, would be to us, if we were not inclined to entertain it, already, nothing but a matter of gratitude —to the poets in particular; for the effect of their writings upon society is more certain, general, and uniform; the moralists, in their love of systematizing, and sometimes, of adapting their theories to the prejudices of society, being too apt to reason of virtue and vice as abstract qualities, and not as greater or less degrees of knowledge and genial habitude. Our writer, from his love of Shakspeare and the other great poets, is one of the last persons whom we should have suspected of bringing a railing accusation against them, and of reviving the ancient spleen of the Fathers, and others, who made them lineal descendants of the Devil,

the first
Artificer of fraud.[3]

Shakspeare, at least, he might have excepted, according to his own interpretations of him; but perhaps his moral offences in other female characters came across him; and even in the present instance, we do not think the intended compliment well founded. The difficulty of getting at the real opinions of dramatic writers is notorious, unless they deal in declamations and Esopian morals, or go out of their characters to talk in their own persons, as Dr. Johnson does in his *Rasselas;* but this is not a foible of our great poet's; and though the character is a reasoning one, and there is sometimes a disposition to conclude that the darker the view of human nature, the more profound, there is no more reason to imagine that he thought with *Iago* than that he did with *Falstaff,* or *Romeo,* or *Sir Andrew Aguecheek.* The character thought like itself, and that was enough for him. If his own opinions are to be gathered from any part of his writings, it is from his miscellaneous pieces, his songs and sonnets. The writer of the article on *Iago* once quoted a passage from the latter in aid of an argument that Shakspeare had no desire of posthumous fame. We promised an answer to that argument, but were prevented by illness. We have not lost sight however of the promise, and perhaps may be enabled materially to assist our view of the subject by these very sonnets. At present, we shall conclude with one of the most beautiful of them, which, if it proves anything, is certainly not on the other side of the question. It seems, by the commencement, as if Shakspeare himself had been engaged in some such argument, and the conclusion is remarkable.

Sonnet 116

Let me not to the marriage of true minds
Admit impediments. Love is not love,
Which alters when it alteration finds,
Or bends with the remover to remove:
O no! it is an ever-fixed mark,
That looks on tempests and is never shaken;
It is the star to every wandering bark,
Whose worth's unknown, although his height be taken.
Love's not time's fool, though rosy lips and cheeks
Within his bending sickle's compass come;
Love alters not with his brief hours and weeks,
But bears it out even to the edge of doom.
If this be errour, and upon me prov'd,
I never writ, nor no man ever lov'd.

ON RESUMING OUR THEATRICAL
CRITICISM

January 1, 1815

In taking the old and favourite subject into our own hands again a few weeks before we are at large,[1] we are, of course, not going to imitate certain preternatural-sighted vagaries that we have formerly witnessed, and criticise plays and actors without having been at the Theatre. What we are going to say in this, and in the two or three articles that will follow, the readers will be good enough to consider as so much prefatory matter to the more particular criticism that we shall afterwards be enabled to make. We wish to put them in possession, in the first instance, of our general opinions on the stage; and accordingly, after making a few still more prefatory observations in the present number, shall proceed in our next papers to give critical notices of all the performers now at both Theatres, whom we were accustomed to see before we came to prison.

These prolegomena however are chiefly intended, as far at least as any direct novelty may go, to readers whom we may have acquired within these two years. To others, some of whom we have retained by the occasional criticisms of a friend as well as by their own good will, and some of whom we fancy we can see stealing back to us (the rogues!) now that we are getting "critical" again, they may be little more than a sort of pleasant putting in mind—a reminiscence of old times and associations, such as companions delight in after having been long asunder.

Indeed there is scarcely any one thing which will strike us with a fresher sense of our return to liberty, than this particular subject. It was the first on which we commenced writing for the public; [2] it is connected with our ideas of youth, of enthusiasm, almost of boyhood; it makes us view over again a thousand novelties, to which absence has almost given their original charm and sparkling wonderment; in fine, it presses upon our conviction that early and passionate love of truth (if we may say as much) which at least shared, if it did not overbalance, the youthful vanity of being considered an arbitrator, and which has still accompanied us, and we trust will do so to the end of our lives, though a better knowledge of human nature and our own infirmities may have taught us to value ourselves upon less than some may imagine.

But who becomes grave at the thought of issuing forth to the theatre? Perhaps the critic; but at the present moment of anticipation, we are not critics, or at least not full grown and self-possessed ones. We imagine ourselves, years back, dancing off to Covent-Garden or Drury-Lane, either on foot (but keep that a secret:) or in a hackney-coach (but let that be hushed up:)—some ladies are of course with us, in all the propriety of fans and white gloves, the younger ones able to speak only at the top of their breaths for expectation, the older ones (if of a lively cast) almost as eager, but affecting to be wise and staid; the coach tumbles away, through narrow street and through broad, with the lamps every now and then illustrating our faces —another turn down a street—a noise and a throng—the coach heaves with a swing and stops—the theatre! After descending safely from the insidious steps that seem as if they would run under the coach with you, and from watermen, linkboys, and all the rest of the affectionate bye-standers, who shew such a passion for being "remembered" by you, how pleasant to let go the first self-shutting door, and feel the lightsome warmth of the staircase hall, with its lamps and marble steps; then to ascend the said steps, to enter other doors and cross other lightsome halls silent as yet, to pass by the statue of Shakspeare (not very fine perhaps, but still Shakspeare), to enter at last the final lobby, to communicate with that ready and civil person- age, sometimes expostulatory but always disinterested, the box- keeper, to hear the dashing key turn about in the twinkling of an eye, to see the theatre open upon, to take your seat! What an idea of space all over the house! Darkness and vacuity seem lingering in it in spite of the light and the spectators; the pit seems below the light, and the gallery, in their proper celestial char- acter, speak out from a lofty obscurity. But now the musicians come in lingeringly, one by one, with looks of indifference at the audience, and an utter contempt of the galleries; they commence those horrid scratchings and tweakings of the fiddle-strings, which seem to make the very instruments complain: the stage-lights arise "like an exhalation," and throw brilliance upon many a young and answering eye before them; the music stops, up rolls the curtain, the play has begun, enter—whom shall we say!—Miss O'Neil: [3]—we feel our prison walls again, and have done.

There is only one thing more we shall say of ourselves in this prefatory matter, and that is, that with the addition of some qualifications perhaps for the better sort of criticism, we retain one, without which the very best is sure to be rendered futile. The rock upon which theatrical, like all other criticism, is too apt to split, is personal acquaintance with the men criticised. This at least will not be our fate: the land in which it lies neither presents an aspect formidable enough to make us go nicely beside it, nor contains anything like metal attractive enough to draw us towards it. In short we know still less, if possible, of actors than politicians; we are not acquainted with a single one of them.

THE COMIC ACTRESSES

January 8, 1815

WE ENTER on this subject according to promise, and shall begin, as in gallantry bound, with the ladies.[1] It might have appeared as well to some, had we prefaced our notices of the players with remarks on the present dramatic writers; but not to mention that it is doubtful whether any such persons exist in the real sense of the word, nothing has appeared of late to excite a new interest in the comparative merits of those who are so called; and to say the truth, we are happy to escape as long as possible from a renewal of our griefs on that score.

Of all the actresses whom we were in the habit of seeing before we came to prison, and who still keep possession of the stage, the truest and most native is unquestionably Mrs. Jordan. Her talent lies in the expression of a warm, unsophisticated heart, full of kindly impulses, and quick as a child to everything new and pleasurable. Her range, in consequence, is not extensive. In sentimental comedy she is particularly poor; and she is all deficient in the *lady;* though as everybody must have their blindness of some kind, she does not appear conscious of it, and is sometimes injudiciously praised for the reverse by those who confound gentility with flirts of the fan and a fine dashing manner. In fact, the principal secret of gentility is a certain graceful orderliness, an habitual subjugation, more or less, of impulse to manner: and Mrs. Jordan is deficient in this respect, not because she is impudent or vulgar-minded—for apparently, as well as by all account, she possesses those generous and affectionate qualities upon which the truest good breeding is founded—but because from circumstances perhaps not to be found out, she seems never to have been in the habit of controlling her impressions externally. We do not believe, with the world in general, that great powers of a different nature may not unite in the same person; but some, we believe, are less likely to do so than others, particularly if they depend upon everyday habits; and of these kinds is the talent possessed by Mrs. Jordan, and that which Miss Farren [2] is said to have exhibited. If Mrs. Jordan were what she ought to be in the lady, we more than doubt whether she could be what she is in the boarding-school girl or the buxom woman.

But then how true to the life is she in characters of that description! In the girl, what hey-day vivacity, what bounding eagerness, what tip-toe spirits and expectation, what exquisite ignorance of received habits! In the woman, what generous confidence, what a flush of mirth and tenderness, what a breath-suspended and then blurting kind of pleasantry, relieved from coarseness by a delicious voice!

There are some primitive expressions of feeling to excel in which implies, at once, a taste for nature. Miss O'Neil, we are told, is pre-eminent in what is elegantly termed "a cry": and Mrs. Jordan always appeared to us unrivalled in a laugh. A stage-laugh generally follows the speech which it should accompany, and is as good a set Ha, ha, ha! as the author has put down in his book; but the laughter of Mrs. Jordan, in all its branches, from the giggle to the full burst, is social and genuine; it clips, as it were, and tickles the dialogue; it breaks in and about her words, like sparkles of bubbling water; and when the whole stream comes out, nothing can be fuller of heart and soul.

The last time we saw this charming actress she was of a size which, however convenient for the widow, certainly obstructed a little the dancing vivacity of the hoyden; but such is the effect of native feeling, vivacity, and a tone of generous temper, that even a portly young girl of forty hardly appeared an extravagance; and we had scarcely to shut our eyes in order to fancy ourselves in the middle of a school-room when the governess had gone out of the way.

Mrs. Jordan is not only the first living actress in comedy, but we fear that, when our readers consider the matter nicely, she will be found to be the only actress, since the retirement of Miss Pope,[3] who can any way be reckoned great and original.

There are some other clever actresses no doubt, but they fix upon one's mind no idea of themselves which we may not connect with that of another. We shall therefore be very brief with the remainder.

Mrs. Davison, for instance (lately Miss Duncan), is a very useful as well as clever actress, and may be said to partake in some measure both of Mrs. Jordan and of Miss Farren, though with a greater portion of the former; but she has not enough of either to dispute the palm with them, and of course is still less able, in point of reputation, to set up for herself. There is something too hard and robust in her manner for the lady, something too theatrically conscious for the woman of nature; but where she is to *descend* a little from the lady, or to *affect* nature and simplicity, there her theatrical feeling comes in aid of her better talent, and she receives a great deal of just applause. We do not know whether we are contradicting a little work which we published some years ago upon the Performers, and which we do not happen to have by us; but the two characters, if we recollect rightly, in which Mrs. Davison has pleased us most, are *Miss Hardcastle* in *She Stoops to Conquer,* and *Maria* in the farce of the *Citizen;* [4] and these will exemplify the remark we have just been making.

Mrs. Edwin,[5] though still a clever and a useful actress, and such as the stage, we should think, could ill afford to miss, is a kind of inferior Mrs. Davison, and that too only in the lady. She is prettier than the latter, though not so striking or well proportioned. Her most obvious fault is that of an over-earnest and syllabical enunciation, which inclines her to speak on all serious occasions as if she were reading some one a lecture.

Mrs. Charles Kemble [6] is a still more useful actress than either of those ladies, and, we suspect, a much more intelligent woman. There is no description of character, tragic, comic, or pantomimic, old or young, speaking, singing, or dancing, which she cannot undertake, and for which she would not gain a certain degree of applause; but notwithstanding the effect she has had in some characters, and the display she gives to most, we are inclined to attribute her success more to the superior intellect above-mentioned, and a certain general readiness of apprehension, than to any actual talent for the stage. She seldom performs, we believe, now; and had latterly got into some parts which tended to lead the natural vigour of her temperament into the masculine; but they who remember her not many years back in the parts of romantic heroines and melodramatic nymphs and goddesses, will not easily forget the graceful pomp of her action, her striking features, her beautiful figure, her rich profusion of hair, and her large black eyes looking upon you with a lamping earnestness.

Another very useful actress, and one who is touched, we think, with a more real feeling of nature than any whom we have yet seen, after Mrs. Jordan, is Miss Kelly. She seems to have little however to accompany and bring out that single feeling; and whatever genius may be, it does not seem, after all, that mere organization, or a liability to impressions, is enough to procure a name for it, though perhaps it is nine-tenths of the requisites. There is a first cause in everything, which eludes our researches. We remember seeing Miss Kelly one evening in a trying character—we believe, that of a youth who is put in danger of his life on a false charge—and everybody, as well as ourselves, was forcibly interested in the truth and vehemence of her agitation. Her performance ended in a fainting fit. Miss Kelly is evidently an actress of great sensibility; and what is more, without that perverter of it, affectation. She has a pleasing person, and a face which, though not handsome, and apt to pout a little too much, is intelligent and has a sort of domestic air about it.

We know not that there are any other actresses in these departments worthy of particular mention. Both Mrs. Sparks, however, and Mrs. Davenport,[7] are praiseworthy in motherly old women and gossips, the former with the greater leaning to farce, and the latter, who by the way digs at her words as if she were rooting up horse-radish, to comedy. Mrs. Harlowe [8] is commendable for her scolding and chambermaid airs, and makes an excellent *Mrs. Sneak*. We have seen her work up a fit of angry crying to a climax not to be contemplated by the most

determined husband without trepidation. Mrs. Orger [9] is reckoned pretty, and meets with a considerable degree of applause,
if not in the house, at least in some of the Daily Papers. To our
taste, she is too mincing and over-conscious.

THE TRAGIC ACTRESSES

January 15, 1815

THIS IS NOT a very lively subject, and we are afraid we cannot recommend our seriousness upon it by any redeeming enthusiasm.[1] It rather indeed overpowers us with a general sense of its wants and insipidity; and we look at it with a sort of indifferent despair, like a painter who has a dull family brought him to sit for their portraits.

We have the consolation however of foreseeing that, if we are unentertaining, we shall be equally brief—which is not always the talent of dull fellows; so without any more ado, we take another desperate dip of ink, and begin.

The reader will be good enough to recollect, that we have not yet seen Miss O'Neil; but for some time past, the actress who has been most before the public eye is Mrs. Bartley,[2] lately Miss Smith. We are afraid that her pre-eminence was owing more to the want of merit in others [3] than to the possession of it herself. Mrs. Bartley is at the head of what are called respectable actresses, that is to say, of actresses who are not particularly respectable *as* such, but who have a certain art of decorum and good sense, and whose performance altogether presents us with the idea of persons who have sufficiently thumbed, in their time, *Dr. Enfield's Speaker.*[4] Her figure is indifferent, her voice pretty much of the same description, her face and eyes good, and promising more than they perform. Her style of acting, like that of mediocrity in general, may be called external; if there is surprise, she stares; if joy, she smiles; if horror, she shudders—but we get little or nothing else, nothing deep or replenished; or what we do get, is a sort of washed-down imitation of Mrs. Siddons. What is most remarkable about Mrs. Bartley is a certain fatality attending her appearance in point of age, whether old or young; if she is to represent, for instance, a matron, she seems too flippant-voiced and young; if a young woman, too matronly and old. We have heard, it is true, of some changes or attempt at change in her style lately, which are supposed to be in honour of Mr. Kean; but of these we are bound, of course, not to speak till we see them.

So barren of female performers is this department that on looking round for another tragic actress, or one even called so by courtesy, we can hardly find her. Mrs. Glover,[5] who ought not to have been left out of our last week's paper, is a better comedian than tragedian; and though almost as void of simplicity in her mode of acting as dressing (and by the way, it is better to enjoy the credit of having once had a beautiful figure than to make such an edifice of her shape as she does) is by no means deficient in a hearty feeling and humour. She dashes away, efficiently enough, in the fine lady, real or affected; and by the help of her laughing round face and half-shut eyes almost over-whelms us sometimes with her exhibition of pigsnye merri-ment. But her tragedy, though really striking us now and then with a look of deeper feeling than her admirers in comedy can discover, is, upon the whole, coarse and turbulent. Her features and shape, too, as we have just hinted, are totally unfit for it; the former remain comic in spite of herself—comedy in pain; and as she appears to be fearful of this, she endeavours, like other comedians in the same predicament, to throw into them a double portion of seriousness and being-in-earnest, which pro-duces nothing but a ludicrous and blubbered effect. Upon the whole, Mrs. Glover is a very useful and painstaking actress, not without a considerable portion of ingeniousness.

Of the tragic actresses now performing, she who has been longest in possession of the stage, and of a certain level, middle walk of performance, is Mrs. Renaud,[6] lately Mrs. Powell. With the same face, and the same voice, she goes up and down over the blank verse in the smoothest undulatory monotony imagi-nable, and is, we suspect, just such an actress as forms the *beau ideal* of a boarding-school. We wish we could speak better of her, because she appears of a more unpresuming character than most of her theatrical sisters. She is however a very useful per-former, and still retains the marks of having been a very hand-some woman.

The rest of the tragic or sentimental actresses whom we can recollect, we notice perhaps more in honour of their sex than anything else. Mrs. H. Johnston [7] used to be interesting sometimes with her delicate person and face, though her voice and manner were equally weak, and her countenance had an awkward trick of mistaking vixenishness for gravity. Mrs. Humphries is a pretty woman who masticates a blank verse just as she might a parsnip; and Mrs. St. Leger, in tragedy at least, is a sort of inferior Mrs. Glover, a head and shoulders taller, and with a still more portentous manner of dressing herself. She walks a part however in a very sufficing manner, if she does not act it; *incedit regina;* and there are not wanting persons who, carrying the Homeric taste in beauty farther than we do, think her figure a fine one.

THE COMIC ACTORS

January 22, 1815

Our BELOVED COUNTRY, fertile in all sorts of good things but a decent atmosphere and a regular encouragement of the spirits, contrives to extract good out of its evil; and with the assistance of these very drawbacks, as well as of its political freedom, produces that variety of character and personal humour which renders it equally celebrated for wit and melancholy.[1]

It is thus that many of our pains and pleasures spring up together, the antidote by the poison; and hence, in some measure, that stock of merry fellows, really or apparently so, who have abounded on our comic stage, and who repay us so pleasantly now and then for a rainy morning.

With these, whatever may have been the case with tragedians, our stage has never been unsupplied. We have always been secure of our grin at a reasonable price, from the days of Tarleton[2] in Shakspeare's time, who chatted and joked with the spectators between the acts, down to Munden and Grimaldi,[3] who keep up the intercourse all the rest of the evening. This we learn not only from books, but from the successive generations also of old gentlemen, on the relief of whose particular cases by these means, it is impossible not to reflect without a retrospection and anticipation equally agreeable; for they are sure to have living comedians to amuse them, while at the same time they find still more entertainment in the recollection of those who are dead. Thus in the time of the Stewarts, the venerable part of the pit had their Tarleton to recollect and their Nell Gwyn to enjoy; then came the Nell Gwyns and Nokeses, the Cibbers and Macklins,[4] &c., &c., and now we are told of the Garricks, Dodds, and Kings:[5] our elderly friends will soon be talking of the Popes[6] and the Lewises; and we, by and by, shall have no mercy on our grandchildren with the never-to-be-rivalled excellences of the Listons, Dowtons, and Bannisters.[7]

There is only one department in which the supply appears to have been at all deficient; and this (if we may whisper it without calling up the indignation of all the unobjectionable performers who may happen to be seated at this minute in taprooms or tilburies) is the Gentleman. To begin, for instance, with the comedians before us, the only comedian, truly to be called so, who at present performs in genteel parts is Elliston, an actor whose name we never mention without regret, because he has been spoiling himself very fast of late years in theatrical pursuits and companies beneath him, and because to add another truth, he galls our self-love with the recollection of certain enthusiastic things we formerly said of him, which by such conduct he has been doing his best to make ridiculous. He had always a tendency to overdo his part; and the consequence of his Circus vagaries, added to the flattery of those who could not distinguish between any species of success and the best species, is that he has become little better than a mere declaimer in tragedy, and degraded an unequivocal and powerful talent for comedy into coarseness and vulgar confidence. We remember the time when his *Duke Aranza* in the *Honey Moon* [8] was one of the few performances that might absolutely be termed complete; but between this and his present style of acting it, we understand there is now as much difference as between a nobleman himself and a noisy fellow in front of a booth. We are afraid to think what may have become, in like manner of his *Ranger,* his *Benedict,* his *Sir Harry Wildair,* his *Charles Surface,* &c., and his part (we forget the name) in that pleasant little afterpiece *Matrimony,*[9] where he and Mrs. Jordan used to play at such delightful cross-purposes. Still, however, —unless he has been going on more precipitantly than usual during the last two years, we look upon Mr. Elliston as an actor of no ordinary rank. A man's pretensions to more than he can perform are apt to lower the effect of his real ones; but in rakish characters, in hey-day lovers, in carriers on of a genteel equivoque, and for dry pleasantry in general, we know not that the present stage can shew anyone that approaches him. Neither is he at all equalled in the more sentimental parts of comedy, where a proper and affectionate manliness, rather than any ideal softness, is required. His approaches to women are particularly good; and have at times a tremulous cordiality of voice and manner, which is indicative of more feeling than his declamation in tragedy gets him credit for. The general fault of his style is an affectation of energy; and by the *Times* Newspaper of yesterday, we find that he has not got rid of his old trick of catching his breath and buzzing, like one who is being punched in the ribs.

The greatest living comedian out of the direct pale of gentility, though we by no means mean to insinuate that he is vulgar, appears to us to be Dowton. We recollect this growing more and more upon us in proportion as we became better acquainted with human nature; and we may say the same of Bannister, and (what may surprise some who think him a mere droll) of Liston.

Dowton's genius lies in the expression of strong feeling, open or subdued, at the middle period of life. He can smooth over an habitual vehemence, indulge himself in the most delightful cordiality, and be carried away into the uttermost transport of rage, with equal felicity. Of this, his three several parts of the *Hypocrite*,[10] of *Sir Oliver* in the *School for Scandal,* and of *Sir Anthony Absolute* in the *Rivals,* may be considered as finished specimens. The *Hypocrite* indeed is one of the few perfect pieces of acting on the stage; and after that long exhibition of smoothness and affected humility of which everybody has spoken in praise, nothing can shew the greatness of this actor more (if he still plays it as he used to do) than his foregoing the temptation to rant in the concluding scene, and braving the scorn of those who have detected him, not with the ordinary outcry of stage desperation, but with a rage too deep for violence, and a black, inward-breathing, quivering malignity. It amounts to the awful. On the other hand, *Sir Anthony Absolute,* a mere self-witted old gentleman, is indulged in the usual comic transports; and the actor's art is shewn almost as much in these, by carrying them to their full extent, even to a hoarse voice and an indication of absolute kicking, without giving us an idea of their being caricatured. Between these two, and with all the strength but none of the unamiableness of their feelings, is *Sir Oliver;* and in this, though altogether quiet, he is just as true to the life, with his cordial and unaffected benevolence. With powers of this kind, it will easily be seen that Mr. Dowton must be alive to all the other impressions of his nature; and so he is; though there is a barrier of mind and manner drawn between tragedy and comedy in general, which the finest susceptibility, without other requisites, will not enable an actor to get over. He can reach all the pathetic feelings which are out of the range of direct tragedy; and we need not inform our readers that a great comedian of this kind is infinitely superior to the common run of serious actors and only yields to the very first of tragedians.

January 29, 1815

Mr. Bannister [11] is an excellent comedian who has as little need of grimace as Mr. Dowton, and would probably fail in it about as much if he condescended to use it. There is a fine stout air of frankness and simplicity about him that takes you at once and is excellently borne out by his jovial person, his honest countenance, his intelligent dark eyes, and his manly, melodious voice. There are no two persons on the stage who look so completely English as he and the performer just noticed. You might take Fawcett for a German, Munden or rather Mathews [12] for a Frenchman, and Kemble for an Italian; but Dowton and Bannister would remain Englishmen all over the world. With this aspect, Mr. Bannister is particularly excellent in sailors and other hearty, unaffected characters; and, like Dowton, he has a true taste for what may be called the homely pathetic. His *Job Thornberry*, in *John Bull*,[13] is as much superior to Mr. Fawcett's as tears are to blubbering, though the latter performer, after all, is by no means deficient in feeling. His *Walter* also in the *Children in the Wood* is very deep-felt and effective, and has, in one particular part,[14] a mute wretchedness in it as striking in its way as the loftier fixedness of Mrs. Siddons. At the same time, Mr. Bannister has a great talent for mimicry and low humour of the most laughable cast, which, when we consider his freedom from grimace, must strike us with its infinite superiority to the more external drollery of others. His very farce is comedy compared with theirs. There is no actor, excepting Liston, who can play the *butt* so well—with such an admirable mixture of unconsciousness and good temper. His *Marplot* [15] has hitherto been unrivalled. In mimicry, as in the part of *Colonel Feignwell*, for instance, in the *Bold Stroke for a Wife*,[16] he is as various and effective as Mathews, with a more equable spirit of self-possession; and, in general drollery, nothing can surpass the tall-boy airs, the mixed ignorance and cunning, and the mischievous perversity of his *Tony Lumpkin*, in *She Stoops to Conquer*. It is one of those sort of performances which set people upon the full enjoyment of their ease and merriment and make the laughter come away as heartily and companionably as over a round game at cards or a play at forfeits.

At the name of Liston we think we see our readers involuntarily smiling and calling up to their minds that face of irresistible drollery, those helpless airs, those half-conscious, half-unconscious looks of assumption, that exquisite languor of appeal, and all those inimitable, indescribable somethings which hang about the aspect and person of this creature of humour—for this is his proper appellation; he seems to belong and to be made out of humour itself, and not a person assuming particular characters and putting on just as much humour as suits him; he always looks as if he could not help his own drollery: it seems interwoven with all the good-tempered particles of his nature; and for these reasons, one is sometimes in doubt whether to call him an actor at all, and whether the part which he pretends to act is not rather a vehicle for Liston than Liston for the part. There is indeed a distinction in his several performances; *Jacob Gawky* [17] with his awkward gestures and inexperience, and his oh fie looks, is not the beauish, flattering, and exhibiting *Caper*; and *Caper* is not *Grizzle* in *Tom Thumb*;[18] but still he, in a manner, overdoes all his characters with an exuberance of personal humour, and the audience are still thinking of Liston and content to give up the character, as it were, for his sake. He is decidedly a pet of their own, and may be reckoned the most fortunate performer now living. We shall take the first opportunity of saying more on the popularity of this actor's humour, the investigation of which will demand a little more time and room than we have at present to spare.

We used formerly to contrast Mr. Liston and Mr. Emery,[19] chiefly where they came in contact in rustic characters; but there is no real ground for such a comparison. Mr. Emery is an excellent actor, of an entirely different cast; he is not of so genial and comic a nature, and identifies himself in a most remarkable manner with his respective characters, though they are of a confined class, and he ought never to step out of a certain rusticity. His common town characters, old or young, are as bad as Mr. Dowton's face-making, Mr. Bannister's genteel parts, or Mr. Liston's *Octavian*.[20] But the countryman at all periods of life, and in all sorts of humours, comic or serious, sullen or good-tempered, placid or full of passion, is exclusively and entirely his. His robust look, his thick, round features, his I-tell-you-what sort of manner, and something altogether between a cunning and clod-hopping air, admirably fit him for his favourite Yorkshire characters; and like several other of our best comedians (which, by the way, is a favourable thing to say of the general sensibility of their countrymen) he unites a considerable feeling of the serious and pathetic with his drollery and, we remember, electrified the audience once with a burst of absolute tragic passion. It was in the character of a profligate rustic, who had been sentenced to be transported and who described his old father standing wretchedly on the shore when the ship was going off. We believe it is in a piece of Mr. Morton's [21] and that it is still one of the favourite parts of this performer.

Mr. Mathews sometimes appears in rustic characters, and does them very well after the usual nature of his style of acting —that is to say, as pieces of mimicry; for all his performances are more or less of this description, and we are afraid that the exception which we formerly made in favour of his *Sir Fretful*

Plagiary [22] will not hold good, unless inasmuch as it includes more of mental expression than usual. But as a direct mimic, he is upon the whole unrivalled. The more bustle and assumption he has got to manage, the better he becomes; and in proportion as this is wanting, it is curious to see how he relapses into a want of self-possession. At one minute, putting your head in at a box-door you might take him for an uneasy simpleton, when at the next you will find him keeping it up, as the phrase is, in the most confident manner, and being the life of the evening. Mr. Mathews is excellent in a hey-day song, and has latterly, among his other mimicries, shewn himself a great adept in the slang of our fashionable coach-drivers, the cut of whose intellects and greatcoats he imitates with equal felicity.

One of the most amusing comedians living, if not the most amusing of all in certain characters, after Liston, is Mr. Munden. He is not so great a one perhaps as the lovers of broad farce may think him; but on the other hand he is a much greater than the indiscriminating objectors to grimace may allow. Certainly the work he makes with his face is equally alarming as well as droll; he has a sort of complicated grin, which may be thus described: he begins by throwing aside his mouth at the corner with as little remorse as a boy pulling it down with his fingers; then he jerks up his eyebrows; then he brings his mouth a little back again with a shew of his teeth; then he pulls down the upper lip over the top-row, as a knight might his vizor; and finally consummates the joke with a general stir round and grind of the whole lower part of his face. This accompanied with some dry phrase, or sometimes with a single word, the spectators always find irresistible, and the roar springs forth accordingly. But he is a genuine comedian nevertheless, with a considerable degree of insight into character as well as surface and with a great power of filling up the paltriest sketches. We have known him entertain the audience with a real as well as sophisticated humour for five or six minutes together, scarcely speaking a word the whole time, as in the part of a sailor in the opera of the *English Fleet*,[23] and in one, we think, in an afterpiece called the *Turnpike Gate*,[24] where he comes in and hovers about a pot of ale which he sees standing on a table, looking about him with ludicrous caution as he makes his advances, half-afraid and half-simpering when he has got near it, and then after circumventing it with his eyes and feelings over and over again, with some more cautious lookings about, heaving a sudden look into it in the most ludicrous manner imaginable and exclaiming, in an under voice of affected indifference and real chuckling, "Some gentleman has left his ale." Mr. Munden is remarkable for dressing as well as acting old age, and is equally good in the two extremes of generous old men and mercenary—the warm-hearted admiral, and the close-fisted city hunks. His cordiality would be still better, if his propensity to grimace did not interfere, a propensity always dangerous from the success it has.

The only remaining comedian whom our recollection points out to us as worthy of distinct mention is Mr. Fawcett, who may be called a vigorous actor with a tendency to farce, like Mr. Munden, though rather in general broadness than grinning. His talent lies chiefly in vehement middle-aged gentlemen, in boisterous eccentricities of all kinds, and in merry-hearted footmen; and he almost beats the orchestra itself in the strength and rapidity with which he can run through a song. *Pangloss,* in the *Heir at Law,*[25] and *Caleb Quotem,* in the *Wags of Windsor,*[26] are almost identified with his manner of acting them and are of that order of performances which, as the phrase goes, makes one die with laughter. Mr. Fawcett is at the same time harsh as well as vigorous, and this too in every respect, for his voice is harsh, his manner is harsh, and his face is harsh. In the Brazier, in *John Bull,* he and his commodities seem cut out of the same metal.

THE TRAGIC ACTORS

February 5, 1815

IT IS IMPOSSIBLE to mention the word tragedy [1] without being struck with the exceeding barrenness which the stage has exhibited of late years in everything that concerns the tragic department. Mrs. Siddons is the only real tragic genius with whom the last and present generation can be said to have been acquainted; and it may be asserted, not only that Mr. Coleridge's *Remorse* has been the only tragedy touched with real poetry for the last fifty years, but that there has been no complete production of the kind since the time of Otway. But more on this subject in an approaching number.

Since the retirement of Mrs. Siddons, and before the appearance of Mr. Kean,[2] Mr. Kemble has been in undisputed possession of the tragic throne; and it must be confessed, even by those who think least of his genius, that he occupied it with a regality which it was not easy to approach without respect. Of the Roman cast in his person and features, well read in the drama, and of a temperament perhaps to turn everything coolly about in his mind, he has a remarkable air of self-possession, and never fails to look, walk, and deliver his blank verse with an effect which to some is curious, to more is imposing, and to all, in a certain degree, striking. But the want of the real grandeur of genius is to be detected in that leisurely detail, that syllabical slowness of enunciation, that frigid reservation of himself for particular passages—that general preference, in short, for effect rather than expression, and that want of all genial impulse and extemporaneousness which have been the actual grounds of his success with his admirers, and have imposed upon them, just as mere gravity does upon people in general. It is thus that his verbal knowledge of his author has sometimes degenerated into pedantry, and his dignity into mock-heroic. With the same solemn deliberation and the same loftiness of aspect, he has issued his commands, divided a word into two syllables, and taken out his pocket handkerchief. He is always in a dress of ceremony. He feels, as it were, in externals, and speaks in hyphens.

On the other hand, the same faults of style that prevent him from being a great general tragedian, particularly in characters of sensibility and variety, are of assistance to him in certain parts of loftiness and austerity which he has almost exclusively made his own. Of this description are *Coriolanus,* and the misanthropic character of *Penruddock* in the *Wheel of Fortune.*[3] The haughtiness and rigidity which are only disagreeable intrusions upon most of his tragic parts here come in aid of the actual characters to be represented; the statue is on its pedestal again, in all becoming attitude and condition; and no longer renders us insensible to its real merits by pretending to walk about like one of ourselves.

If Mr. Kemble's style of acting was optional with him,—if, as some would have us believe, it was the result of choice and deliberation, his faith in its excellence may have been shaken a little by the success of Mr. Kean—that is to say, if the latter performer answers to what is said of him.[4] At any rate, it would seem that he is in something of the same situation with Quin, when Garrick, like the tip-toe day, made his first appearance and scattered the ghastly tones and air-sawing nonentities of declamation. But still he is not to be dismissed by the most passionate admirers of natural acting as a performer of no account. He may fall in reputation, not because his individual talent has fallen, but because his style of acting was of a description either to keep out nature entirely, or to fall before it. He is still at the head of the artificial manner; he has done wonders, in his way, with an inefficient voice and a mind rather led perhaps to the stage by circumstances than any natural genius for it; and it must not be forgotten, that his dramatic reading, his taste in private life, and the general superiority of his demeanour have added a respectability to his profession of which it has too often stood in need.

We know not that anything particular is to be said of the other actors in this department, not one of whom perhaps (and the case is remarkable) had any original genius for the stage. Mr. Young is a most respectable performer as well as gentleman, and has one element of good acting in him superior to what is possessed by Mr. Kemble—sensibility. From the want however of this original genius, he cannot put it to the best account; he has unluckily formed himself upon the artificial style lately in vogue; and his manner in general is over formal, and his enunciation laboriously syllabical. A part of strong feeling however sometimes lifts him above his usual style, as is the case in his performance of *Cassius;* and in scenes of tenderness, his heart now and then seems to flow forth from him with a tremulous softness. His face, which has considerable marks of care for a man in his prime, relaxes at these times into a very sweet expression; and his voice is always fine. Mr. Charles Kemble, who is most probably an actor because the rest of his family were actors, is another very gentlemanly and useful performer, with a most handsome face and person, and a general air of the graceful and romantic. With a dress fitted to his shape, a cloak thrown behind him, and a feather in his cap, we have seen him without speaking a word make an impression upon the spectators which nobody need be ashamed of who admires a portrait of Titian or a cast from the antique. Nor does the rest of his performance disgrace, though it does not perhaps add to, this winning appearance; it is always pleasing, and would be still more so could he leave off a trick of frowning, which he appears to mistake for dignity.

The remaining tragic actors (if actors they are to be called, who are scarcely to be called so, except in Partridge's sense of the word) are distinguishable by little but their deficiencies. Mr. Brunton is a most namby-pamby person, with an air nevertheless of good sense at bottom. Mr. Barrymore [5] is a useful performer and very sufficing in a Turk, though he ought by no means to talk about music as he does in that exquisite opening of *Twelfth-Night.* He speaks of "a dying fall" and "the food of love," just as he might order a Lord Mayor's dinner. Mr. Claremont is a useful performer also in under parts, and seems a good-tempered man with an inordinate passion for neckcloths. As to

Mr. Raymond, he has revenged himself upon us every time these seven years for some hopeful things we formerly said of him,[6] by getting every day more noisy and presumptuous, and refuting every word we uttered with all his might and main.

SINGERS, &C.

February 12, 1815

IN ORDER to give a completeness, such as it is, to the subject before us,[1] we shall conclude our Sketches with notices of the principal singers, pantomime-actors, &c. and with a glance or two at such performers as have escaped us in the preceding articles.

Mr. Braham[2] is the first living singer in England, perhaps in the world. He has a melodious and powerful voice, correctness, taste, passion. It is curious to observe how the orchestra inspires him; and what a difference there is between the tame, indifferent, vapid creature that gets rid of his words with a hasty, half-breathing imbecility when speaking, and the firm, ardent, intelligent being that throws them hither and thither with masterly power during a song. He has, however, considerable drawbacks on his power of pleasing; and in a country where fine singers abounded, would, we suspect, be comparatively set aside, like a precious stone that had flaws in it. The general tone of his voice has a nasal twang, which to our ears is very offensive, and involves, like the same thing in speaking, a kind of meanness and innate vulgarity; and his general style of singing is meretricious; and not only is the general style of his singing meretricious, but the ornaments with all their exuberance are frequently misplaced, and so far he wants the common taste even of floridness. He wears bells on his toes as well as rings on his fingers. He will run divisions upon the most insignificant words, and trill, quaver, and roll about at you without remorse. He lights up, as it were, fifty wax candles to exhibit a nut shell; or resembles a fantastic fellow, who instead of approaching you by the ordinary path and in a straight manner, should come up with all sorts of fluttering gestures and meanders, and accompany his concluding bow with a shake of the head and cheeks of five minutes duration. One of his most disagreeable tricks is that of swelling out and iterating his voice like a mail-coach horn—which is all very well on proper occasions, but, when it comes forth upon a word that does not call for it, is as ridiculous as if he were to ask you, in the same manner, how you did. At the same time, it must not be denied that he can divest himself now and then of all this absurdity, and give you a simple ballad or piece of pathos in its native beauty; but then the very applause which rewards him for so doing and would encourage him to persist in it tends to lead him astray again, and off he goes into some ridiculous catching and quavering. The mode, for instance, in which he sings the well-known ballad of *Robin Adair*, is for the most part exquisite, but if he begins and proceeds well, a cadence is generally his stumbling-block; he must ring out a kind of triumph at having done so well, must reward his virtue, like the man in the old story, with a dram; and nothing can be more mean or unnatural, and more destructive of the touching simplicity of the original, than his twitching up his voice on every syllable in the words "Robin Adair"—

Rŏ–ō—bĭ–ĭn———A–ā—dair.

It is generally said in his behalf that simplicity and the true style of singing are his real talent, and that the rest is only put on for the sake of effect. We were of the same opinion ourselves formerly; but we very much doubt the thing at present, and are inclined to think vice versa—that floridness is his talent, and simplicity only his occasional virtue. True geniuses are not so apt to accommodate themselves to inferior ones, and if they do, it is not with a *predominance* of the worse taste: the vice is occasional, and the virtue predominant. The appeal too which the bad taste must make to the grosser multitude, and the kind of suspicion it involves with regard to vulgarity of intellect and the love of money-making, go very much against the better inference in these matters. Milton wrote for posterity; but Mr. Walter Scott writes for the booksellers.

The other living singers are not to be called great in any sense of the word, either as leaders of a good or a bad taste.* Mrs. Dickons is the best we have after Braham, and is perhaps as

* The writer has not yet heard Miss Stephens. [Catherine Stephens, later the Countess of Essex (1794–1882).]

correct a one as any living: she has also considerable power, and may be called upon the whole a very useful and effective singer, a pitch above mediocrity. By many indeed she is thought to possess a good deal of taste; but this we conceive to be one of the impositions arising from the bravura and florid style. To us, besides her unpleasant reediness of voice, there is a coarse, flaunting air in her very best manner; and on no account should she ever undertake to be fascinating. Mrs. Mountain [3] is a pleasing singer in the upper rank of the mediocre, and is a better actress than most of her profession. Mrs. Bishop,[4] to our ears at least, is sharp and glassy. Mrs. Liston [5] has a sweet voice, and is by no means deficient in taste of the ballad kind; but she is inferior, we think, in both to Mrs. Bland, whose style has a sort of gentle-hearted, dairy-maid simplicity with it, that would set all the people in a village listening to nothing else every summer's evening.

Of the remaining male singers, Smith [6] has mere depth and plainness; and Sinclair [7] (though the phrase is rather man-millinery) is a pretty singer with a pleasing, sweet voice, and no great powers of any kind. The best of them is one who has been celebrated in his time—Incledon. He has a fine, manly voice, and once united the two extremes of strength and sweetness. He has been reckoned indeed a true specimen of an English singer; but we confess, he does not appear so to us. He may have the force, and even the sweetness; but he wants the dignity and expressiveness, or, in other words, the intelligence. He is not a fit singer, for instance, for the true English composers, such as Arne and Purcell, except where they get into their most inferior ballad-style. Mr. Bartleman,[8] who does not come under our present stage view, leaves him and everybody else, in this respect, at an immeasurable distance. There is in fact a vulgar slang about Incledon's style, which is not at all relieved by his trick of gabbling and of licking his lips. And yet notwithstanding all his defects, and even his inferiority in point of talent, we have oftener perhaps heard him with satisfaction than Braham himself—so charming is simplicity, even in its least charming undress.

It would be unpardonable, in this summary of our actors, to omit one who, though he scarcely ever utters a syllable, is a more entertaining and even elegant performer than many who talk well enough. We allude to Grimaldi, but must not indulge ourselves on the subject, or we should have no end in describing his tricks and devices, his grins and shoulder-shakings, his pleasantries equally excellent, whether taken from nature or otherwise, his expressions of childish glee in gigglings and squeaks, his facile dislocation of limbs carried about with an air as if he did not know it, his short and deep snatches of laughter like what we read in the poets of Robin Goodfellow, and his Ho! ho!—in short, all those perfections of the clown which before his time perhaps were confined to the Italian stage, and which indeed may be said, after all, to have come to him through the same medium, if his stock, as we believe, is Italian. We shall only say, that at Christmas, we are as great boys as any that go to see him.

Among the performers who have been omitted in the course of these sketches, and of whom our correspondents have reminded us, may be mentioned, in conclusion, Mr. Lovegrove, a pleasing and useful actor on a small scale, though with a voice approaching the nasal Knight,[9] an actor of rustics, whom we remember for nothing but a sort of muscular little strength and a straightforward voice, but who has improved, it is said, very much within the last two years, and Oxberry,[10] a comedian by no means deficient in humour, with a strange mixture of manliness in his general appearance, and a sort of gossiping, old-wife look in his face. Mr. Pope also must not be omitted, who though a very false and bombastic actor in general, acts at least one character well and even perfectly, and that is Henry the 8th. His mode of looking and dressing this part is excellently correct, and rivals the laudable and historical accuracy of the French stage, which, by the way, is the only thing it has got in tragedy that is worth rivalling. In fine, we ought not to have forgotten Johnstone,[11] who has made the Irish character, or at least the stage idea of it, his own; and who is, or has been, a very good singer as well as actor, with a true quiet style of humour, and an exquisite, lack-a-day sort of trusting repose on his audience. As to Mr. Raymond, to whom we unwillingly revert in consequence of what a correspondent has written to us, we are sorry that we cannot give a more gratifying answer to a letter so well-tempered; but for his "noisy" style of acting we must again refer to all the tragic characters we ever recollect him to have performed, and for the epithet "presumption," to his mode of addressing audiences during a play, and his preface to a drama that was published some three or four years back by a person much superior to himself, of the name of Lake.[12] Mr. Raymond may be as pleasant and intelligent a man in private as his advocate represents him; but our business is with his theatrical character, and we have only to regret that he is not equally so in public.

[RICHARD III]

February 26, 1815   *Drury-Lane*

THE EDITOR for the first time since his imprisonment went to the Theatre on Monday last, when he saw Mr. Kean; [1] and it must not be imputed to the fastidiousness of criticism, if he confesses that upon the whole he was disappointed. Indeed it is but proper, and may in some measure perhaps account for the disappointment, to mention that his expectations had been raised to a very high pitch by the reports in favour of that performer, [2] expectations to which he gave way the more readily, inasmuch as he had been in the habit, for years, of objecting to the artificial style of the actors lately in vogue; so that he had enthusiastically concluded that he was now going to realize, on the sudden, all that had ever appeared to him natural and desirable in theatrical representation. It is right to mention also (thanks to the magnificent inconvenience of these fine theatres!) that he was not as near to the stage as he ought to have been; and it should not be omitted that many of the most intelligent as well as ardent admirers of this gentleman think him much fallen off from what he was the last season.

Neither of these circumstances, however, can account, in his mind, for the *sort* of deficiency which Mr. Kean appeared to exhibit. It was not that the actor seemed to want only to be perfectly seen and heard, or to be inferior in degree to what he might have been a season before; but that the general run of his style was not of the cast that we had been led to anticipate. It seemed too artificial to be a mere falling off from nature. It was artificial in the general, and natural only in the particular; its native parts were the exceptions; in other words, and to state at once our conclusion respecting him, as far as this one character can enable us to come to any, Mr. Kean appeared to us, during the greater part of his performance, to be nothing but a first-rate actor of the ordinary, stagy class, and to start only occasionally into passages of truth and originality.

To come a little more to particulars. We expected to find in Mr. Kean an actor as little artificial as possible; we expected to find no declamation, no common rant, no puttings forth of the old oratorical right hand, no speech-making and attitudinizing at one, no implication, in short, of a set of spectators; but something genuine and unconscious, something that moved, looked, and spoke solely under the impulse of the immediate idea, something as natural in its way, with proper allowance, of course, for the gravity of the interests going forward, as the man who enters his room after a walk, takes off his hat, pinches off one glove and throws into it, then the other glove and throws into it, gives a pull down to his coat or a pull up to his neckcloth, and makes up the fire-place with a rub of his hands and a draught of the air through his teeth. If this should be thought too much to demand in tragedy, it is only because we have been accustomed to the reverse—to art instead of nature. We are persuaded that it is quite practicable, that it would take, as the phrase is, immediately, and that it wants only a daring genius, with the genuine boldness and unaccommodating self-respect of enthusiasm, to push it to its utmost.

Such was the actor we expected to find in Mr. Kean; but his *Richard,* for one character at least, does not prove him to be the person. In the ordinary scenes, for instance, such as those with *Buckingham,* with his mother, with the young Princes, and in all the more level parts of the dialogue, he was no better than Mr. Kemble; that is to say, without meaning any invidious allusion to that gentleman, he was no better than the best kind of actor in the artificial style; he dealt out his syllables, and stood finely, and strutted at the set off of a speech, just as other well-received performers do; and he is much farther gone in stage trickery than we supposed him to be, particularly in the old violent contrasts when delivering an equivoque, dropping his voice too consciously from a serious line to a sly one, and fairly putting it to the house as a good joke.

On the other hand, he has occasional bursts, and touches of nature, such as might be expected from the actor we had fancied to ourselves, and such as would go near to make us think that the general run of his style was really different from what it used to be, were those who are once in love with nature, genuinely and heartily, apt to let an inferior habit get the better of them. We wish the reader to keep in mind that we look upon him to be equal, at all times, to the best actors in vogue; but in particular passages, he undoubtedly goes far beyond any of them, and makes us regret that he who can be so natural, so nobly familiar, in half a dozen instances, should not conduct himself with the same nativeness throughout. Nothing, for example, can take leave, with better effect, of the usual solemn pedantry of the stage than that action of rubbing his hands, to which he gives way occasionally in his part when he thinks his views are succeeding. In some characters there might be a vulgarity and an over-excitement in it; but people of *Richard's* cast of ambition are seldom very refined, and their joy is not bound to be philosophical. His other gestures too, now and then, and the turns of his countenance, tend in a very happy manner to unite common life with tragedy—which is the great stage-desideratum; and it would be impossible to express in a deeper manner the intentness of *Richard's* mind upon the battle that was about to take place, or to quit the scene with an abruptness more self-recollecting, pithy, and familiar, than by the reverie in which he stands drawing lines upon the ground with the point of his sword, and his sudden recovery of himself with a "Good night."

The more we think on his passages of this description the more we regret our disappointment upon the whole, and the happier we should be to unsay any of our unfavourable remarks upon seeing him in another character. Of his bad voice, we should think little or nothing if he met our wishes in other respects, though, to say the truth, it grew deplorable enough towards the conclusion, and resembled a hackney-coachman's at one o'clock in the morning. It is not, we suspect, essentially bad; and it is to be wished he could find some means of keeping it in proper tone. While he was about mending himself in this particular, we would also suggest that he ought not to get under such a large hat and feathers as he seems fond of; and it might be as well

also, if he would contrive to get a little handsomer deformity
—to inflict a reasonable lump on his leg—instead of the enormous and bolster-like pad which he puts into his stocking for
that purpose.

SOME ACCOUNT OF THE ORIGIN
AND NATURE OF MASKS

March, 1815

As THE SPECIES of dramatic production called a Mask[1] has been unknown among us for a long time,[2] the reader may not be unwilling, before he enters upon the following pages, to hear a few words respecting it. Not that the author pretends to instruct everyone on the subject who may happen to take up his book; but it is possible for persons well acquainted in general with our elder and nobler poetry to have missed this particular branch of it, which, as it was chiefly used for ornament on temporary and private occasions, was at the same time of the most irregular turn and the most carelessly cultivated. The Mask with which poetical readers are most familiar —*Comus*—has less of the particular nature of the composition than any other; and those which have most of it either form parts of other dramas, as in the *Tempest*, and are too short to fix a separate recollection, or happen to be so poor in themselves, like those of Ben Jonson, as to be occasionally omitted in the writer's works.

The Mask, with regard to its origin, is dismissed by Warton in his *History of Poetry* as "a branch of the elder drama";[3] and its nature is defined by Dr. Johnson to be "a dramatic performance written in a tragic style without attention to rules or probability."[4] These accounts appear equally vague and incorrect. It is more than doubtful whether the Mask had any connexion with the drama in the first instance; and there have been Masks in a comic as well as tragic style. The definition would even include a number of tragedies.

On the other hand, it is not easy to settle the distinct nature of a composition the lawlessness of which is confessed. Some Masks have been without supernatural agency, others without scenery, others without a machinery of any kind; but an intermixture of songs, and especially some kind of pomp or pageant, seem to have been features in all of them—in all, at least, that pretend to a dramatic form; for the title, in some instances, appears to have been warranted by the exhibition, real or descriptive, of a piece of dumb show; and this, together with the name itself and the mention of the word pageant, may lead us to its true origin and definition, the former of which is otherwise lost amidst a multitude of shows, mysteries, and musical dramas.[5]

The Mask then, as far as its actors and in-door character were concerned, seems to have grown more immediately out of the entertainment called a Masquerade, and as far as its gorgeousness and machinery, out of the Pageants or Public Shows with which it was customary in the reign of the Tudors to welcome princes and other persons of distinction. From the latter it took its deities and allegorical persons, and from the former its representation by families, or by parties of the gentry and nobility.

Both of these kinds of exhibition, with a remote relationship perhaps to the Greek stage, and a nearer one to the festive compositions of the Provençals, had their birth in Italy,—the soil in which every species of modern poetry seems to have originally sprung up. The first appearance of one of them, or perhaps combination of both, undoubtedly took place at Florence, in the time of Lorenzo de' Medici, when a party of persons, during a season of public festivity, made their appearance in the streets, riding along in procession and dressed up like reanimated dead bodies, who sung a tremendous chorus, reminding the appalled spectators of their mortality.* Spectacles of this nature were clearly the origin of the Trionfi or Triumphs of the Italian poets; and under different aspects, and with more or less assumption of a dramatic air, soon spread all over Italy, now contracting themselves into domestic and gorgeous congratulations at the nuptials of great men, now splitting from a

* See the History of Lorenzo de' Medici by Mr. Roscoe, to whom the lovers of Italian literature are so much indebted. [William Roscoe, *The Life of Lorenzo de' Medici, Called the Magnificent* (Liverpool: Printed by J. M'Creery, and sold by J. Edwards, London, 1795), I, 305.]

particular purpose into the scattered and individual freaks of carnivals and masquerades.

It is true, the fondness of the Inns of Court for this species of performance may be referred to the old theatrical exhibitions in monasteries and colleges; but the connexion with masquerades in general seems easily traceable. The masquerade, in this country, as a particular entertainment, was for a long time confined to the houses of the great and to the celebrations of births, marriages, and the higher description of festive meetings; and as the Masquers, who sometimes went visiting in a troop, would now and then come upon their host unawares, it may be conjectured that, finding themselves encouraged by success to give their compliments a more prepared and poetical turn, they gradually assumed characters in honour of the day's celebration, and accompanied their appearance with songs and dialogue: in a short time, the Pageants that were every day occurring, and the very nature of the exhibition itself, easily suggested the addition of allegory and personification; by further degrees, a scene and a stage arose; the composer and machinist were regularly employed: and at length the Mask took its place as a species of fanciful drama, which the poet was to render as agreeable and surprising as he could.

The Mask, therefore, in its proper character, and such as it flourished in this country during the finest times of our poetry, may be defined—a mixed Drama, allowing of natural incidents as of everything else that is dramatic, but more essentially given up to the fancy, and abounding in machinery and personification, generally with a particular allusion.

To some critics, the license which such a species of composition allows is intolerable. They see in it nothing but the violation of rules and probabilities; and turn aside from the most charming fancy, when it comes to them in a dress which the French have not authorized. Give others again the fancy, and in a piece professedly supernatural they will be content to overlook rules and probabilities; they go whithersoever the poet leads them, provided he does it with grace as well as imagination; and when they find themselves among summer clouds or enchanted gardens, do not quarrel with him for being out of London or Paris. Undoubtedly, that work is the noblest, which can produce the greatest quantity of fancies and probabilities at once, or in other words, the greatest pleasure under the greatest difficulty. A Mask, it is confessed, is not a great drama, nor an epic poem. But when the poet chooses to take leave of the probable, it does not follow that he must abandon the tasteful or even the natural, whatever has been the assertion of those whose taste, if they could have found out the truth, was of as small a range as their imagination. Even the improbable has its rules, and does not mistake mere exaggeration for greatness, the shocking for the terrific, or the puerile for the tricksome. In short, taste as well as fancy, has a very extensive province, even of the most legitimate kind; and the wildest imagination may be found there, and is, so long as it carries with it two things which may be called the poet's passports, and which our critical friends on the other side of the water would be in vain called upon to produce—primitive feelings, and a natural language. Let the reader just look at a passage, almost a random one, from the *Tempest*. It is where Prospero tells Ariel to bring in some of the inferior spirits for the Mask.

> *Ariel.*   Presently?
> *Prospero.* Ay,—with a twink.
> *Ariel.* Before you can say Come and Go,
> And breathe twice, and cry So, so,
> Each one tripping on his toe,
> Will be here with mop and mowe.
> *Do you love me, Master? No.*
> *Prospero.* Dearly, my delicate Ariel.[6]

Here are freaks of the fancy; but do they hinder the properest and most natural language, or even an appeal to the affections? The half arch, half pathetic line in italics comes across our nature with a startling smilingness, and finds us at home when we most seem to have gone out of ourselves.

It is observable, that in proportion as the critic possesses something of poetry himself, or the poet rises in the enthusiasm of his art, he gets above this kind of prejudice. What are styled "fooleries" by Warburton [7] are called "liberal and elegant amusements" by Warton; [8] and what were neglected by the wits of Charles the Second's day for French rhetoric, rhyming tragedies, and the conceits of the corrupted Italian school (for when writers talk of the conceits of the Italians, they are speaking of what the Italians themselves condemn), were praised and practised by the men, who, by universal consent, are at the head of our native poetry.

Had our great poets indeed stopped short of actual practice in this instance, it would be clear from a variety of passages in their works what hold these gorgeous and fanciful exhibitions had taken on their minds. Pageant and Mask are common terms in Shakspeare and Spenser for something more than ordinarily striking in the way of vision; they often furnish them with resemblances and reflections; and a great deal of the main feature of the *Faerie Queen* has with great probability been traced to the influence of these congenial spectacles. Milton, it is true, who objected to kings on earth and filled heaven with regalities, who denied music to chapel-goers [9] and allowed it to angels, who would have had nothing brilliant in human worship and sprinkled the pavement before the deity's throne with roses and amaranths, has a passage in which he speaks contemptuously of

Court-amours,
Mix'd dance, or wanton Mask, or midnight ball *;

but it was after he had learnt to quarrel with the graces of the world, as something which Providence had sent us only to deny ourselves. He is speaking here, too, of the entertainment in its abuse rather than its proper character. In his younger, happier, and it may be added, not less poetical days, he counted

. . . Masque and antique Pageantry

among the rational pleasures of cheerfulness, and gave them perhaps the very highest as well as most lovely character of abstract and essential poetry, by calling them

Such sights as youthful poets dream
On summer eves by haunted stream.**

* Parad. Lost, Book V. [Erroneous. Book IV, 767–768.]
** L'Allegro. [128–130.]

In short, *Comus* had been the result of his early feelings; and it was curious that he who inveighed against Masks in his more advanced age should have been fated to leave to posterity the very piece by which this species of composition is chiefly known.

Comus, however, though an undoubted Mask in some respects, as in its magic, its route of monsters, and its particular allusion to an event in the noble family that performed it, is more allied, from its regularity of story and its deficiency in scenic show, to the Favole Boschereccie, or Sylvan Tales of the Italian poets, which had just then been imitated and surpassed by the *Faithful Shepherdess* of Fletcher. A Mask may be pastoral or not as it pleases, but scenic show and personification are, upon the whole, its distinguishing features; and Milton, with the *Faithful Shepherdess* on his table (his evident prototype), was tempted to deviate more and more from the title of his piece by the new charm that had come upon him.

On the other hand, Spenser, who appears at one time to have written a set of Pageants, has introduced into his great poem an allegorical procession into which Upton conjectures them to have been worked up,* and which the author has expressly called a "Maske," though it is in the other extreme of *Comus* and has nothing but show about it. It is in Book the third, Canto the twelfth, where Britomart, in the strange Castle, and in the silence and solitude of night, is awaked by a "shrilling trumpet," and after a storm of wind and thunder, with the clapping of doors, sees the "Maske of Cupid" issue from the Enchanted Chamber and pace about her room. The whole scene is in his noblest style of painting; but as it is only a mute spectacle, and that, too, rather described than acted, it does not include the dramatic character necessary to complete the more general idea of the Mask.

The Mask which is introduced in the *Tempest*, and which Warburton had unluckily forgotten when he thought to countenance his opinion of these "fooleries" by saying that Shakspeare

---

* See a note on the passage. Todd's Spenser, Vol. 5, p. 106.—1805. [Cf. the first paragraph of Upton's note on the Mask of Cupid, *The Works of Edmund Spenser. A Variorum Edition*, ed. E. Greenlaw, C. G. Osgood, F. M. Padelford (Baltimore: The Johns Hopkins Press, 1932–1943), Book III (1934), p. 299.]

had written none,* is a much completer thing of its kind. In addition to supernatural agency, it has songs and a dialogue, and it is called up by Prospero for the purpose of celebrating a particular event—the betrothment of Ferdinand and Miranda. It is not, of course, as the mere contingency of a play, to be compared with the work of Milton, nor is it, though not without marks of a great hand, so lively and interesting as Spenser's Pageant; but it comes much nearer than either to the genuine Mask, and indeed only differs from it inasmuch as it is rather an incident than a piece by itself—rather a Mask in a drama, than a drama in the form of a Mask. Of a similar kind, and not without touches of poetry, is the Mask in the *Maid's Tragedy* of Beaumont and Fletcher, and the spirited little sketch of another, after Spenser, in Fletcher's *Wife for a Month*.

The pieces written for more direct occasions, and altogether presenting us with the complete and distinct character of this entertainment, may be divided perhaps into two classes—those written to be seen only, and those that had the ambition also to be read. Of the former class (for it seems but fair to allow them this privilege) are the Masks of Ben Jonson. It may seem a hardy thing to assert that Jonson was in one respect eminently qualified for this kind of production by the luxuriance and volatility of his fancy; but the ancients, instead of furnishing cordials to his actual deficiency, will be found perhaps, upon a due insight into the more poetical part of him, to have been the bane of his natural strength. A classical education may have given him an accidental inclination towards them, as it will do with most poets at first; but upon comparison of his learning with his fancy, it seems likely that nothing but a perversion of the love of originality, and perhaps a consciousness that he could never meet Shakspeare on equal terms in the walk of humanity, determined him on being a local humorist in the grave cloak of a scholar. What he wanted, besides the generalising power, was sentiment. His turn of mind, doubly distorted perhaps by the thwarting of his genius, was so unfortunate on this score, and appears to have acquired such a general tendency to contradiction, that he almost seems to be playing the Hector

* Note to Romeo and Juliet, act 1, scene 4. [See note 7, p. 311.]

with his own performances, and to delight in shaming the occasional elegance of his fancy by following it up with an additional coarseness and hey-day vulgarity. Of the numerous Masks which he wrote for the court of James the First, those perhaps that contain the most poetical passages are two with very attractive titles—the *Vision of Delight,* and *Pleasure Reconciled to Vertue;* but neither is free from this sort of bitterness. That they are poor in other respects is not to be wondered at. The author probably wrote them with little good-will. Not only was the honour of the inventions partaken by the celebrated Inigo Jones, whom he has frequently endeavoured to gall in his Epigrams, but the King, whose taste, when he was not hunting or disputing, ran upon finery, most likely expressed a greater admiration of the machinist's beauties than the poet's; and to sum up all, the task was an official one. If this cannot excuse the coarseness of the humour, or even the gross servility of the adulation, it may reasonably apologize for the rest: and something of the same kind may be observed for the poverty of Masks in general. A passage in Beaumont and Fletcher will at once illustrate this observation, and show the opinion which two real poets who wrote Masks themselves, entertained of their general awkwardness.

> *Lysippus.* Strato, thou hast some skill in poetry;
>   What think'st thou of the Masque? Will it be well?
> *Strato.* As well as Masque can be.
> *Lysippus.* As Masque can be?
> *Strato.* Yes.
>   They must commend their king, and speak in praise
>   Of the assembly,—bless the bride and bridegroom
>   In person of some god. They're tyed to rules
>   Of flattery.
>   *Maid's Tragedy,* Act 1. Sc. 1
>   [opening passage]

Taste and good temper, however, would make a considerable difference in the merit even of flattery: and it is to be recollected, after all, that the Mask was not of necessity to be complimentary, though it was generally produced on complimentary occasions. Beaumont, in a piece called the *Masque of the Inner Temple and Gray's Inn,* and written in honour of the Elector Palatine's marriage with James's daughter, has exhibited equal delicacy and invention. Carew, in the succeeding reign, when the Prince, whatever political errors he had derived from a bad education, was a man of taste and respectability, complimented the court in a Mask entitled *Coelum Britannicum,* which, contrary to the usual corruptness of the author's taste, is in some parts worthy the dignity of Milton himself; and among the variety of productions of this kind which the gentlemen of the law appear to have got up, as the phrase is, for their own amusement, there is one of a general description, founded on the fable of Circe and written by William Browne, a student of the Temple in the beginning of James's reign, which reminds us of Milton, and has been supposed by some [10] to have been one of the various productions which furnished hints for his *Comus.* Browne, though he was deficient in that pervading taste, or selectness, which can alone bring down a man to posterity, or at least enable him to survive but with the curious, was a true poet, with a luxuriant fancy and great powers of description, and has undoubtedly been imitated by Milton in some instances.

These three pieces, the *Masque of the Inner Temple and Gray's Inn* by Beaumont, the *Coelum Britannicum* of Carew, and the *Inner Temple Mask or Circe* of Browne, are of the more ambitious class that aim to be read; and may be pronounced, perhaps, upon the whole, the best specimens of the Mask, in its stricter sense, that are to be found. They are far below such a work as *Comus;* but considered as an inferior species of composition, of no great extent, and, two of them, with a courtly purpose, they possess no small portion of poetry, and may be characterized, the first by fancy and elegance, the second by a lofty strain of sentiment, and the third by a certain full and reposing luxury.

To complete the sketch on the present subject, a specimen may be quoted, from each of these pieces, of the three principal features of the Mask,—its show, its personification, and its songs. Beaumont has prefaced his with the following "Device

or Argument," which contains an analysis of the entire performance, and will exhibit at once the main fabric of a Mask:

Jupiter and Juno, willing to do honour to the marriage of the two
famous rivers, Thamesis and Rhine (an allusion to the Princess Elizabeth and the Elector Palatine), employ their messengers severally,
Mercury and Iris, for that purpose. They meet and contend. Then
Mercury, for his part, brings forth an anti-masque, all of spirits or
divine natures, but yet not of one kind or livery, because that had
been so much in use heretofore, but, as it were, in consort, like to
broken music; and preserving the *propriety* of the devise—for that
rivers in nature are maintained either by springs from beneath or
showers from above—he raiseth four of the Naiades out of the
fountains, and bringeth down five of the Hyades out of the clouds,
to dance. Hereupon, Iris scoffs at Mercury, for that he had devised
a dance but of one sex, which could have no life; but Mercury, who
was provided for that exception, and in token that the match should
be blessed both with love and riches, calleth forth out of the groves
four Cupids, and brings down from Jupiter's altar four statues of
gold and silver to dance with the nymphs and stars, in which dance
the Cupids being blind, and the statues having half life put into
them, and retaining still some of their old nature, giveth fit occasion
to new and strange varieties both in the music and paces. This was
the first anti-masque.

Then Iris, for her part, in scorn of this high-flying devise, and in
token that the match shall likewise be blessed with the love of the
common people, calls to Flora her confederate (for that the months
of flowers are likewise the months of sweet showers and rainbows)
to bring in a May-dance, or rural dance, consisting likewise not of
any suited persons, but of a confusion or commixture of all such
persons as are natural and proper for country sports. This is the
second anti-masque.

Then Mercury and Iris, after this vieing one upon the other, seem
to leave their contention; and Mercury, by the consent of Iris, brings
down the Olympian knights, intimating, that Jupiter having, after
a long discontinuance, revived the Olympian games, and summoned
thereunto from all parts the liveliest and activest persons that were,
had enjoined them, before they fell to their games, to do honour to
these nuptials. The Olympian games portend to the match celebrity,
victory, and felicity. [This was the maine Masque.] [11]

The fabric was a mountain with two descents, and served with
two traverses. At the entrance of the king the first traverse was
drawn, [and the lower descent of the Mountaine discovered;] [12]
which was a pendant of a hill to the life with divers boscages and

grovets upon the steep or hanging grounds thereof; and at the foot of the hill, four delicate fountains running with water and bordered with sedges and water-flowers.

Iris first appeared; and presently after, Mercury, striving to overtake her. Iris appareled in a robe of discoloured taffeta, figured in variable colours like the rainbow, a cloudy wreath on her head, and tresses. Mercury in doublet and hose of white taffeta, a white hat, wings on his shoulders and feet, his caduceus in his hand, speaking to Iris as followeth:

> *Mercury.*   Stay, stay,
> Stay, light-foot Iris, for thou strivest in vain;
> My wings are nimbler than thy feet.
> *Iris.*   Away,
> Dissembling Mercury! my messages
> Ask honest haste, not like those wanton ones
> Your thund'ring father sends.
> *Mer.*   Stay, foolish maid!
> Or I will take my rise upon a hill,
> When I perceive thee seated on a cloud
> In all the painted glory that thou hast,
> And never cease to clap my willing wings,
> Till I catch hold of thy discoloured bow,
> And shiver it, beyond the angry pow'r
> Of your curst mistress to make up again.
> *Iris.* Hermes, forbear. Juno will chide and strike.
> Is great Jove jealous that I am employed
> On her love-errands? She did never yet
> Clasp weak mortality in her white arms,
> As he hath often done.
>   &c. &c.

All this, it must be confessed, is sufficiently wild; yet the author, we see, thinks of his *proprieties* in the midst of it; and the critic, who is about to cry out against the dancing statues, will probably check himself on the sudden, by recollecting the walking images and peripatetic footstools in Homer. In fact, it is of these very images that the poet has made use. The conclusion of the piece is very quiet and pleasing:

> Peace and silence be the guide
> To the man, and to the bride.
> If there be a joy yet new
> In marriage, let it fall on you.
>   &c.

In the *Coelum Britannicum,* which represents the Pagan heaven as having resolved, out of pure emulation of the British court, to lead a better life and rid the constellations of their unworthy occupants, a variety of allegorical persons come before Mercury and Momus to show the extensiveness of their sovereignty and lay claim to the vacant places. Among others, Poverty and Pleasure appear, the former of whom is described as a "woman of pale colour, large brims of a hat upon her head, through which her hair started up like a Fury; her robe was of a dark colour full of patches; about one of her hands was tyed a chaine of iron, to which was fastened a weighty stone, which she bore up under her arm." Mercury, after hearing her pretensions, which are of the Stoical cast, dismisses her with an invective, which begins thus:

> Thou dost presume too much, poor needy wretch,
> To claim a station in the firmament,
> Because thy humble cottage, or thy tub,
> Nurses some lazy or pedantique virtue,
> In the cheap sunshine, or by shady springs,
> With roots and pot-herbs; where thy rigid hand,
> Tearing those human passions from the mind,
> Upon whose stock fair blooming writers flourish,[13]
> Degradeth Nature and benumbeth sense,
> And Gorgon-like, turns active men to stone.

The picture of Pleasure is that of "a young woman with a smiling face, in a light lascivious habit, adorned with silver and gold, her temples crowned with a garland of roses, and over that a rainbow circling her head down to her shoulders." Poverty's speech is followed with a dance of Gypsies, Pleasure's with that of the Five Senses: but Mercury dismisses her in like manner, commencing, among other images of a less original complexion, with some that are very lively and forcible:

> Bewitching Syren, gilded rottenness,
> Thou hast with cunning artifice displayed
> Th'enamel'd outside, and the honied verge
> Of the fair cup, where deadly poison lurks;
> Within, a thousand sorrows dance the round:
> And, like a shell, Pain circles thee without;
> Grief is the shadow waiting on thy steps,

Which, as thy joys 'gin tow'rds their West decline,
Doth to a gyant's spreading form extend
Thy dwarfish stature.

For the third, or lyrical part of the Mask, nothing can equal in point of richness and harmonious variety the songs in *Comus*, that, for instance, beginning

Sabrina fair,
    Listen where thou art sitting
        Under the glassy, cool, translucent wave,
    In twisted braids of lilies knitting
        The loose train of thy amber-dropping hair: . . .

The lyrics in the *Faithful Shepherdess* are also models of this kind in point of grace and a light touching; nor could Ben Jonson have more completely proved his fitness for writing Masks than by the single production of that most accomplished invocation to Diana in *Cynthia's Revels:*

Queen and huntress, chaste and fair,
    Now the sun is laid to sleep,
Seated in thy silver chair,
    State in wonted manner keep; * &c.

But to conclude the specimens from the more decided Mask, the following passage may be taken from the *Circe* of Browne. The Charme, though falling off towards the conclusion, has been quoted by Warton in his *History of Poetry* * * with a just feeling of admiration.

The Songe of Nymphes in the Wood

What sing the sweet birds in each grove?
            Nought but love.
What sound our echoes, day and night?
            All delighte.
What doth each wynd breathe us, that fleetes?
            Endlesse sweetes.

Chorus

Is there a place on earth this isle excels,
Or any nymphes more happy live than we,
When all our songes, our soundes, and breathinges be,
That here all love, delighte, and sweetnesse dwells?

* Act 5. Sc. 6. [1–4.]
** Vol. 2. Sect. 16. [Thos. Warton, *op. cit.*, III, 321.]

Circe

Yet holdes soft sleepe his course. Now, Ithacus,
Ajax would offer hecatombes to us,
And Ilium's ravish'd wifes, and childlesse sires,
With incense dym the bright aetherial fires,
To have thee bounde in chaynes of sleepe as here;
But that thou mayst behold, and knowe how deare
Thou art to Circe, with my magic deepe
And powerfull verses thus I banish sleepe.

THE CHARME

Sonne of Erebus and Night!
Hye away; and aime thy flighte,
Where consorte none other fowle,
Than the batte, and sullen owle;
Where upon the lymber grasse,
Poppy and mandragoras,
With like simples not a fewe,
Hang for ever droppes of dewe;
Where flowes Lethe, without coyle,
Softly like a stream of oyle.
Hye thee thither, gentle Sleepe,
With this Greeke no longer keepe.
Thrice I charge thee by my wand,
Thrice with moly from my hand
Doe I touch Ulysses' eyes,
And with the jaspis.—Then arise,
Sagest Greeke!

This is the hepta-syllabic measure which Fletcher rendered so attractive in his *Faithful Shepherdess,* and which from its adoption by succeeding writers, particularly Milton, has almost become appropriated to the rhyming speeches of the Mask and Pastoral Drama, as distinguished from their songs and dialogue.

With these writers the Mask may be said to have begun and ended; for though a few pieces are to be found under the same title, or that of Operas, in the works of Dryden and others, yet upon the whole, the distinct species of drama, both in character and mode of performance, had gone by: the witchery that had consented to visit the dreams of an earlier and less sophisticated age, had vanished. The Puritans, who first put an end to them,   .

and who, for the most part, were as disagreeable a body of persons as Liberty could have taken it into her head to make use of, quarrelled with everything they found established, liberal as well as despotic; and the golden age of English poetry, in its feeling as well as its freaks, in its sublimity and love of nature as well as its sports and extravagancies, closed at the very moment when it might have given additional lustre to the rise of freedom.

The harsh and disputatious period that succeeded, and the still more unfeeling debauchery of the one after, effectually prevented the reappearance of genuine poetry. The Muse, it is true, had not quite forsaken the land, nor given it up to the hopelessness of better days. In the person of Milton, she had retired into a sacred obscurity, and built herself, as it were, an invisible bower, where the ascension of her voice, and the mingling of her majestic organ, might be heard at intervals by a few favored ears;—but the rest of the country was occupied with a very different succession of sounds; and after "a sullen interval of war," came in

> The barbarous dissonance
> Of Bacchus and his revellers.

In short, both Puritan and Cavalier, though in different ways and for different objects, did their best to substitute words for things, and art for nature; and hence arose in this country all which has been since understood as *verse* as distinguished from *poetry.*

And here might be discerned the real poetical corruption of which the critics afterwards complained, and which they confounded with every species of exuberant fancy. *Masks,* which though of a lawless nature in their incidents referred their feelings and expressions to nature, were the exuberance of an age of real poets; it was *conceits* that first marked the reverse; and the introduction of satire, of declamation, and of what has been called the reasoning spirit in poetry, has maintained the perversion more or less ever since, or at least till within a very late period.

But not to lose sight of the main subject. It is obvious from what has been seen of the nature of Masks, that they contained a good deal of real poetry, and might have been very entertaining to those who nevertheless knew how to set a proper value on the more regular works of imagination. It is equally obvious, however, at the same time, that from the nature of their object in general, they ran a chance of not living beyond their day, or at any rate of passing unnoticed by the great mass of readers among the larger and more ambitious works of their authors. This has accordingly been the case. The only way to secure them a better fate was to contrive such additional touches of description and human nature as should supply the loss of the particular interest by what was universally and perpetually engaging. We have seen what prevented the writers in most instances from having sufficient zeal for the composition, and what approaches it made to the chance of vitality in proportion as the object of the panegyric was respectable, the subject capable of natural embellishment, or the writer freed from the trammels of a particular allusion. The want of choice and inclination however usually prevailed over the ambition of the author, who was most likely employed in works of more general interest; and while we can trace the best pieces of this description to the circumstances above-mentioned, as in the instances of Beaumont and Browne, yet there is an air, it must be confessed, of constraint and imperfection in all; and we must still return to *Comus*, which was evidently written cheerfully and ambitiously, as the only, and at the same time the least *specific* production of the kind that can truly be said to have outlived its occasion.

The piece now presented to the reader [*The Descent of Liberty*] would endeavour to supply this deficiency in the actual character of the Mask by keeping the scenic and fanciful part of it predominant, while it would still exhibit something more of regularity and human interest than is possessed by Masks in general. But enough of this is suggested by the Preface. It may seem strange to some readers, that a drama professedly full of machinery should be written expressly for the closet, and not even have made an attempt at being performed. In the first instance, the author's intention was otherwise; and an eminent person who relieves his attention to public business by looking after the interests of a theatre, and to whom an application was made on the subject, gave him reason to expect every politeness, had he offered it to the stage. As he proceeded, however, he found himself making so many demands upon the machinist, besides hazarding, *perhaps,* in one or two instances, the disturbance of an unanimity which, above all others, ought to have attended the representation of such a piece, that he soon gave up the wish, and set himself, with no diminution of self-indulgence, to make a stage of his own in the reader's fancy. It is the most suitable one, he is convinced, for the very dramas which appear most to demand a machinist. When a storm blows on the stage without disturbing the philosophy of the trees, when instead of boiling up a waste of waters it sets in painful motion a dozen asthmatic pieces of tin, when Ariel, instead of breaking out of the atmosphere with ready eagerness at his master's ear, comes walking in with his wand like a premature common-councilman—in short, when the lightning lingers, the rain leaves dry, the torrent has a hitch in the gait, and one flat piece of carpeted board performs the eternal part of lawn, meadow, and lea, of over-grown wild and finished garden, who, that has any fancy at all, does not feel that he can raise much better pictures in his own mind than he finds in the theatre? The author is far from intending to ridicule the stage, the truest office of which (and a noble one it is) is the representation of manners. The stage does a good deal, and perhaps cannot afford to do more. He would merely remind the reader of what must have struck himself whenever he went to see a play like the *Tempest.* When Masks were in fashion, the Machinist was an important person, and used the utmost efforts of his art; but it was chiefly in still life and architectural decorations, and even for these no expense seems to have been spared. The rest of the show, however novel and rich, was of as easy a nature as it could be rendered, and subservient rather to the parade of the actors than to the fancy of the poet.

In a word, as the present piece was written partly to indulge the imagination of one who could realize no sights for himself, so it is more distinctly addressed to such habitual readers of poetry as can yield him a ready mirror in the liveliness of their own apprehensions. There is a good deal of prose intermixed, but the nature of a Mask requires it; and if the reader be of the description just mentioned, and shall settle himself with his book in a comfortable arm-chair condition—in winter perhaps, with the lights at his shoulder, and his feet on a good fender, in summer, with a window open to a soothing air, and the consciousness of some green trees about him, and in both instances (if he can muster up so much poetical accompaniment) with a lady beside him—the author does not despair of converting him into a very sufficient and satisfied kind of theatre.

[TIMON OF ATHENS]

November 4, 1816   *Drury-Lane*

THE TRAGEDY of *Timon of Athens*,[1] after a lapse of several years,[2] was revived at this theatre on Monday. The Managers, we suppose, were led to their choice of it, not only by their general desire to bring forward what is good, but by the great success of Mr. Kean in characters of a certain caustic interest; yet although the selection is honourable to both parties, and the performance was received and given out for repetition with great applause, we doubted and still doubt whether it will have what is called a run.[3] If it has, we shall save our self-love by attributing a part of it to the present times, which are certainly favourable ones for giving effect to representations of pecuniary difficulty, and of friendship put to the test.[4] But the parts of this tragedy which contain the dramatic interest are comparatively few; the moral, though strong, is obvious, and in fact too easily anticipated; and when *Timon* has once fallen from his fortunes, there is little to excite further attention in the spectator. The *reader* is still delighted, but he would be still more so in his closet, where he could weigh every precious sentence at leisure, and lose none of the text either by the freaks of adapters or the failure of actors' voices.

Timon's story is short. He is a magnificent liver, who wastes a princely fortune in gifts and entertainments, and finding he can get no assistance from those who devoured it, turns misanthrope, and dies in the woods. Dr. Johnson says that the play affords "a very powerful warning against that ostentatious liberality, which scatters bounty, but confers no benefits, and buys flattery, but not friendship."[5] Professor Richardson too sees nothing but "inconsiderate profusion" in *Timon*, "a profusion," says he, "which is supposed even by the inconsiderate person himself to proceed from a generous principle, but which in reality has its chief origin in the love of distinction."[6] The opinion here given by Johnson is a mere dove-tailing of words, or to speak after his own fashion, a smooth adjustment of alliterative antithesis. *Timon*, in the midst of his squandering, does confer benefits, as in the cases of the man whom he saves from prison, and the servant whom he enables to marry. The Professor is apparently more to the purpose; but we may here remark that it is a much safer way in morals to shew the probable unhappiness that attends a doubtful virtue than to set about proving its selfishness; for by the same process, the tables may be turned on virtues the most securely reckoned upon; and the kindest man upon earth be startled to learn that he saves others from pain, only to relieve himself. Human nature can arrive at no higher idea of virtue than that which makes us seek our own happiness in the happiness of others. The very greatest self-denial is either resolvable into this principle, or it is mere egotism, or want of feeling. If Professor Richardson had resolved to push his criticism to the depth, it would have remained for him to prove how far even "the love of distinction" did not proceed from "a generous principle"—that which leads us to give and to receive a social pleasure. The fact is, that *Timon* is really a generous man, spoiled by habitual good fortune and the enjoyment of his animal spirits. The moral of his tragedy is, not that he conferred bounties only and no benefits, nor that he mistook the love of distinction for generosity, but that human nature will allow of no excess; [7] and that, if we set out in this world with animal spirits which lead us to think too highly of it, we shall be disappointed. Shakspeare never wrote commonplace morals. He flattered virtuous men no more than he did vicious. In the very play we are now talking of, he seems to have been before-hand with the complacency of the dogmatic; and will not allow the cynic philosopher *Apemantus*, who had been bred up in different circumstances and never been flattered, to rail at *Timon*, without a bitter rebuke for the mistakes of his own egotism.

The whole play indeed abounds in masterly delineations of character, and in passages equally poetical and profound; though the latter unfortunately reduced the adapter [8] of the piece to an awkward dilemma; for they constitute its main beauty, and yet he seems to have felt himself obliged to cut them short, either for fear of making it drag with the spectators, or in compliance with a sophisticated decorum. Thus many of the most striking pieces of satire are left out; and we see nothing of the two females who come in upon *Timon's* retreat with *Alcibiades*. Yet the character of *Alcibiades* himself survives and furnishes a singular sort of cooler to the two burning, theoretical spirits of *Timon* and *Apemantus*. Shakspeare seems to have well appreciated this celebrated pupil of Socrates, at least the better part of him, and perhaps to have liked him. He makes him utterly careless of pretension of any sort, brave, open, generous, pleasurable, making allowances for other people, and revenging himself of his enemies rather out of contempt for their not being generous, also, than from any graver self-love of his own, though still he does not affect to be exempt from it. He takes the world as he finds it; and though he kicks a little at the meaner part, enjoys the generous; and is not to be put out, as the phrase is, even by difference of opinion. He has all the knowledge of humanity to which the military profession naturally contributes, and which renders a cheerful and intelligent soldier one of the most amiable men in the world, making the best of evil, and the very best of good. Of all the persons who visit *Timon* in his misery, *Alcibiades* is the only one whom the misanthrope seems puzzled how to abuse. When he came to him in his prosperity, it was not as a flatterer like the others, but as a cheerful friend; and when he sees him in his adversity, he would do him service if *Timon* would suffer it, bears his contumely with silent commiseration, and at last tells the drums to strike up for the march, because "We but offend him."

The play, upon the whole, was well performed. Mr. Kean, as usual, gave touches of natural excellence, such as no other living actor could produce. We suspect however that *Timon* will not not rank as one of his first performances; it wants sufficient variety and flexibility of passion for him. Neither do we think that he succeeded in the first part of the play, where *Timon* is prosperous and indulges his credulous generosity. He was too stately and tragic. It is true this may appear reconcilable with the

ostentation which is charged *Timon;* but as we have before observed, the charge appears to us to be unfounded, as far as the
leading passion is concerned; and *Timon* is a man of ardent
animal spirits, whose great enjoyment is the sense of a certain
glorious fellowship, upon which he thinks he could equally
reckon in a time of adversity, and the disappointment of which
drives him, in a manner, distracted. He smiles at first, when his
steward talks to him of cold friends; finds a reason for the first
disappointment he encounters from the senators in the cold-
bloodedness of their time of life; and, during the banquet in the
second scene, the fullness of his trusting heart fairly runs over
into tears of delight. From all this, it appears to us that the actor's
representation of him in his prosperity should be more easy and
cordial, and that he should receive and entertain his visitors,
not like a prince with a diadem, but like a companion who has
the happy art of being heartily though gracefully one's equal.
If *Timon* had been only ostentatious, he would hardly have
been so willing to borrow, and to think all his friends as generous as himself: he would have run mad for pride; whereas his
misanthropy is really owing, as in almost all instances, to an
unexpected and extreme conviction of the hollowness of the
human heart. We think Mr. Kean also had too great a tendency
in some parts to be violent, or rather to carry the paroxysms of
Timon to a pitch beyond true rage, and too often to mistake
vehemence for intenseness. *Timon's* curses in general should
have been "not loud, but deep": and, where Mr. Kean's acting
was of this description, it certainly had the greatest effect out
of the pale of the galleries, though some of his passionate starts
were deservedly admired also. The finest scene in the whole
performance was the one with *Alcibiades.* We never remember
the force of contrast to have been more truly pathetic. *Timon,*
digging in the woods with his spade, hears the approach of
military music; he starts, waits its approach sullenly, and at
last in comes the gallant *Alcibiades* with a train of splendid
soldiery. Never was scene more effectively managed. First,
you heard a sprightly quick march playing in the distance; Kean
started, listened, and leaned in a fixed and angry manner on his

spade, with frowning eyes, and lips full of the truest feeling, compressed but not too much so; he seemed as if resolved not to be deceived, even by the charm of a thing inanimate; the audience were silent; the march threw forth its gallant note nearer and nearer; the Athenian standards appear, then the soldiers come treading on the scene with that air of confident progress which is produced by the accompaniment of music; and at last, while the squalid misanthrope still maintains his posture and keeps his back to the strangers, in steps the young and splendid *Alcibiades,* in the flush of victorious expectation. It is the encounter of hope with despair.

Alcibiades luckily had a representative in Mr. Wallack who, besides performing the rest of his part with good credit, dressed and looked it uncommonly well. He seemed to have been studying the bust of his hero, as well as the costume of the Greek soldier. Mr. Bengough, in *Apemantus,* made as good a Cynic philosopher as we wished to see; he did not look quite so shrewd or beggarly as Diogenes, but he was wise enough for the part. As to Mr. Holland in the kind and lamenting Steward, he seemed quite inspired. We do not know that we ever saw him in so much advantage: but Mr. Kean's acting, we suspect, has given a great fillip to all the minor performers now-a-days.

With respect to the scenery and other mechanical matters, the piece was excellently got up. One of the scenes was a striking view of Athens, composed perhaps, from the picture in *Hobhouse's Travels. Timon's* solitude also was very leafy and to the purpose; and the splendour of the banquet-scene obtained great applause. We must protest however against the dance of young Amazons, clashing their swords and shields. Shakspeare, we allow, has specified Amazons for the occasion; but if Amazons there must be, they should at least have had lutes in their hands, which he has specified also, instead of weapons. We are at a loss to conjecture why Shakspeare introduced Amazons at all, which seem to be no more to his taste in general than they were to old Homer's; but did he find, anywhere, that an Amazon with a lute was *Timon's* device? We have not the commentators at hand to refer to; but *Timon* in thanking the dancers, tells them that they have entertained him with his "own device"; and devices of this kind were common from time immemorial. A dramatic mask, it is true, was called a device; but the host in the present instance seems to have been taken unawares, and could hardly have spoken as he did, had he himself invented the subject of the dance. At all events, we should like to have as little of these unfeminine feminines as possible: lutes would make them more human, and might act as a sort of compliment to *Alcibiades,* who is one of the guests, or to the spirit of sociality in general, as much as to say—a spirit of harmony corrects what is barbarous. We doubt also the propriety of the diadem and fillet worn by Mr. Kean, as well as the want of another sort of wreath to the heads of him and his guests during the banquets. They should undoubtedly, as was the custom, wear roses, myrtles, or other flowers mentioned by Anacreon and Plutarch, which besides being proper, would also have a pleasing effect, and contribute to the luxury of the scene: not that all this is necessary to Shakspeare, or demanded by him, but that it is as well to complete the costume in all instances, where it is undertaken in most.

We thank the Managers for *Timon,* which for our part we could see over again, were it only for the fine scene before mentioned; though we are afraid they have miscalculated the chances of its long run. We hope their next reproduction will be equally creditable to their taste, and more likely to reward it.

[ON PANTOMIME]

January 5, 1817

WE MUST INDULGE OURSELVES a little this season on the subject of Pantomimes [1]—a species of drama, for which, at whatever hazard of our critical reputation, we must acknowledge a great predilection. There is no such thing as modern comedy, tragedy, nor even farce, since Mr. Colman has left off writing it; but Pantomime flourishes as much as ever, and makes all parties comfortable; it enchants the little holiday folks; it draws tenfold applauding thunder from the gods; it makes giggle all those who can afford to be made giggle; and finally, it brings out the real abilities of our dramatic writers, who would be very pleasant fellows if they would not write comedy.

Yes, there is something *real* in Pantomime: there is animal spirit in it. A comedy may be, and often is, a gross piece of effort from beginning to end, both in dialogue and performance, and so may a tragedy: in either case you have no sensation, very often, but one of the most painful in the world, that of seeing a number of people pretending to be what they are not, the actors affecting an interest, while they are deploring their bad parts, and the author thinking himself wise, and shewing at every sentence that he is foolish. Nobody pleases, and nobody is pleased. But in Pantomime, who so busy and full of glee as the understrappers [2] and the Banbury-cake men? What so clever, in their way as the heels of Harlequin and the jaws of the Clown? And what so gay and eternal as the music, which runs merrily through the whole piece, like the pattern of a watered gown?

Let us recollect the delights of the three principal personages —the *Clown, Harlequin,* and *Colombine.* The others have their merits, particularly *Pantaloon,* who is a prodigiously dull old gentleman, and does not spoil the effect of his native stupidity with unskilful speaking. He is so dull that we lose all uneasy sympathy with him as an animal, and only retain sufficient to give zest to the tripping up of his heels. *Pantaloon*, together with the other characters, originates in Italian comedy, where he performs the part of the old gentleman of the second class in ours. The *Clown*, or as he used to be called, *Scaramouch*, is a descendant of the famous Italian comedian Scaramaccia, who began a sort of dynasty of humourous servants, and gave his name to them as Caesar did to the Roman Emperors. It was said of him that he had a very talkative countenance; and certainly nothing of the eloquence has been lost in that of the present potentate—Mr. Grimaldi, who is assuredly

"No tenth transmitter of a foolish face." [3]

But more of these particulars by and by. The Clown is a delightful fellow to tickle our self-love with. He is very stupid, mischievous, gluttonous, and cowardly, none of which, of course, any of us are, especially the first; and as in these respects, we feel a lofty advantage over him, so he occasionally aspires to our level by a sort of glimmering cunning and jocoseness, of which he thinks so prodigiously himself as to give us a still more delightful notion of our superiority. When he shakes his shoulders therefore at the dullest trick in the world, we laugh with equal enjoyment; when he pilfers from the cake-man, and looks the most outrageous lies in the latter's face, we love the profligate wag who so unambitiously amuses us at another's expense; and when he trips up his poor old master, whose face comes on the ground like a block of wood, we shout with rapture to see the lesser stupid thus overturn the greater. Nor is all this to be quarrelled with. We have a right to enjoy a good notion of ourselves in a pleasant way, and as long as we are all merry together; and here we enjoy it with all the advantages of harmlessness. We imagine our superiority, and that is enough; and we can relieve ourselves at any time from the more tragic delights, by calling to mind that the trips up and thumps are not real. Nay, even if they were, we reflect that they would be but so many fugitive bodily pains, with which no human spirit is wounded. But our philosophy will be getting grave.

See then who comes here to give us a new kind of pleasure, in which animal spirits are everything! It is the party-coloured descendant of the famous Arlequin, another real comedian, who has bequeathed his name to a class of theatrical beings. *Harlequin*, in the Italian comedy, is generally a servant, messenger, or other person in low life, active, cunning, and impudent. In the English pantomime, as perfected by Rich [4] and others, he is always a lover who has eloped with his mistress, and this gives him a tastier and pleasanter air with us, while it not only leaves him all his activity, but gives him every possible reason for it. Activity indeed at least shares his passion with love. He is the perpetual motion personified. At his very first appearance, he seems ambitious to shew you all his powers, from head to feet. He wriggles about, he capers, he takes a circuit, he nods, he wags his wooden sword, as a dog does his tail, he draws and prophetically flourishes it, he gives a jump sideways with both his knees, like a toy; and lastly, to convince the uncharitable that those who have good heels have good heads also, he begins grinding about his pericranium in that remarkable manner, gradually getting it into proper rotatory persuasiveness, till the whole head is whirling like a ventilator. Who does not wish such a fellow success with his mistress, and see moreover that he must gain it?

And here whirls in the damsel herself, fit companion for that vivacious fugitive, and an epitome of all that is trim and chaceable. What an amiable airiness, slender without weakness, and plump without inactivity! "Sir," as Dr. Johnson might have said, after having taken his bottle of wine at the Mitre, "these are such figures as we may imagine Pan or Phoebus to have hunted in the woods." *Colombine* in the Italian comedy is the mistress of *Harlequin,* as well as in our Pantomime, and performs the part of lady's-maids or the sprightly servants. Her name signifies the little dove; and such she is in her beauty, her ready flight, her elegance, and her amorousness. The Managers should always select as graceful a girl for this part as possible, who could indulge in all the feats of activity and dancing without trenching on the lady-like; for all the above qualities should lift her into that. We remember seeing the late Mrs. Heathcote a few years back in the character, when Miss Searle; and then for the first time began to wonder what the world and its axis had been at, since its inhabitants had made a fable of the Golden Age, and turned from the best things and virtues in it to the pursuit of all sorts of imaginary possessions, which only serve to set them against each other.

(*To be continued.*) [5]

ON PANTOMIME, CONTINUED
FROM A LATE PAPER

January 26, 1817

THE THREE general pleasures of a Pantomime [1] are its bustle, its variety, and its sudden changes. We have already described the unceasing vivacity of the music. The stage is never empty or still; either Pantaloon is hobbling about, or somebody is falling flat, or somebody else is receiving an ingenious thump on the face, or the Clown is jolting himself with jaunty dislocations, or Colombine is skimming across like a frightened pigeon, or Harlequin is quivering hither and thither, or gliding out of a window, or slapping something into a metamorphosis.

But a Pantomime, at present, is also the best medium of dramatic satire. Our farces and comedies spoil the effect of their ridicule by the dull mistakes of the author; but the absence of dialogue in Pantomime saves him this contradiction, and leaves the spectators, according to their several powers, to imagine what supplement they please to the mute caricature before them. Thus the grotesque mimicry of Mr. Grimaldi has its proper force; and the bullies or coxcombs whom he occasionally imitates come in one respect still nearer to the truth than in the best dialogue, being in actual life very dull persons who have little or nothing to say. Harlequin's sword also, besides being a thing very pleasant in the imagination to handle, is excellent at satirical strokes. Lissom as a cane, and furnishing all that little supply of conscious power which a nervous mind requires, and which is the secret of all button-pulling, switch-carrying, seal-twirling, and glove-twirling, it is not possible to witness its additional possession of a magic power without envy. We always think, when we see it, what precious thumps we should like to give some persons— that is to say, provided we could forget our own infirmities for the occasion. We would have a whole train of them go by at proper distances, like boys coming to be confirmed—the worldly, the hypocritical, the selfish, the self-sufficient, the gossiping,

the traitorous, the ungrateful, the vile-tempered, the ostentatious, the canting, the oppressing, the envious, the sulky, the
money-scraping, the prodigiously sweet-voiced, the over-cold,
the over-squeezing, the furious, the resenter of inconvenience
who has inconvenienced, the cloaker of conscious ill by accusation, the insolent in return for sparing. What fine work for a
winter's morning, with a good broad set of backs to operate
upon! We would have looking-glasses put before the patients,
in order that they might know themselves when transformed
into their essential shapes; after which they might recover; and
then the wisest, the least presuming, and most generous person among the spectators, such a one as was agreed by his
most veracious companions to know himself best, and to be
the most able to bear objection, should set the glass before
ourselves, and give us a thump equally informing.

[DON GIOVANNI]

August 17, 1817   *Italian Opera*

THIS THEATRE closed for the season on Tuesday with *Don Giovanni*,[1] the ballet of *Figaro*, and a *Rejouissance* (there is no English word, it seems, to express such a thing) in honour of the Prince Regent's birthday.

We cannot mention *Don Giovanni* again without again expressing the delight it has given us.[2] The Managers have shewed their taste, as well as a sense of their true interest, in getting it up so well, and repeating it so often. Our objections to the marble Ghost (always begging the reader to keep in mind that we speak with very unaffected deference on the works of this great Master) still remain; but it appears that some have mistaken the nature of them, and we cannot afford to let their error continue. It is the *noise,* and the noise only, of the music in which the Ghost is concerned, that we find fault with, not the chords, or the rest of the feeling. But to the noise we have very strong objections, and we think they are founded in reason, and in the practice of Mozart's brethren, the poets. We have not our former criticism by us, but we believe we there stated, though briefly, that loudness on such an occasion was contrary to the finest idea of the supernatural, which is that of power in its most powerful shape, and consequently its least vehement and assuming.

We ought therefore to have mentioned before that the first scene in which the statue speaks is that in which he affects us most. The cemetery by moonlight, the gleaming in it (which by the way is very finely managed) of the statue on horseback, the air of deathlike repose, the solemn and mute inclination of the statue's head, when *Don Giovanni* asks him if he will come to sup with him, and then the terrible words it utters—

Di rider finirai pria dell' aurora—

Thou shalt have done with laughter before morning—

in which every word is syllabled out with so awful a monotony, till there comes a drop on the *o* in *aurora*—present a combination than which nothing can be more grand or fearful; but then nothing at the same time can be more quiet, and full of a conscious power.

Now when Mozart got his statue off the horse, and set him in motion, it appears to us that he spoiled him; and we think Wieland or Schiller would have told him so, had he known and been in the habit of talking with them on his works; just as Raphael made use of his friend Ariosto, and Ariosto perhaps did of Raphael, when he wrote his picture of Alcina. All the great professors of the arts profit by this sort of communication with each other. They exchange, as it were, their experiences. There is no necessity for the Ghost to make a noise. He is not a pretender, and therefore he need not resort to the arts of human ones; and all power is great, and commanding, and awful, in proportion to its ease. The loudness, the crashing, the slamming thumps, are all comparatively vulgar. We rouse ourselves instinctively against them: we seem to say—"Oh, is that your mode of proceeding? —Well, I can be as noisy as you." There is a feeling of equality in it, as well as a reference to common human terrors, extremely hurtful to the ideas of the supernatural and the potent.

It is on these principles of our nature that the great poets, ancient and modern, have always represented power as quiet in proportion to its strength; and to ghosts they have given an especial dimness and obscurity, as beings that least of all require ordinary appearances in order to affect us.

With regard to mere power, for instance, look at the noble difference made by the ancients between Mars and Jupiter, the former a much inferior god to the other, and extremely given to noise. His shout in Homer makes the two armies start, a very sublime fancy, no doubt; but yet nothing compared with the solitary nod of Jupiter, at which the whole universe trembles. And there was something still greater and more powerful than Jupiter himself, which was Fate, a thing, or being, or whatever it was, that lay hidden in the silence and darkness of infinitude. The sublime thought of Moses is well known: "And GOD said,

let there be light; and there was light." He does not say, "And
a grand and mighty noise ensued, with shouts of cherubim and
seraphim, &c." but we are to imagine the calm utterance of
power issuing from the darkness; and light *is*. In the Psalms of
David, it is observable that wherever the author gives way to
the more violent and warlike part of his character, and makes
the characteristics of the Deity loud and shewy, or the effects
of his appearance tumultuous, his taste is by no means at its
best—his effect is not greatest. When he says, for instance, that
the Divine Being breaks people in pieces "like a potter's vessel,"
that he consumes them in fire "like the fat of lambs," that he
breaks Rahab in bits, "like one that is slain," that he will cause
"the righteous to bathe their legs in the blood of their enemies,"
and that he will "dash the heads of little children against the
stones," we are only shocked; but when he talks of the "pesti-
lence that walketh in darkness," and of fear and terror coming
upon men, and when he says, that God sits with "darkness under
his feet," that "his pavilion round about him is dark waters and
thick clouds of the skies," that his lightnings enlighten the world,
which sees and trembles, that he gives out his voice, that he
stills the seas with it, that his eye is upon his creatures, and that
if David could take "the wings of the morning and remain in
the uttermost part of the sea, even there also his hand would
be"—we acknowledge that these indeed however faint in the
comparison, are something like ideas of the great and wonderful
Spirit of Nature.

There is a very fine passage in the 1st book of *Kings* (chap.
xix) where the union of power with quietness is remarkably expressed, being contrasted, as if it were on purpose, with various
striking pieces of violence, so that it has an air of complete climax. Not that we mean to say it was at all written critically;
but such are the instinctive feelings of our nature in all ages.
The passage is as follows: "And he said, Go forth, and stand
upon the mount before the Lord. And behold, the Lord passed
by, and a great and strong wind rent the mountains, and broke
in pieces the rocks before the Lord: but the Lord was *not* in
the wind; and after the wind an earthquake, but the Lord was

not in the earthquake; and after the earthquake a fire, but the
Lord was not in the fire: and after the fire a *still small voice.*"
The voice was the mighty Being. This is very magnificent, and
appears to have given rise to a fine passage in the Koran, where
there is a succession of similar agitations, after which comes a
small voice, saying, "Peace be to the righteous!"

And this brings us more particularly to the idea of power as
connected with apparitions. And first observe the very word
apparition; it is a something noiseless, and only visible, an appearance. All the other words are of similar import, or still more
shadowy. Thus the word *Ghost* is the same as *Spirit,* which is
nothing but *Breath;* there is also a vision, a visitation, a spectre,
a sight, a goblin, a shape, a phantom, a phantasma. Milton has
used the force of this indistinctness to wonderful advantage in
his introduction of Death, whom he calls the shadow, the monster, the goblin, the grisly terror, the hellish pest, the execrable
shape, the "shape, if shape it might be called": he defines nothing:

> What *seemed his head*
> The *likeness* of a kingly crown had on;— [3]

and yet this indescribable something was "fierce as ten furies,"
who are the most raging and violent of all supernatural beings";
and the phrase "fierce as ten furies" is not a tenth part so dreadful
as that other one, "Black *it* stood as night." There is another passage in Milton which instantly came into our minds when we
were thinking of that speaking, as it were, in *hyphens,* which we
have mentioned above, and with which Mozart makes his spectre
dole out his terrible words. It is in the same awful and shadowy
style. It is where the *Lady* speaks in *Comus,* when she is be-
nighted in the forest:—

> A thousand fantasies
> Begin to throng into my memory,
> Of *calling shapes,* and *beckoning shadows* dire,
> And aery *tongues* that *syllable* men's names,
> On sands, and shores, and desert wildernesses.[4]

It is gratifying to notice this point of contact between Mozart
and Milton, the latter of whom was more than fond of music,
which he both played and composed. But we must not indulge

ourselves with all the poetical passages that present themselves to our recollection. Suffice it to say, that the greatest Greek and Latin Poets, that Dante, Camoens, Spenser, and Shakspeare, and all other writers whose imaginations have been of the loftiest and whose feelings of the intensest order, have agreed to place the height of the terrible or the powerful in the indistinct, the solemn, and the quiet. The Ghost in *Hamlet*, who "revisits the glimpses of the moon, making night hideous," and who walks "slow and stately" by his dumb-stricken beholders, who are

Distilled
Almost to jelly with the act of fear,—

is alone a complete specimen of the overpowering nature of the quiet supernatural. When it moves, it is slowly; when it speaks, it is slowly also, and with a hollow voice; when it goes away, it *fades*.

We cannot however help concluding our observations on this subject with an extract from the sublimest book in the Scripture, the Arabian story of *Job*. It is another curious proof of what has been felt on these points in ages when the feelings of mankind were in all their ruder freshness, and when they were prepared to resist the ordinary appearances of terror and violence, as things within everybody's power to inflict or to resent. It is Eliphaz, Job's friend, who is speaking. "In thoughts from the visions of the night, when deep sleep falleth on men, fear came upon me, and trembling, which made all my bones to shake. Then a spirit passed before my face; the hair of my flesh stood up:—it stood still, but I could not discern the form thereof: an image was before mine eyes—*there was silence*—and I heard a voice, saying, "Shall mortal man be more just than God? Shall a man be more pure than his maker?"

Now from all this we infer that however fine Mozart's Ghost is in one scene, it is very inferior in another, and, as far as the loudness and clatter are concerned, is a mistake. Doubtless, something of a more distinct nature than in general, as far as *form* is concerned, may be allowed a *marble* ghost: and the idea of "the man of stone," the "white man," as *Leporello* in great horror announces the Statue when it comes to supper, is very fearful; but the noise—the noise—it is the noise only with which we quarrel; and we cannot help thinking that had the music in the orchestra been all in an undertone, the Ghost undertoned also, and the whole house comparatively silent, leaving at the same time all the chords as they are, the effect would have been twenty times finer, not to mention the double force that would have thus been given to the subsequent despair and outcries of *Don Giovanni.*

As to the "*Grand Rejouissance* in commemoration of the PRINCE REGENT's birth-day, sung by all the vocal performers, accompanied by thirty Prussian trumpets, and composed by Mr. KELLY [5] expressly for the occasion," we cannot say much for it, whatever pains it took to impress upon us the merits of his Royal Highness. It presented us, first, with a raised orchestra at the back of the stage, containing the said 30 Prussian trumpets; there were some steps from the side in front, and down these steps descended a troop of flag-bearers, with G.P. on their flags; after which the vocal performers descended likewise in stage dresses, and sung an anthem written in Italian, in which the "powerful REGENT" is said to be in possession of the "gentler virtues," to have the scissors,—we beg pardon, the fate of England, in his hands, to be great in peace and war, and to give laws both to sea and land! The music was common-place to the last degree. Yet we think better of some of Mr. Kelly's compositions than many do. If he stole them, as it is alleged, we should like to see the originals: and then we shall maintain that he has been a very tasteful thief; but till then, we must maintain that he has some-times shewn himself a very tasteful composer. But whether his subject overpowered him in the present instance, or whatever else was the cause, certainly there never was a business at once more noisy and more dull. The thirty trumpets brayed away at a prodigious rate, after the newest fashion of a trumpet-song in a flute-book; but Mr. Kelly, we see, was resolved to have some-thing surprising in his words; and in order, we suppose, to mus-ter up something more, his Commemoration exhibited a singular medley of national associations. There was a French title, Italian words, French and Italian singers, Prussian trumpets, and an English composer. A feast of Welsh rabbits and German sausages, crowned with a politer heap of trifle, would have completed this many-tongued and metaphorical exhibition.

We cannot take leave of the Opera this season, without expressing our sense of the very great merits of the Band. It is a masterly one, ready, powerful, tasteful, with one hand and one feeling; and whether its business was to be playful or serious, loud or soft, whether it had to wait upon the voice of a fine singer, or make the best of that of an inferior one, was sure to do just what it ought. It was of itself a treat to the lovers of music throughout the whole of the evening.

We ought not to forget that we have omitted to do justice to the performance of Signor Angrisani [6] in the Opera above mentioned. He is very natural and pleasant in the part of *Masetto*, and turns himself to stone, nevertheless, with great effect in the Ghost. The Performers indeed altogether have done well; and the Managers, if they go on as they have begun, will deserve riches as well as get them. It is understood, we believe, that there has hardly ever been so excellent a season, or one in which the public attention has been so forcibly awakened to the beauty and merit of this graceful kind of entertainment.

[DRURY-LANE REDECORATED]

September 7, 1817   *Drury-Lane*

DRURY-LANE THEATRE was to open last night,[1] and Covent-Garden opens tomorrow. The improvements or alterations which the former has been making we saw on Friday evening, and can promise our Readers much satisfaction with the gas-lights, which are introduced not only in front of the stage, but at the various compartments on each side: Their effect, as they appear suddenly from the gloom, is like the striking of daylight; and indeed, it is in its resemblance to day that this beautiful light surpasses all others. It is as mild as it is splendid—white, regular, and pervading. If the Italian Ambassador, as he entered London in the evening, took the ordinary lamps in the street for an illumination and an elegant compliment, what would he have thought had he passed through the lustre which is shed at present from so many of our shops? In some of them, where the gas is managed with taste and shot out from a slender pipe, it is no extravagance to say that it puts one in mind of what one fancies in poetry, of the flamy breath at the point of a Seraph's wand:

> And in his hand a reed
> Stood waving, tipt with fire.[2]

The Theatre has not the advantage of this part of the beauty, as the lights are enclosed in glasses and blinded from the audience by side-scenes and reflectors; but the result in every other respect is excellent, and a very great improvement; and, if it is managed as well as we saw it on Friday, will enable the spectator to see every part of the stage with equal clearness. If the front light could be thrown, as day-light is, from above instead of below (and we should like to hear the reasons why it cannot) the effect would be perfect.

The rest of the house (always excepting the bad gilt figures on the stage boxes, which spoil a pleasant subject) is very neatly coloured and ornamented, and maintains the old reputation of this theatre for a certain airy elegance, a something of the lightness of comedy in its very appearance.

But we protest vehemently against the Saloon. They have absolutely filled it with Chinese pagodas and lanthorns, a series of the former occupying the middle, and a profusion of the latter being hung up on all sides, *adorned* with monsters and mandarins, and shedding a ghastly twilight! Nothing can be more puerile or tasteless. All the world knows that though the Chinese are a shrewd people in some things, they are very stupid and disgusting in others, matters of taste included; and if all the world did not know it, yet as it is of course to go and see the new Saloon, these Chinese lanthorns would be sufficient to enlighten it. What mummeries and monstrosities! On one lanthorn, a man like a watchman; on another, a dragon or some unintelligible compound of limbs; on another, some Chinese pothooks and hangers! Then the pagodas rise one over the other, like the card-houses of the little boys; and as if there were not monsters enough on the lanthorns, a set of huge tyger busts, or some such substitutes for Grecian sculpture, gape down upon you from the sides of the ceiling, and only want some puppet-shew men to ventriloquize for them and make them growl, to render this exquisite attraction complete. What is the meaning? Some libelous fellows say that it is a complimentary imitation of the Prince Regent, who, it is averred, has whole rooms full of such lumber in his palaces, and holds Phidias exceedingly cheap and illegitimate. Others suspect that the light has been made thus coy and shadowy, to save the blushes of such Ladies as may chance to look in, and might feel their conscious modesty disturbed by too great a glare—

> Illa verecundis lux est praebenda puellis,
> Qua timidus latebras speret habere pudor.[3]

Others conclude that the seductive horrors are intended to rival the more natural though less wealthy novelty at the Lyceum; and others again, who are attached to the doctrine of mixed motives, have made up their mind that all these reasons co-operate more or less. Be they what they may, there never was

a more graceless or absurd piece of business. It is really humiliat-
ing to the national taste. If the Prince Regent or the loungers
put up with the compliment, we cannot imagine any other
human being within the civilized pale who would admire it,
except indeed the Chinese themselves, who hustled us out of
doors the other day.

Now the Saloon at the Lyceum, though a poor business compared with what a shrubbery ought to be, and much humbler
of course in point of size, is really, in our eyes, a thousand times
more attractive; that is to say, there is something attractive in
the very idea of green leaves and walks, in the least piece of
nature, and nothing but what is repulsive in these monstrous
abuses of art. But Mr. Arnold,[4] if he is not rich enough to make
his shrubbery as good as we would have it, or to treat us with a
regular green-house, should contrive to let his plants have some
means of keeping themselves alive; for though young trees are
much cheaper than many imagine (and how infinitely cheaper
than they imagine is *real* taste, of all sorts), yet the recurrence
of dusty and dying plants every season would subject him to
something of a losing nature—which is ridicule. Above all, he
ought not to puff so, and make so many pompous announcements. The shrubbery for instance, about which he so repeatedly
flourished his triumpets, is in fact nothing more than some ranges
of shrubs in pots on each side the saloon, pleasing enough certainly when fresh, and much better than Chinese deformities,
but nothing to warrant such exceeding proclamations on the
house-tops. Well, suddenly, amidst his eternal announcements,
he informs us of "a novel and interesting feature," or some such
thing, which is the delight of all beholders: the readers of the
play-bill are kept in attractive suspense, and then informed that
this novelty is a "Chinese walk"; and what is the Chinese walk?
Nothing but the usual walk up the Saloon, with a trumpery
Chinese tap-room or tea-room at the *end* of it, over which is
daubed on a board *"Thè a-la-Chinoise,"* and where (stupendous
to think of!) you can buy cakes.

The sage Fum Hoams who contrived the Drury-Lane Saloon,
moved admiringly, we suppose, towards this "interesting fea-

ture," and passing by the firs and poplars, emulated the pagoda! They will find their account in it, we dare say, at first; but surely there is too much taste diffused now-a-days not to make them repent it ultimately. Now if they would emulate the Lyceum in a *shrubbery*, and adorn it with a few specimens (which they might do very cheaply) of ancient sculpture, or take the opportunity of encouraging modern, they would do themselves a lasting service, and give the public a pleasure full of the most beautiful associations both of Nature and Art.

We know not whether anything has been done with the Saloon at Covent-Garden; but we trust when we see it to find that the taste of Siddons and Kemble has not departed with their persons.[5]

CIBBER'S COMEDY OF "THE REFUSAL"

AUTHOR'S CHARACTER. OBSERVATIONS ON THE CANT AGAINST LEARNING IN WOMEN. THE NEW ACTRESS IN BELVIDERA.

October 12, 1817   *Drury-Lane*

CIBBER'S COMEDY of *The Refusal, or The Ladies' Philosophy,* has been revived here.[1] *Sir Gilbert Wrangle* (Mr. Dowton), a good-natured old Gentleman, perverted by the spirit of money-getting, has bargained away the choice of one of his two daughters (Mrs. Alsop and Mrs. Mardyn) with *Witling,* a flourishing city-fop, who has a prodigious notion of himself (Mr. Harley).[2] He chooses *Charlotte,* the latter; but in the meantime she has fallen mutually in love with *Frankly* (Mr. Stanley); and the main plot consists of the schemes of her, her lover, and her father (who has too much sense and good nature not to prefer her marrying a sensible man), to render the bargain of no effect, provided the old gentleman is not to compromise his "honesty." *Charlotte* therefore so works upon the vanity of *Witling* that in the closing scene, when *Sir Gilbert,* seeing him resolute, appears uneasy with his bargain and *Frankly* and his friend *Granger* (Mr. Penley) offer to pay down the forfeit to a lawyer who has come to perform the marriage ceremony, the unlucky and trusting coxcomb, in order to give a final proof of his mistress's attachment to him, returns the bond to *Sir Gilbert;* upon which, *Charlotte* being called on by all parties to pronounce whom she will take for her husband—*Frankly* looking confident and *Witling* more so—makes a formal declaration ending with—*Thomas Frankly, Esquire:* and springs accordingly into the latter's arms, to poor *Witling's* utter dismay.

The rest of the piece is taken up with the quarrels of *Sir Gilbert* and his wife, with the pedantic airs of her and his eldest daughter, and with the disputes of the three ladies respecting *Mr.*

Frankly, with whom they are all in love. There is a very pleasant scene between all four, in which they contrive to ask him, one by one, which of the *other two* he prefers, in order to bring him to a declaration; but he baffles it by some pretty equivocal speech. His love for the youngest however is soon discovered; and the lovers have much to undergo from the intriguing resentment of the mother-in-law, who contrives to injure him as much as possible, and from the pettier jealousy of *Miss Sophronia,* who in the course of her walking about the house with her book in her hand is always interrupting them, and whose mistaken notion of learning indeed lost her this very lover; for his attachment was to her in the first instance; but she trifled with it so, and in such a prudish and lofty manner, that he turned to more unaffected flesh and blood. She is consoled however towards the conclusion by the love of *Granger,* who contrives to cure her of her pretended Platonism by affecting such excessive admiration of that system himself that she takes alarm, and fairly acknowledges, at last, that bridegrooms are not to be so treated.

There is also a prominent scene in which *Lady Wrangle,* having missed a translation of hers from Ovid, of the loves of Byblis and Cannus, and asking her maid in a rage what has been done with it, discovers that John the cook has snatched it out of her hand, and skewered his roast beef with it. A great hubbub ensues; John the cook is sent for: and in he comes with his cap and floured face, holding the much-injured manuscript on the skewer itself. The Lady's rage then redoubles; but the cook does not choose to stand it, and gives her warning with equal vehemence, upon which the maid, seized with a disinterested resentment in John's behalf, pronounces her determination to go also; and so they leave the stage to the disconsolate termagant, her half-frightened husband, and her "roasted poetry." Some Ladies, who keep cooks, will perhaps think this low; but if they think so, angrily, we are afraid they are lower themselves.

The reader will see that if a comedy with this kind of plot is not ill written, it may upon the whole be a very pleasant one; and it is so.[3] There is nothing very great or new in it; but there is nothing flat or very old; and what is much better than even artificial greatness, there is a flow of natural sprightly humour, which takes one quite at one's ease along with it. This was the chief merit of Cibber, who possessed in his person a great flow of animal spirits; and though they were not delicate or informed enough to give him sentiment, or elevate him above a certain pitch of coxcombry himself, yet they were sufficiently genial-blooded and good-natured to be extremely pleasant as well as continuous. Pope's mistake about him, or rather wilful change of tone (for he had done justice to his *Careless Husband*) is well known; as well as the recoil which he has suffered from his own satire in consequence. Cibber has something of the same natural charm in comedy and artificial life as Allan Ramsay has in the pastoral. There is no comparison, it is true, between the two styles; and Ramsay has much the greater sentiment; but all we mean to say is that the talent of both the men is left quite free to itself, and speaks its own language; and that therefore the principle of the charm in both is the same. But Cibber had nothing to do out of his sphere, any more than Ramsay with grave English verses. In the piece before us he has attacked learned ladies; and though he has done it pleasantly enough, it is clear he knows nothing of the matter, and only followed the common-places of men who were learned themselves and ought to have known better. There was a cant in those days against learning in woman; but they did not see that instead of ridiculing the mistakes into which beginners fall, and confounding the sex with the mistake, they ought to have paid a juster compliment to the sources of what they thought their own superiority, and shewn how delightful and unaffected women could be *in proportion* to their learning, not how foolish they (*as well as men*) could make themselves with a smattering of it. Indeed, there was more jealousy in the ridicule than the men were aware of; and a most ridiculous jealousy certainly; for the real knowledge which they ought to have taught and shared with the other sex, and which they would have understood the better for so sharing it, would have taught the women what it is to be truly wise and delightful, without at all averting them from those accomplishments which it is the mark of an uncultivated understanding to despise. Neither is it by any means certain that the pedantry attributed to women of learning has ever existed, whatever may have been the case with the smatterers of either sex; and it was not their smattering, be it observed, that it was intended to ridicule, but something particularly anti-feminine and disagreeable which was to result from women's reading the classics themselves instead of bad translations! But Lady Wortley Montague, so praised by Mr. Pope while she appeared to think him as charming as he thought her, was a learned and most sprightly woman, whose letters beat his own hollow in unaffectedness, as well as everything else. Madam Dacier too, his antagonist, and the most learned woman of the time, made an excellent unaffected wife. Then in the previous age, there was Mrs. Behn, who translated from Latin for the book-sellers, and whom nobody will accuse of being prudish and crabbed. And in the age or two before that—Shakspeare's age —it was as common a thing as it will be, some time hence, for ladies to know quite as much Latin and Greek as their lovers— perhaps more. It was Queen Elizabeth's station, and not her learning, that made her masculine. Sir Thomas More's daughters were excellent every way, as well as in scholarship; and Lady Jane Grey is to this day equally famous for her learning, her misfortunes, and her feminine sweetness. The philosophy of the present age is rapidly doing away this notion against women's knowing as much as men. We are intimate with more than one lady who reads Latin, and whose manners are in no way affected by it, unless a gentle reserve at first, and no obtrusion of the fact at any time, be the results. The wisest and best men whom we know, are also advocates for this right in women; and we are acquainted with the head of one excellent family in particular, which is in the sphere both of rank and fashion, and yet all the girls learn the ancient as well as modern languages, not omitting the accomplishments more usual with their sex; and from what little we have seen of them, we cannot pay them a higher compliment than by saying that they have all the ease, good taste, and affectionate simplicity of their parents.[4]

But to resume. The comedy is excellently performed. Dowton is, as usual, full of a certain fatherly humour, and of admirable bye-play. No man fills up the outline of a pleasant sort of passionate old temperament as he does. His repeated turns round to *Frankly*, when his daughter is opposing his pretended wishes, his bursts of self-congratulating giggles, half suppressed, and the convulsive twitchings up of his knee, made the house laugh over and over again. We never saw Harley also to better advantage. He is greatly improved, and does not confine himself to his favourite nod of the head—which we are glad to find; for there seems a good deal of comedy both in his face and voice, though the latter has one or two tones in it that are apt to clatter on the ear too much, and drown the remainder. Mr. Smith,[5] in the cook, was very oratorical and independent and made out his case extremely like "a sarvant," that will "take the law." Of Mr. Stanley, we can only say, as before, that we heartily wish him in some other range of characters. Lively gentlemen are really not fit for him, and we are sorry for it; for he has some expressions in his face that we would give a good deal not to be obliged to say Nay to. Mrs. Glover, who was always a good actress, seems to us to get better and better every day. Her style grows very natural and powerful. We do not think the character of a pedantic lady suited to Mrs. Alsop. She has too much of her charming mother in her and evidently wants to be more at her ease. Mrs. Mardyn danced and shook her curls about with much effect, as *Miss Charlotte*. She has a great notion, by the way, of a good head of hair. She has also, we think, more notions of true acting than some suppose; only a sense of what nobody can be blind to, her beauty, interferes perhaps a little too much and prevents her from using her eyes and her attitudes as moderately as she might. Yet we would not constrain her, if constraint is to do away her animal spirits. They are things too precious to lose. She twirled herself most delightfully into the arms of *Frankly*.

With respect to the new actress in *Belvidera*,[6] Miss Campbell, we would rather see her again, before we give our opinion. The effect of her first appearance on us was certainly not very favourable; but then it is to be recollected that we think it right to judge by a high standard. The audience applauded very much; but this tells little for a performer, as they naturally feel for the situation of a person in a first appearance, and applaud with all their might, not very wisely perhaps, whether the stranger appears to want encouragement or not. Miss Campbell seemed in full self-possession. She has at least many physical qualifications for a tragic actress—a face and person tending to the large, and a powerful and not unmelodious voice. But she used the latter unmercifully; and the whole character of her performance on Wednesday night was robust and overdone. *Belvidera* is a heroine of strong passions, but they are founded on great tenderness; and Miss Campbell exhibited all the former, and little of the latter. Tenderness did not inspire her in her fondness, nor check her in her resentment. When she threw herself into *Jaffier's* arms, it seemed at his peril not to be very fond; and when she reproached him with leaving her as his pledge among the conspirators, it was real, bitter taunting of the most unequivocal description—that is to say, like that of a person habitually violent, instead of occasionally warm. The reader may conceive what the mad scene was. It was terrible certainly; but of a sort of terror not to be expected even from raving, in such a character as *Belvidera*. It was muscular plunging, and hoarse convulsion.

Our old theatrical acquaintance, Mr. H. Johnston, has come to this theatre and performed for the first time in *Pierre*. He is not a first-rate performer, and deals too much in stage trick, in high and low tones, and strutting off; but he has some good ideas too, and is undoubtedly an acquisition.

Mr. Kean recommenced his operations on Monday. We shall attend both to him and Miss O'Neil, when the immediate novelties have gone by a little.

ACCUSATION OF SEVERITY MADE
AGAINST THE "EXAMINER"

October 19, 1817   *Drury-Lane*

"Now," says the Manager, holding our wet newspaper to
the fire, and seeing the steam roll up from it, as the mist in the
Arabian Nights did, before the goblin was discernible, "let us
see what that cursed fellow——says of Miss Byrne." [1]

A word or two, by the way, before we proceed, respecting
these notions on the part of Managers. We omitted to notice,
the other day, the compliment paid to our talents at the expense
of our kindness in the Lyceum Address; for to us, we understand, it alluded; and most likely it did, as we were the only
critics, we believe, who took any regular notice of Mr. Arnold's
Shrubbery.[2] We happened however, the same week in which the
address was published, to take occasion of the unpleasant necessity we were under in condemning some new performers, of
making some observations on this very subject—this notion of
our being so very severe.[3] It was there, we believe, observed
that, if a paper did not speak what it thought on these occasions,
it only tended to lower its own character, to make the public
impatient and resentful, to lead the Managers into a number
of dilatory and costly experiments to no purpose—in short, to
do no good to any party, and harm to all. We have now three
further remarks to make: 1st, that in proportion as the censure
of a journal is formidable, its approbation is valuable; 2d, that
if by "severity" the Managers of theatres mean ill-nature (as
it seems they do), they make a great mistake with regard to the
nature of us all; and 3d, that the public, and even the critics,
are to be considered, as well as the new performers. Do the
Managers think that nobody has feelings or mortifications out
of the pale of a theatre? Does not a performer some times hazard

voluntarily the charge of presumption? Is it no annoyance to a critic to be compelled in consequence to pronounce an unfavourable judgment? And would the Manager think himself justly accused of ill-nature, if the very same performer should propose to sell him bad lights or bad furniture for his theatre, and have his offer rejected? Ill-nature wishes to inflict pain; severity, or what is so called in this instance, is nothing but a wish to speak the truth belonging to its office, to consider many interests instead of one—nay, to consider that one also, and eventually to save pain. We do not pretend to any particular self-knowledge. We are very sceptical with regard to its existence in anybody, and therefore ought to doubt it in ourselves, as we very sincerely do; but we speak of the case in general; and our friends, we believe, would acquit us readily enough of any propensity to speak ill of others in private. Again, were the alleged severity of our criticisms a mere supererogation on our part, or were we slow, or frigid, or even infrequent, in expressing our praise also, we might be liable to the charge. But the public require notices of plays; chance, and a general love of poetry and the arts connected with it, made us critics some years ago; and certainly we stumbled upon a most unfortunate period of the stage, both for the reputation of the drama and of our own good-nature. But there have always been good and natural actors, and have we not praised these? Had Lewis, or Bannister, or Miss Pope, or Mrs. Jordan anything to complain of us? Has Kean, Dowton, Knight, Emery, Liston, Mrs. Davison, Miss Kelly, Miss Stephens? Do we not always speak of them with praise, often with great admiration, sometimes with transport? Some of them, so far from having any abstract tendency to give sentence against new performers, we happen to have spoken more highly of from the first, than any other journal. We believe such was the case with Mrs. Davison, then Miss Duncan. Of Miss Kelly, we believe we were solitary, for some time, in speaking and auguring highly; and the late Mr. Cumberland,[4] who introduced that excellent actor Dowton to the stage, did us the honour of saying that we corroborated his judgment of him. It is said indeed that performers are not content unless the praise is in every instance excessive and unqualified. We do not mean to insinuate that we know this to be true of any of the persons here mentioned; but we can believe it of performers in general, because they stand in the thick of so much personal panegyric, which at once stimulates their vanity and is the excuse for it. It is not to be expected, therefore, but that Managers, who are sometimes actors themselves, sometimes writers, and always come under criticism in some way or other, should partake of a good deal of the same irritability. Mr. Fawcett once spoke an epilogue at us, written by Mr. Colman; and now Mr. Bartley [5] speaks an address, written, we suppose, by Mr. Arnold. We bow, with due gratitude and gravity, to the compliment of being "a celebrated critic, equally well known for his severity as his talents" (we believe those were the words); but we should have been more touched with it had Mr. Arnold, instead of giving the audience to understand that we had been the only objectors to his Shrubbery, told them that we had only been objectors to his giving the said Shrubbery too many puffs and too little water; and furthermore, that we had been praisers, perhaps the only critical praisers, of the principle of such an ornament. We even recommended it to Drury-Lane, in preference to the dragons and paper lights; but hold—the dragons will think it severe of us if we attack them twice.

To drop the subject therefore, and turn to a much pleasanter one, we have the hearty satisfaction this week of being able to hail a new performer, who is indeed an acquisition to the Theatre. On Tuesday evening Miss Byrne from the Dublin stage made her first appearance here, as *Adela* in the *Haunted Tower*.[6] She is young; and is of a prepossessing appearance, with fine dark eyes and hair and a little lady-like figure. Indeed, we think we have not seen an actress for a long time so genteel in her air and natural deportment. Her mouth is her least handsome feature, being somewhat too prominent under the lip, though the chin itself recedes; but her smile redeems it in an instant; and this is one of the best things that can be said of a face. She has the ease and unaffectedness of conscious ability, and yet, at the same time, apparently the true kind of good breeding, a disinclination to make herself over-conspicuous, and a consideration for others. In one scene, where there was a vehement *encore* evidently directed to her alone, she kept unaffectedly at the side among the rest, looking easily about her, as much as if she would have said it was a general call upon them and she waited their determination. Now let us have actresses of this sort, and see if we cannot praise them.

We have involuntarily been speaking of Miss Byrne as an actress; and the truth is, she is a very promising one, and decidedly the best we have yet seen among the professed singers. She has a feeling for by-play, as well as for dialogue; and taps her fan on the palm of her hand with a very natural sprightliness.

Her voice has one considerable defect in the quality of the louder tones, which are reedy; but she has some sweet ones among the softer, both high and low; her ear is excellent; and the general style of her singing is sensible, correct, and powerful. Her taste is so good that she will doubtless get over a certain hardness of outline, or over-distinctness in the enunciation of her notes; yet this was most observable in her first song, "Whither, my love," and was perhaps summoned up by her in order to hinder her timidity from going to the opposite fault of overslurring; for she was at first much agitated, though she soon recovered herself. The execution however of this song, which is Paesiello's air of *La Rachelina* (one of the sweetest in the whole circle of melody), was upon the whole a very promising announcement of her powers, and told us at once that we had no common singer before us. We liked her also exceedingly in her more trifling part in the duet with her lover; and suspect she could dance very nicely as well as sing, if she were to set about it. Drury-Lane has certainly now got a singer, as well as Covent-Garden; and though Miss Stephens remains unrivalled among our native performers, for sweetness of tone and a touching plaintiveness, yet Miss Byrne, we guess, will have her exclusive reputation too, of no mean order. They are both correct and powerful singers; and will perhaps take their respective stands in the estimation of the town, the one as a kind of mild tragedy singer, not without her feeling of the pleasant, and the other as a well-bred comedy one, not without her feeling of the grave.

"CHARACTERS OF SHAKESPEAR'S PLAYS," BY WILLIAM HAZLITT

October 26, 1817

WE TAKE SHAME TO OURSELVES for not having before given a regular notice of this work.[1] It is on a favourite subject; falls in directly with one of the chief objects of our paper; and is the production of a writer of whose talents we have every reason to express our admiration. What is the reason then we have not noticed it, except in passing?[2] Why, partly because we have been occupied and dilatory, and partly because the work is all that we have said it is. It is full of thinking and penetration; and when a critic comes to handle such a work (unless he is very ignorant of himself indeed, or has an unconsciousness of another sort which critics are very unlikely to have) he is apt to perplex himself with his own vanity (or modesty, call it which you will), and to fear lest he should commit himself in the eyes of the author by comments unworthy of the text.

However, the work has in the meantime been criticised by the *Edinburgh Review;* and if we still think that a good deal more might reasonably be said upon it, it only shews how little we need perplex ourselves with the fear of not saying enough. Indeed, it is not easy to do justice to such a book as Mr. Hazlitt's in any limited piece of criticism, much less a newspaper one; and therefore we shall not trouble ourselves or the reader any further with our dilemmas, but speak what little we have to say at present after our usual straightforward fashion. There are some points of notice which we reserve for another time, especially the masterly exposition, in the Preface, of Dr. Johnson's Shakespeare criticisms.

It may be said to be the object of Mr. Hazlitt's book to explain the characteristic features of Shakspeare's genius, and to illustrate what he explains by reference. Now criticism on such a picture involves of necessity great admiration of it; and as depth and variety of knowledge are among the most remarkable of Shakspeare's properties, so much so as to affect the most careless reader, it may be fairly asserted that, in proportion to anyone's unaffected perception of this depth and variety, will be his enthusiastic praise of his author. It is the reverse therefore of a fault, in our eyes, that Mr. Hazlitt's criticism is so repeatedly raising its voice into eulogy and rapture. Love, in this instance, is knowledge.[3] Admiration of great writers, like every other proper feeling, is undoubtedly injured by the cant of the pretending; but so much the more incumbent is it on those who can give "a reason for the faith they have" in such men, to proclaim their worship. Every fresh lover of a great poet, or of Nature, is a proselyte from trusting slavery. It is the want of wisdom and of a wise enthusiasm which makes the world what it is. Men have long enough admired foolish things to no purpose; but they have so often been told so that they begin to think there is some truth in it; and the objects of their false attention instructively feel it necessary to bind them ever to their admiration by law—"*legitimate's* your only wear." Let them persist however in turning their minds towards those who have thought and felt for them; and the more they know and admire, the sooner they will laugh down the pretensions of the unthinking and the unfeeling. "Knowledge," says Lord Bacon, "is power." It is: but a little knowledge cannot make head against a great deal of folly already in possession; and power has too often pretended to be knowledge. Let us enlarge the growing sphere of our wisdom, our enthusiasm, and our love of humanity, and the world will turn to that finer light, and move round it.

But Mr. Hazlitt is talking of Shakspeare, and we are interrupting him. Mr. Hazlitt goes through the whole of the plays, making a chapter of each. It is not easy to say which of these chapters is the best, or which three or four of them. The first thing that strikes the reader is the novelty [4] of having Shakspeare so well understood as well as admired, and the pleasure of being shewn a metaphysical reason for every beauty he has felt himself. The second is the appreciation and display of Shakspeare's most beautiful and impartial spirit of humanity, which shines like the sun of heaven "on the just and the unjust." The third is not only the general enthusiasm of Mr. Hazlitt for his author, but the very striking susceptibility with which he changes his own humour and manner according to the nature of the play he comes upon; like a spectator in a theatre, who accompanies the turns of the actor's face with his own, now looking eager, now withdrawn, now staring, now subsided, now cheerful-mouthed, now sad, now careless, now meditative, now wound up by social merriment, now relaxed by solitary despondency. Thus in the plays that deal chiefly with the knowledge of life, he is all excited to speculation; in those of which women are the chief ornaments, he reposes upon their trusting nature and tenderness: in the political ones, he is—a politician; in *Romeo and Juliet,* he is inclined to be all hope and enjoyment, he has "eyes of youth"; in *Twelfth Night,* he is one of the party that riot in "cakes and ale," and *Malvolio's* absurdities; in the *Midsummer Night's Dream,* he is off, and fantastics it equally well with the clowns and the fairies; in *Henry 4th,* he sees the soul as well as body of *Falstaff,* and swims round his corpulence as to a merry planet; in *As You Like It,* he sits and hears the wind in the trees; in *Macbeth,* he looks about him, and feels in strange places; in *Hamlet,* he is over-conscious and hypochondriacal, he sees all things in their anatomy; in *Lear,* he is shrunk up.

We are at a great loss how to commence our extracts, or which to chuse; and we are hampered with this difficulty quite as much by the exuberance of the criticism, as by the necessity of putting what we gather from it into very small limits. It will be better to refer the reader at once to the book itself, for a just appreciation of it; and to profess to do nothing more than sharpen his inclinations by some passages taken almost at random. We shall condense our remarks upon them as much as possible, avoiding at the same time the passages which have been extracted in the *Edinburgh Review,* under the presumption that most of our readers are intimate with that celebrated publication. Yet we are much tempted to begin with what has been extracted there of Mr. Hazlitt's remarks on the women of Shakspeare, and of what he has said on *Hamlet*. The first paragraph of the latter, at any rate, has been unquoted; and we shall begin with this, as a striking specimen of the tendency we have just noticed in this author to give himself up to his poet. What the *Edinburgh Reviewer* very elegantly says of Shakspeare's having "*peopled* the fancies of English readers," could not be better exemplified. Mr. Hazlitt contrives to make the very name of the play at the top of his chapter take a sort of air and attitude of personification.

November 2, 1817

This [5] is that Hamlet the Dane, whom we read of in our youth, and whom we seem almost to remember in our after-years; he who made that famous soliloquy on life, who gave the advice to the players, who thought "this goodly frame, the earth, a steril promontory, and this brave o'er-hanging firmament, the air, this majestical roof fretted with golden fire, a foul and pestilent congregation of vapours"; whom "man delighted not, nor woman neither"; he who talked with the grave-diggers, and moralized on Yorick's skull; the school-fellow of Rosencrans and Guildenstern at Wittenberg; the friend of Horatio; the lover of Ophelia; he that was mad and sent to England; the slow avenger of his father's death; who lived at the court of Horwendillus five hundred years before we were born, but all whose thoughts we seem to know as well as we do our own, because we have read them in Shakspeare.—P. 103.

In addition to the passages extracted by the *Review*, may be quoted the following:

It is not for any want of attachment to his father or abhorrence of his murder that Hamlet is thus dilatory, but it is more to his taste to indulge his imagination in reflecting upon the enormity of the crime and refining on his schemes of vengeance, than to put them into immediate practice. His ruling passion is to think, not to act; and any vague pretence that flatters this propensity instantly diverts him from his previous purposes.—P. 109.

We can only refer to the comparison of *Macbeth* and *Richard 3rd*, which is too long to extract whole, and too good to abridge. Of *Othello.* we shall speak by and bye, and of passages in the chapter on *Troilus and Cressida*.

CHARACTER OF CORIOLANUS, *And the reason why he does not like praise*

Coriolanus himself is a complete character: his love of reputation, his contempt of popular opinion, his pride and modesty, are consequences of each other. His pride consists in the inflexible sternness of his will: his love of glory is a determined desire to bear down all opposition, and to extort the admiration both of friends and foes. His contempt for popular favour, his unwillingness to hear his own praises, spring from the same source. He cannot contradict the praises that are bestowed upon him; therefore he is impatient at hearing them.—P. 76.

CLEOPATRA

Cleopatra's whole character is the triumph of the voluptuous, of the love of pleasure and the power of giving it, over every other consideration. Octavia is a dull foil to her, and Fulvia a shrew and shrill-tongued. What a picture do those lines give of her—

> Age cannot wither her, nor custom steal [*sic*]
> Her infinite variety. Other women cloy
> The appetites they feed, but she makes hungry
> Where most she satisfies.

What a spirit and fire in her conversation with Antony's messenger who brings her the unwelcome news of his marriage with Octavia! How all the pride of beauty and of high rank breaks out in her promised reward to him—

> There's gold, and here
> My bluest veins to kiss!—

She had great and unpardonable faults, but the beauty of her death almost redeems them. She learns from the depth of despair the strength of her affections. She keeps her queenlike state in the last disgrace, and her sense of the pleasurable in the last moments of her life. She tastes a luxury in death. After applying the asp, she says with fondness—

> Dost thou not see my baby at my breast
> That sucks the nurse asleep?
> As sweet as balm, as soft as air, as gentle.
> Oh Antony!

It is worth while to observe that Shakspeare has contrasted the extreme magnificence of the descriptions in this play with pictures of extreme suffering and physical horror, not less striking—partly perhaps to excuse the effeminacy of Mark Antony, to whom they are related as having happened, but more to preserve a certain balance of feeling in the mind.—P. 98, 99.

The little paragraph by itself at the conclusion of the criticism on *Antony and Cleopatra* is in the deepest style of criticism, and combines a local and a general feeling worthy indeed of the subject:

Shakspeare's genius has spread over the whole play *a richness like the overflowing of the Nile.*

CALIBAN

The character of Caliban is generally thought (and justly so) to be one of the author's master-pieces. It is not indeed pleasant to see this character on the stage any more than it is to see the God Pan personated there. But in itself it is one of the wildest and most abstracted of all Shakspeare's characters, whose deformity, whether of body or mind, is redeemed by the power and truth of the imagination displayed in it. It is the essence of grossness, but there is not a particle of vulgarity in it. Shakspeare has described the brutal mind of Caliban in contact with the pure and original forms of nature; the character grows out of the soil where it is rooted uncontrouled, uncouth and wild, uncramped by any of the meannesses of custom. It is "of the earth, earthy." It seems almost to have been dug out of the ground, with a soul instinctively superadded to it answering to its wants and origin. Vulgarity is not natural coarseness, but conventional coarseness, learnt from others, contrary to or without an entire conformity of natural power and disposition; as fashion is the common-place affectation of what is elegant and refined, without any feeling of the essence of it.—P. 118.

ARIEL

Shakspeare has, as it were by design, drawn off from Caliban the elements of whatever is ethereal and refined, to compound them in the unearthly mould of Ariel. Nothing was ever more finely conceived than this contrast between the material and the spiritual, the gross and delicate. Ariel is *imaginary* power, *the swiftness of thought personified.*—P. 121.

Our readers are already acquainted with the exquisite appreciation of the actors in the *Midsummer Night's Dream,* which has also been extracted in the *Edinburgh Review.* It is as full of enjoyment, as it is critical; and *Bottom,* "the most romantic of mechanics," has for the first time "had justice done him." Indeed, it has been a singular stain on the national character hitherto, that as far as criticism is concerned, Mr. Hazlitt has been the first to do justice to Shakspeare's characters in general. Perhaps *Falstaff* is to be excepted, who won Dr. Johnson's heart with his taste in jokes and good dishes, as Wilkes did at the bookseller's table in the Poultry. Yet Johnson, after all, could not well explain his liking of *Falstaff*, and rises into an antithetical apostrophe, which exhibits a singular struggle of his declamatory faculties with his pleasanter ones. Mr. Hazlitt's praise might have been relished by *Falstaff* himself; but with all due regard to the Doctor (whom we like and respect very sincerely nevertheless, all sorts of differences of opinion not excepted), *Sir Hugh Evans*, we suspect, would have been most taken with his.

But we must check ourselves here, both in reverence to the Doctor and to the limits of our paper; for we have not yet got through half Mr. Hazlitt's book, and there are points of notice which we have also left on the road. We shall therefore conclude our extracts next week, together with some further general remarks, a character of Mr. Hazlitt's style, and such objections as we venture to make to one or two particulars in his philosophy.

But though we quit Mr. Hazlitt's book for the present, he has left the subject still in our heads; and we feel as if we were stopping at a half-way house on a beautiful road, with the pleasantest of the poet's characters to supper. What? Shall we sup royally, or aristocratically, or romantically, or only humanly? Shall we have cannon to accompany us; or say "Nay, my lords, no ceremony"; or shall we feed with the fairies

On purple grapes, green figs, and mulberries; [6]

or shall we cry,

A hall! a ball! give room, and foot it, girls;—[7]

or "shall we make the *welkin* dance? Shall we rouse the night-owl in a catch, that shall draw three souls out of one weaver?" [8] Anything but "go round about the cauldron," [9] and sup with the witches: we will leave them out of doors; and listen to them, in the intervals of the wind, just before we are going to bed.

November 23, 1817

THE FOUR NEXT PLAYS,[10] which Mr. Hazlitt notices in succession, are *Romeo and Juliet, Lear, Richard the 2d,* and *Henry the 4th.* We mention them together, because, in turning over the leaves to see what was coming for us, they happened to strike us as affording a singular specimen of the unparalleled variety of Shakspeare. In *Henry the 4th* is *Falstaff.* What a succession! A pair of young lovers, full of hope and joy; an old king, whom the habitual impatience of royalty and the ingratitude of his children have driven mad; another King (*Richard 2d*) of an impatient and royal temperament also, but as unlike in his wretchedness as difference of sentiment can make him; *another King* (*Henry 4th*), fond of royalty also, and unhappy with it, but upon quite different impulses, and with a totally distinct character; princes, and noblemen, and gentry, and plebeians, of all sorts, sizes, and humours; and lastly, that Corpus Facetiarum, the very mention of whose name is as big with humourous associations as his body—*Falstaff.* Then again comes another sort of king (*Henry 5th*), then *another* totally different (*Henry 6th*), then *another* equally so (*Richard 3d*), then

> Another yet? a seventh? * I'll *look* no more;
> And yet an eighth † appears! [11]

It is astonishing to see what a task the critics have had of late, and still have indeed, though not so much as before, to vindicate the most natural productions of poetry from the charge of being unnatural; and what is very curious, it made no matter whether the language was natural, or even naturally, that is to say characteristically, artificial. Quin was quite petrified when Garrick introduced for the first time, from a true copy of Shakspeare, the violent and familiar piece of abuse with which *Macbeth* receives a messenger of bad news. The French school could not tolerate Shakspeare's familiarities of any sort; and yet its followers in this country contrived to find out that the language of the lovers, *Romeo* and *Juliet,* was too *artificial!*

> Oh that I were a glove upon that hand— [12]

* Henry 8th.   † King John.

And a multitude of other passages, which would have been pedantry in the mouths of middle-aged lovers, were pronounced for that reason to be the same in those of romantic youth. Nature was always in the wrong. If upon a true ground of art, her language was natural, it was too inartificial; and, if upon the very ground of nature, it was artificial, then it was not natural enough.

Mr. Hazlitt, we see, has not noticed this mistake. Indeed he does not seem to be aware of it, or feels so intensely the reverse fact that it never occurred to his recollection. He says, as a matter of course, that "their courtship is not an insipid change of sentiments lip-deep, learnt at second hand from poems and plays"; nor is it. Heaven knows; though we may here observe that both the lovers bring into play the association of their reading hours, perhaps we should rather say their school recollections; and this, which mere scholars, or mere critics, or conscious pretenders to sentiment, mistook for cant and common-place, is only an additional instance of the thorough and never-failing nature of all that Shakspeare does.[13] One of the commonest marks of an enthusiastic and imaginative boy at school is the making the most of all that he has read and heard of, or in other words, the feeling and applying all that he acquires in the shape of intellectual gracefulness to himself, his thoughts, and his very diversions. He is Hector in the play-ground, Epaminondas or one of the Gracchi in a dispute with the upper Powers, Nisus of Pylades in friendship, and somebody in Ovid, or in Shakspeare himself, when he makes love. There was a boy at our school who has declared that when he saw his friend's face turn upon him for the first time in the day round a cloister, the sun or the finest kind of daylight literally seemed to make its first appearance too: and we believe he felt so. It may be imagined what poetical fancies such a boy would paint to himself as realities, when he fell in love. Now *Romeo* is a youth of this kind, only, of course, with all the superiority which a mind like Shakspeare's must give him.

Mr. Hazlitt has answered an objection to *Romeo and Juliet* equally unfounded as this, and still more philosophically absurd. We need not point out to our readers the fine mixture of conversational and rhetorical language with which the writer shews at once his strong conviction of the truth of what he is criticising, and his relish of the beauty of it:

We have heard it objected to Romeo and Juliet, that it is founded on an idle passion between a boy and a girl, who have scarcely seen and can have but little sympathy or rational esteem for one another, who have had no experience of the good or ills of life, and whose raptures or despair must be therefore equally groundless and fantastical. Whoever objects to the youth of the parties in this play as "too unripe and crude" to pluck the sweets of love, and wishes to see a first-love carried on into a good old age, and the passions taken at the rebound, when their force is spent, may find all this done in the Stranger and in other German plays, where they do things by contraries, and transpose nature to inspire sentiment and create philosophy. Shakspeare proceeded in a more strait-forward, and, we think, effectual way. He did not endeavour to extract beauty from wrinkles, or the wild throb of passion from the last expiring sigh of indifference. He did not "gather grapes of thorns nor figs of thistles." It was not his way. But he has given a picture of human life, such as it is in the order of nature. He has founded the passion of the two lovers not on the pleasures they had experienced, but on all the pleasures they had not experienced. All that was to come of life was theirs. At that untried source of promised happiness they slaked their thirst, and the first eager draught made them drunk with love and joy. They were in full possession of their senses and their affections. Their hopes were of air, their desires of fire. Youth is the season of love, because the heart is then first melted in tenderness from the touch of novelty, and kindled to rapture, for it knows no end of its enjoyments or its wishes. Desire has no limit but itself. Passion, the love and expectation of pleasure, is infinite, extravagant, inexhaustible, till experience comes to check and kill it. Juliet exclaims on her first interview with Romeo—

My bounty is as boundless as the sea,
My love as deep.[14]

And why should it not? What was to hinder the thrilling tide of pleasure, which had just gushed from her heart, from flowing on without stint or measure, but experience which she was yet without? What was to abate the transport of the first sweet sense of pleasure, which her heart and her senses had just tasted, but indifference which she was yet a stranger to? What was there to check the ardour of hope, of faith, of constancy, just rising in her breast, but disappointment which she had not yet felt? As are the desires and the hopes of youthful passion, such is the keenness of its disappointments, and their baleful effect. Such is the transition in this play from the highest bliss to the lowest despair, from the nuptial couch to an untimely grave. The only evil that even in apprehension befalls the two lovers is the loss of the greatest possible felicity; yet this loss is fatal to both, for they had rather part with life than bear the thought of surviving all that had made life dear to them.

The home argument which is put to Mr. Wordsworth and the Mystics at p. 139,[15] we shall notice hereafter. Of the two garden scenes, Mr. Hazlitt thinks "it would be hard to say which is the finest, that where he first converses with his love, or takes leave of her the morning after their marriage. Both are like a heaven upon earth; the blissful bowers of Paradise let down upon this lower world." After quoting *Juliet's* "apology for her maiden-boldness," "to shew the perfect refinement and delicacy of Shakspeare's conception of the female character," the critic extracts, as "of the same sort, but still bolder in virgin innocence, her soliloquy after her marriage with *Romeo*." "Gallop apace, you fiery footed steeds," &c. &c. He then proceeds thus, in a strain of sentiment, which it would be worth the while of the gross exclaimers against a voluptuousness founded on a sense of the beautiful and the sympathetic to attend to:

We the rather insert this passage here, inasmuch as we have no doubt it has been expunged from the Family Shakespeare. Such critics do not perceive that the feelings of the heart sanctify, without disguising, the impulses of nature. Without refinement themselves, they confound modesty with hypocrisy. Not so the German critic, Schlegel. Speaking of Romeo and Juliet, he says, "It was reserved for Shakespear to unite purity of heart and the glow of imagination, sweetness and dignity of manners and passionate violence, in one ideal picture." The character is indeed one of perfect truth and sweetness. It has nothing forward, nothing coy, nothing affected or coquettish about it;—it is a pure effusion of nature. It is as frank as it is modest, for it has no thought that it wishes to conceal. It reposes in conscious innocence on the strength of its affections. Its delicacy does not consist in coldness and reserve, but in combining warmth of imagination and tenderness of heart with the most voluptuous sensibility.

Mr. Hazlitt has described the tragic part of *Juliet's* character in a sentence. "It is the heroic," says he, "founded on tenderness and delicacy."

We do not think, that when he says "*Romeo* is *Hamlet* in love," he is so happy as in saying that the play in general is "Shakspeare all over, and Shakspeare when he was young." *Hamlet*, we conceive, had a greater preponderance of the thinking faculty in him than *Romeo;* or rather, *Romeo* would not have given up *Ophelia* to brood exclusively over his father's death and to dally with the punishment of his uncle. His animal faculties were in as full perfection as his mental; whereas, though *Hamlet* always appears to us a most elegant and handsome person, we suppose something over-delicate of his constitution. It is from this difference perhaps, that *Romeo* is as much in a hurry in some respects as *Hamlet* is always the reverse. The former kills himself, because, as Mr. Hazlitt justly observes, "though the only evil that even in apprehension befalls the two lovers is the loss of the greatest possible human felicity, yet this loss is fatal to both, for they had rather part with life than bear the thought of surviving all that made life dear to them." Now *Hamlet* might have killed himself also on the sudden; but he might also have brooded over his sorrow, and thought on, and thought on,[16] till his death resulted from the exhaustion of pain rather than the loss of pleasure. In a word, *Hamlet's tendencies*, besides being rendered somewhat lonely and exclusive by his princely rank, we think, were less pleasurable than *Romeo's;* his imagination did not lean so much that way, or sail over so merry a current of blood. He was a Dane; and *Romeo* was an Italian.

But see what it is to get upon Shakspeare, and with such a companion too! We were to finish our observations on Mr. Hazlitt's book in one article, then in two, *then* in three; and here is a whole one upon his chapter of *Romeo and Juliet*. We must make no more promises; but fairly chatter away in future till we have done, sure at any rate that we are upon a subject pleasant to our readers.

A word before we conclude for the present, respecting *Romeo's* first love. "*Romeo's* passion for *Juliet*," observes Mr. Hazlitt, "is not a first love: it succeeds and drives out his passion for another mistress, *Rosaline*, as the sun hides the stars. This," continues our author, "is perhaps an artifice (not absolutely necessary) to give us a higher opinion of the Lady, while the first absolute surrender of her heart to him enhances the richness of the prize. The commencement, progress, and ending of his second passion are however complete in themselves, not injured, if they are not bettered by the first." Now what Mr. Hazlitt conceives to "enhance the value of the prize," contains, we suspect, all the secret. *Romeo's* first mistress did not return his love; the second does; and a young love, unless under very remarkable circumstances or other passions mix with it, can seldom be long content to play all the part itself; though when once it meets with a sympathy, it is equally difficult, if generous, to be torn away. The very idea of *two* and of a return, is necessary to it; but the idea of the sex in general, and the easiness with which it attributes imaginary qualities to an object, prevent it much chance of solitary martyrdom. We think therefore that Shakspeare perfected the *youth* of *Romeo* by representing him as having had a previous love; [17] not to mention that so young an enthusiast will sometimes, out of mere fancy or vanity, think he has fallen in love, and only find his mistake when he does so in reality.

We will make a conjecture here as to the effect that *Romeo and Juliet* has upon an audience, which is this: that nine parts out of ten think the love scenes but poor maudlin work, and find all the interest of the play in the quarrels of the two houses and the more tragic parts in general. And we will make a conjecture, which we think equally well founded, as to the cause of this. It is, that although love is here really and exquisitely pourtrayed, and in such a manner as to enchant all those who have been in love, very few persons, comparatively speaking, *have* been in love. In some the passion is prevented by early and unlimited intercourse with the sex; in a great many by the money-getting part of education; and in a great many more by want of imagination. All have doubtless had their inclinations and preferences, the latter for the most part merely accidental and negative; but love—love is as different a thing from all this! as fascination is from voluntary eyesight, or—*Romeo* from Hopkins.

[RICHARD, DUKE OF YORK]

December 28, 1817 . *Drury-Lane*

A PIECE called *Richard Duke of York or the Contention of York and Lancaster* was produced here on Monday.[1] It is "altered from Shakspeare's *Henry 6th*," and contains almost the whole serious strength of the company; and yet somehow or other, there is very little in it to arrest the attention; and Mr. Kean, in *Richard*, is far from making his usual impression. The general run of the actors here indeed are ill calculated to elevate the middle characters of tragedy into importance; and unfortunately all the characters in the present piece are of this description. Thus we have no impression from Mr. Penley's [2] acting as the *Duke of Somerset*, but that he walked about with robes that hung ill upon him; or from Mr. Bengough's, but that he was a largish old gentleman who was killed, or from Mr. Wallack's, but that he took up the said lusty deceased on his shoulders, and walked off with him. There were fine passages in Mr. Kean's *Duke of York*, but the character wants abruptness and intenseness for him. Besides, he always consents to use a great deal more declamation and common-place than is becoming a great actor; or else he really is only a great actor by fits and starts. Why does he not oftener use the same natural tone with which he begins one of his speeches in answer to *Somerset* before the King? If he thinks it would not strike, he may depend upon it he is mistaken; people do not admire a passage merely because it is unlike others, but because it is like Nature. But if he really does think so, his general greatness is indeed very doubtful; nor is there much hope that he could do it if he would. The best passage, of any continuance, was the farewell scene with his little son *Rutland*, which was very deep, natural, and quiet. We did not admire so much the closing scene, where he stands in a dying state, and *Margaret* (a dreadful incident!) gives him the handkerchief dipped in his boy's blood, to wipe his face with. A certain monotony in it was perhaps suited to his feeble condition; but we wonder he let slip a fine opportunity of turning a familiar phrase to one of those pathetic and exalted accounts which such phrases have in the midst of sorrow:

> See, ruthless Queen, a wretched father's tears:
> This cloth thou dipp'st in blood of my sweet boy,
> And lo! with tears I wash the blood away.
> Keep thou the napkin, and go boast of this:
> (*He gives back the handkerchief.*)
> And if thou tell'st the heavy story right,
> *Upon my soul*, the hearers will shed tears;
> Yea, even my foe will shed fast-falling tears,
> And say—Alas, it was a piteous deed!

If Mr. Kean had lain twice the emphasis he did upon the words in italics, it would have given them double the nature and effect.

We do not think this compilation from Shakspeare will last long.[3] In truth, it is not a good one; nor, however paradoxical the assertion may appear, is it likely that a good compilation will be ever made from the works of a great dramatist: for in proportion as his work is good, and coherent, and finely coloured, this cutting up into piece-meals must inevitably spoil it. Imagine a selection from Rafael's pictures, put together into one picture; or an opera made out of scenes of different operas of Mozart, Paesiello, and Cimarosa. A true painter or musician would laugh in your face at such a proposal. What would become of all the harmonies and gradations of colour, of all the suitabilities to this or that situation or person? The absurdity is self-evident. In the piece before us, for instance, the compiler has made a strange feeble compound out of scenes and characters, which are excellent in their own places, and where they are heightened with those entire specimens, either of great strength or great weakness, with which Shakspeare has set them off. But the hero of this piece is a middle character; *Warwick* is not made prominent enough to take the place of him; other stout and striking characters which vary the three parts of *Henry 6th* are omitted, or could not be brought into a piece that mainly concerns the *Duke of York;* and the compiler, in abridging the part of *Henry* himself, did not see that a character of great and remarkable weakness had better have been made the prominent one at once, than the middle character just mentioned. In short, we must protest vehemently against the irreverent rashness as well as other impolicy of disjointing a great poet in this manner, putting his scattered limbs together, and sending them forth to display an awkward and unnatural vitality, upon the strength of their individual beauty and excellence. It is turning beauty to deformity, and strength to weakness. It is mocking and making nothing of the great writer (ignorantly no doubt) at the very moment when the greatest homage is pretended; it is indeed want of sentiment as well as understanding. Have compilers of this sort never heard of such a thing as context as well as text; and do they think that a poet like Shakspeare puts his scenes and characters in such and such a place, and unites and modifies them in such and such a manner, for nothing? For heaven's sake, let us have no more of such anomalies. Let us see Shakspeare himself, and not a degraded composition of noble limbs, with a piece besides here and there cut from other poets—an eye from poor Chapman, and a knee-pan from Webster: for such also is the case with the present!

If the compiler would make us amends, let him revive some of the plays of those other great poets at once; for though he has introduced them awkwardly to us on the present occasion, his acquaintance with them does him credit; and the evident admiration of the audience at both the passages alluded to is a good earnest that he might succeed better in that speculation than his present one.

[FIGARO]

THIS HOUSE has opened again for the season; and the night we saw it, was very fully attended.[1] It is now lit up with a magnificent chandelier containing a double circle of gas, which hangs like a crystal sun in the centre of the roof, and throws a fine light all over the house, though by contrast the pit and lower boxes look darker than before. But this, we believe, is what the ladies prefer; and for that matter, perhaps the men too, soldiers and statesmen not excepted. We observe that the gas chandeliers have been withdrawn from the boxes at Covent-Garden. The light is found, as was expected, too powerful for the complexion, when brought so near; and certainly there is no reason why the ladies' faces should suffer from it; for as to the notion that a really good complexion ought to be able to stand the most searching light, it is doubtful whether the very best would look at its best under such circumstances; and as the whole matter, even in nature, is a business of deception (health always excepted) it is to the benefit of the beholders to have as many good countenances as possible seen to the best advantage. The true charm of a face is in sweetness and intelligence—in expression; and if it be innocently and unaffectedly assisted, so much the better. Any complexion or mere surface would fly to atoms before a microscope; but soul, and taste, and the beauty of cheerfulness or kindness are another thing. If a lady would look at her best at the Opera, she should take exercise in the morning, and be in a good humour all day; and then if her face has not all the assistance that a proper disposal of the lights and shadows can give it, why it is very ungratefully treated; and if it has, we are prodigiously silly not to be the better pleased.

It was supposed at first, that the gallery must suffer by this hanging of the light; but this, we believe, is now contradicted. The only sufferers are the four painted groups on the ceiling,

representing Music, Painting, Dancing, and Poetry; and they
certainly are a good deal afflicted. They were executed, we understand, by M. Zarra, from the designs and under the inspection of M. Casimir Carbonnier, a young artist, and pupil of
David. We are also informed that the inequality which has been
observed in the execution is owing to the whole work's having
been composed and finished in the course of less than three
weeks. We are loth therefore to pronounce upon the merits of
either of these gentlemen, who are not to be expected to rival
the rapidity of Rafael. Some of the figures are very spirited,
but others are much the contrary; and if M. Carbonnier has any
invention, he requires more time to shew it; for he has drawn
pretty unequivocally upon the most well-known compositions
of Rafael and Michael Angelo, especially the School of Athens,
and the Prophets in the compartments of the Vatican. The
prominent figure of Architecture, for instance, is almost a fac-
simile from one of them; and by the side of the imitations in the
group of music there is introduced the figure of a girl sitting,
so very French-like and artificial as to form a singular contrast.
M. Carbonnier's recollections, however, of his pretty countrywomen, are excusable; but we know not what to say for his
less warrantable nationality, in making Aristophanes, Terence,
and *Molière,* the three prominent names in the label of his group
of poetry, and leaving Sophocles and *Shakspeare* fluttering off
into a dark cloud in the back-ground. Besides, it would have
been better to have made the names of Corneille, Racine, and
Voltaire more prominent than Molière's; and, in an opera-house
perhaps, Quinault's would have been better than all. Even the
name of Tasso does not come forward into notice like that of
Molière; and yet, most unquestionably, the Italian poets should
have been the most prominent in an Italian theatre. Metastasio,
an opera poet, is even, we believe, omitted. But *next* to the
Italian, it would have been better taste in M. Carbonnier, considering where he was, to put the English, or at any rate *not* the
French.

We are glad to see that the Manager has been so quick to
treat us with *Figaro.* It is perhaps the most delightful work of

a most delightful author. *Don Giovanni* [2] disputes the palm with it; but the best things in *Don Giovanni* are of the same nature as those of which *Figaro* entirely consists. Mozart here gave himself up to the intoxication of his animal spirits, not in their noisiest, but in their most graceful and enjoying moments; and we listen, as we might have done at a feast given by young Anacreon, with our senses crowned with roses. All is a smoothing interchange of enjoyments—a series of sprightly turns of lapping pleasures. He reduces us, as usual, to nothing but smiling surprises and exclamations. What can be more airy and yet sufficing than *Se a caso Madamo?* What more pettishly ironical, and then indignant, than *Via resti servita, Madama brillante?* What more hurried, mysterious, and occupying, with a leaning to the pleasurable, and with those little fretful notes at intervals, than *Non so piu cosa son,* or than *Voi che sapete?* What more elegantly raillying, and then strutting off into a military air, with its accompaniment of a really noble march, than *Note piu andrai?* What more sweet-voiced and feeling, what more consuming, what a more delicate and melodious utterance of passion, a more intense mixture of feebleness and strength, than *Porgi, amor?* What more expressive of suspicious questioning than the movement of *Conoscete Signor Figaro* in the Finale of Act 1st; or more petitioning, or anticipative of the consent and harmony which it requests, than *Deh! signor, non contrastete,* which is as soft and gently bending as the smoothing of two cheeks? What more sweetly yet fervently complaining, than *Dove sono i bei momenti?* What more simple and shepherdesslike than *Ricevele, padroncina?* What more exquisitely childish, more prettily sobbing, than *L'ho perduta, me meschina?* What more lightsome and insinuating than *Su Taria?* What more glowing and expectant than *Deh vieni non tardar?* What more perfect in skill, taste, smartness, sweetness, courtship, and triumph, than the duet of *Crudel perche finora,* which is perhaps the very finest effusion of this great master of transport? The three chords in the symphony alone announce an inspired hand.

Madame Camporese [3] does not appear this season; and her part of *Susanna* the Lady's Maid is performed by Madame

Fodor,[4] that lady having kindly given up the *Countess,* as the bills say, to a new singer. The former change seems to be regretted by some of the papers; but we must confess it is not so by us. Madame Fodor may be somewhat too portly for the airy *Susanna;* but she has animal spirits, and a more social look than Madame Camporese; and to say the truth, the latter, to our ears, is rather a correct and powerful than delightful singer. She will be missed however, we suspect.

Of the new singer, Miss Corri, we ought not to pronounce a decided opinion at once, she suffers under such evident agitation. Her acting, partly perhaps on this account, is at present a non-entity; but singers are not expected to excel in this particular, though they have more need of it in Operas like the present than most; and the better performers they are at any time, the better effect it gives to their singing. As a mere singer, Miss Corri shews undoubtedly great promise. Her voice is sweet and distinct; she has an excellent ear; and displays even through her trepidation a facility and power worthy of her reported instructress Madame Catalani. Her deficiency seems to be in the intellectual part of her art—in propriety of expression. She throws her lights and shades too indiscriminately, now dropping her voice and now darting it forth like Catalani, but not, like the latter, upon the proper places. She is said however to be very young, and appears so. But we shall report further in a week or two. Miss Corri's personal appearance, though not remarkable, is lady-like; and she seems so modest as well as clever, that it is impossible not to wish her success heartily.

We cannot reconcile ourselves to Miss Mori as the page. Madame Pasta [5] was not very clever in the character, but she at least looked more like the bashful and amorous boy. Naldi,[6] whom it is a pleasure to hear pronounce Italian, appears to have got rid, at least in this character, of the extremes to which we ventured to object last year. He is quite as intelligent as before, and as active as he need be, but does not fling himself so much about the stage, nor waste such a quantity of threatening gestures upon *Se vuol ballare.* We are glad to see Angrisani again, —and Ambrogetti,[7] who is more full of meaning than ever,

and luckily has a character in this opera that enables him to ex-
patiate, like *Don Giovanni*, instead of his being tempted to
deviate into those unaccountable gestures and elaborate point-
ings to the moon, which he baffled us with in *La Molinara*. His
duet with Madame Fodor, *Crudel père*che, he renders what it
ought to be, and what Mozart made it—a lively dialogue as well
as a beautiful composition. The momentary alarm which he exhibits at *Susanna's* saying *No* instead of saying *Yes*, and *vice
versa*, is excellent, and well appreciated by the audience. It is
observable, by the way, that this little piece of coquettishness
and variety is introduced by Mozart himself, the writer of the
dialogue having given no play upon the words *Yes* and *No*.

Covent-Garden

A TRAGEDY, called *Retribution*,[8] which does not require any
particular notice, has been brought out here. It is not destitute
of dramatic effect; but is of the artificial school, and abounds
with those common-places which acquire, by the usage of scholars, a sort of classical air, and are easily mistaken by a young
writer for ideas instead of words. If the author, however, is as
young as he is said to be, he may become a good writer, especially as he appears to have amiable feelings; which, by the way,
will teach him one day, we hope, that Retribution is not so good
a thing as he seems to think it.

The Editor has been very unwell for two or three weeks past,
till within these few days; or he would have noticed in this Paper
one or two minor novelties.

[THE BARBER OF SEVILLE]

March 22, 1818   *Opera*

AN OPERA, entitled *The Barber of Seville* (*Il Barbiere di Siviglia*), from the pen of Signor Rossini, a young living composer at Rome, has been produced here for the first time in this country.[1] High expectations were entertained of it, especially as it had been performed with great success at various theatres in Italy; but we were among those who thought that the author's having taken up an opera to set to music, which had been already composed by so fine a master as Paesiello,[2] was not a piece of ambition in the best taste, or a very promising symptom of excellence. We expected that we should find little genius exhibited, at least on the score of sentiment; and we conceive that we were not disappointed.

The great excellence of the Italian school (which with all our admiration of Mozart appears to us to be much undervalued now-a-days, partly owing to undoubted merit in the German school, and partly to a court fashion for that school) consists in fine melody and expression.[3] They take up one passion after another, and give you the genuine elementary feeling of it, as if they were undergoing and totally occupied with it themselves. Paesiello's compositions are special instances of this power of expression. His melodies are exquisitely graceful, touching, and original; and his recitatives always appear to us so extremely to the purpose as to be superior even to those of that delightful German by nation, and Italian by nature, Mozart.

In neither of these main qualities, will Signor Rossini's Opera, in our opinion, bear any comparison. We should be loth to speak so decidedly, after only one hearing; but what renders an Opera most delightful, and makes one recur to it over and over again and grow fonder on acquaintance, is a succession of beautiful airs; and of these the new *Barbiere di Siviglia* appears to us to be destitute. We do not recollect one. The passages most resembling them struck us as being traceable to Haydn, Mozart, and to Paesiello himself; and the recitative is singularly bald and common-place. You might always know the comment which the fiddle-bow was going to make. An intelligent daily critic notices, we observe, the resemblance to Haydn of *Zitti, zitti, piano, piano,* the most favourite passage in the Opera.[4] On the other hand, the piece is not destitute of merit, or even, considering the author's youth, of great promise, though not on the higher sides of genius. Its good qualities are a sort of sprightly vehemence, and a talent for expressing oddities of character. We have unfortunately lost our copy of the book; but we have a strong recollection of the most striking passages. Some of them fairly beat it into us. They were the more hurried parts in general, the entrance of the *Count* in the disguise of a singing master, the groans of old *Bartolo,* and the scene where *Figaro* and his master have so much difficulty in getting rid of a set of fellows who have a pro-digious pertinacity. We never met with a composer who gave us such an harmonious sense of discord, who set to music with such vivacity what is vulgarly called a *row.* The rest of the opera is of a piece with this kind of talent, not good in the graver, more sentimental, and graceful parts; but exceedingly promising in the ardent, vehement, and more obviously comic. The general effect is raw and inconsistent. Sometimes, for instance, there is hardly any accompaniment, sometimes a numerous one; some-times the stage is all in a bustle, and sometimes unaccountably quiet. One feature is particularly worth notice; which is, that the young author, in a sort of conscious despair of a proper quantity of ideas, dashes his crotchets about, as it were, at random: and, among a number of grotesque effects, gives now and then a fine hit. He resembles, in the latter respect, the ancient painter, who in a fit of impatience at not being able to express foam at the mouth of a hound, dashed his spunge against the animal's jaws and produced the very thing he despaired of.

We have taken it for granted all this while that Signor Rossini is young, as reported. If not, he will hardly become eminent; but if he is, he undoubtedly may be so; provided he is not as noisy and vehement as his music, and does not get his wild head broken some day, for some over-vivacious serenade.

["BELLAMIRA" AND "THE JEW

OF MALTA"]

April 26, 1818   *Covent-Garden*

THIS HAS BEEN a rich week in theatrical novelties, especially as they have all been successful.[1] Covent-Garden has produced a new tragedy; and Drury-Lane has revived a tragedy of Marlowe's, a musical opera composed by Hook, and produced a new burlesque interlude. Here's a piece of anticlimax, natural to lists of things!

The new tragedy is entitled *Bellamira, or the Fall of Tunis,* and is from the pen of Mr. Shiel,[2] author of the *Apostate. Manfredi,* a Neapolitan Nobleman (Mr. Charles Kemble), is a captive at Tunis, and conspires with his fellow-prisoners to regain their freedom. During his efforts for this purpose, he suddenly encounters, to his great astonishment, his wife *Bellamira* (Miss O'Neil), who has been made captive also with her infant, and who, after undergoing with him some agonizing delays and hindrances, obtains the sympathy of the renegade Governor (Mr. Young), who, partly from weariness of his own offences, partly from regard for his countrymen, and partly from love of the very name of *Bellamira,* which was that of his own child, assists and urges them to escape. Their flight, however, is prevented by the interference of *Amurath,* another renegado Italian (Mr. Macready),[3] who, on account of the Governor's doubtful disposition towards the slaves, is appointed in his room and ordered to put the principal among them to death. *Amurath,* a violent vindictive man, has seen in the condemned list the name of the man he hates most upon earth, *Manfredi;* for the woman he loved had chosen the latter in preference, and it was for an attempt to seize her by force that he was beaten down by his rival, and branded by the executioner in the public place at Naples. To his double delight—the delight of what he calls his love, as well as of his malice—he finds this very woman a prisoner also; and the main part of the piece is occupied with his endeavours to make the one a victim of his lust, and the other of his revenge. In the former attempt he is prevented by the heroism of *Bellamira* herself, who in a struggle with him snatches a dagger from his girdle, and defends herself; he rushes out for the purpose of killing *Manfredi,* but the deposed Governor, who has in the meanwhile found out that *Bellamira* is his child, has in the meantime set the Christians free; and though the conspiracy is discovered, and he and others thrown into prison, yet the city is successfully attacked by Christian troops; the prisoners, who with the exception of the Governor had been led out to death, join them, and assist in the victory; *Amurath,* going in his rage to the dungeon, mortally stabs the Governor, and, after going out again to fight, returns staggering with his wounds, and finds *Bellamira* and her infant with her father. All the flood of his passions rushes back with bitterness on his heart; and though wishing to think for a moment that he could not do harm to an infant, his habitual vindictiveness prevails; he crawls towards the mother and child, in spite of her outcries, in order to sacrifice the latter, when *Montalto* the father, who was not yet dead, totters between them, and returns the mortal stab. At this crisis, the others come in victorious, and the piece ends with the deaths of the two unequal renegades, and the salvation of the husband, wife, and child.

This piece is far from being destitute of merit; and as the author, we understand, is young, has still more promise in it. There is a good deal of interest and suspense in some of the incidents; the language, though not marked with originality, and tending to declamation, is nevertheless instinctively kept under by a lurking better taste; and the sentiments are not only excellent, but the author has given proofs that they are sincerely felt by him: first, by the instinctive better taste just mentioned, which always feels that truth can do without declamation; and second, by an animated burst against the cold-blooded neglect of Captives in Africa by common-place conquerors in Europe —an obvious allusion, which though appealing to the natural impulses of humanity, and pretty sure of the approbation of a

mixed audience, might nevertheless have excited individual
enemies among them, who might have done the author mischief
in other passages. Now we like this sincerity and defiance of
petty chances, exceedingly. It is what the time has wanted, and
is another mark of its growing intellectual power. It does honour
to Mr. Shiel, his country, and even his species.

The fault of the new tragedy is the fault of a young ambition,
ardent for its purpose, without the experience requisite to obtain it; it is a tendency to mistake improbability for interest,
vehemence for strength, the impatience of lowness for the at-
tainment of height, and excessive tragic effect, physically overpowering, for real effect at once carrying away and sustaining.
Mr. Shiel might have selected even from the very dagger-room
of Italian story—the novels of Giraldi Cinthio—a story of Tunis-
ian captives, which might have suggested a less convulsive
set of incidents than his present one. The repeated trick of
controlling a woman's movements by shewing her child or her
husband to her and threatening his life, and a continual putting
in play of daggers, denunciations, villanies, bodily and mental
agonies, and shrieks, mean nothing but that the author has not
yet got the abundance of ideas which can enable him to dispense with the common property of horrifiers. The mother, in
fact, would not have survived such an outrageous set of trials.
The child is almost made a tragic doll of in this piece, for the
purpose of snatching up and laying aside when the mother
pleases; and very like a doll it behaves accordingly, acquiescing
in every thing with a truly waxen passiveness; and sitting, when
not wanted, on the first bench or parapet wall next it, with a
face as indifferent to the storms in front of it as the head of a
ship. Some of these superfluities have, we dare say, been subsequently retrenched. We have not time to say more; but Mr.
Shiel has quite sense and spirit enough to know how to pursue
the hints we give him and to avail himself of them. Let him
earnestly cultivate his reading, and still more his observation of
human nature and the love of the external world, the former
of which is the flesh and blood of genius and the latter its beauti-
fier; and he will neither require so many violent incidents an-

other time, nor have any that he retains without the reconciling graces which repay us for what we suffer.

We have scarcely room to say any thing of the performers, albeit they are great people now-a-days, and sometimes, we believe, insist upon giving the finishing hand to an author's scenes and conceptions, which is one cause perhaps of so many damnations: but in the critic's hands, at any rate, they must be content to take their station below dramatists. The part of *Bellamira* is well suited to the habitual tragic nature of Miss O'Neil's style; and she was excellent in particular passages, particularly in those of sudden emotion. Her very best touches perhaps are those in which she deprecates and protests against anything. Her No, no, no! for instance, is very natural, hurried, and absorbing; but she should take care how she uses it too often. Mr. Young was very judicious as well as powerful in the Governor, especially in the sullen and gathered-up despondency of his latter moments in the dungeon. Charles Kemble is not at his best in a part that indulges him too much in frowning; but he always looks well, and in passages acts well. The most striking actor in the new piece is Mr. Macready, who has got rid of more of his tendency to declamation than we expected so soon and gave the malignant villainy of *Amurath* its best because most quiet effect. We are very glad to see this proof of his better knowledge; for actors are too apt to be seduced by a notion of *what tells,* as the phrase is; whereas it is not what tells at the moment that is to be desired, but what tells in the long run. Mr. Pope's declamation *tells*—but it is a very poor story; Mr. Kean tells to some tune.

Drury-Lane

A MUSICAL OPERA, called the *Lady of the Manor,*[4] with new music by the original composer, Mr. Hook, was revived here on Thursday. We know not the author. It is something in the mediocre but mild and pastoral taste of the dramatic writings of Bickerstaff and Mrs. Brooke.[5] The story is that of two ladies (Miss Kelly and Miss Byrne) who disguise themselves to try the nature of two gentlemen. Miss Kelly performs her part with her usual address and meaning. The music, like the general run of this venerable composer's writings, is in some parts very pleasing, in others very common-place. The difference seems to depend upon whether he has the Italians or Vauxhall in his mind. We do not know which were the new or the old pieces. One of them, a song for several voices on Rural Hospitality, sets out with a delightful movement; but is Mr. Hook the author of the Scotch air of *Down the Burn, Davy, Love?*

Marlowe's *Jew of Malta* was acted on Friday with great success. The reader is probably acquainted with this piece, in consequence of the great and laudable republication of our old poets by the better part of the lovers of black-letter. The story is that of a Jew, who having been oppressively treated by the leading Christians in Malta, has an outrageous hatred for the whole sect, and besides a multitude of indiscriminate murders which he sums up to a servant of his with great satisfaction, contrives that two lovers of his daughter, one of them the Governor's son, shall be killed by each other's hand; strangles a friar who comes to tell him of his daughter's consequent death and to remonstrate with him; poisons a courtesan, a bully, and his own servant who had conspired with them against him, escapes from prison and delivers up Malta to the Turks, and in fine, turns every machination of his enemies upon their own heads, till the final scene, when having undertaken to betray the Turks to the Governor, and at an entertainment blow them up, the latter contrives that he shall be killed instead, in the presence of the invited guests. The performance is said in the play-bills to be *founded* on Marlowe's tragedy,[6] but we do not see the reason of this word; the tragedy is the old tragedy itself with only a few alterations in the nature of the Jew's crimes and catastrophe —poison in wine being substituted for a poisoned flower (and we think not for the better) in the scene with the Courtezan, and *Barabas* being blown up or rather fetched down from a gallery with shots, instead of being tricked into a burning cauldron, a piece of consideration certainly for our nerves, and extremely well managed. Mr. Kean's performance of the Jew is in his very best taste of self-hugging revenge and triumphant Machiavelism. He also delighted the audience with a song, somewhat too much in the manner of Braham perhaps for an amateur, but very sweet and even scientific in the undertones and graces.

We find ourselves inclined to say so much on the subject of Marlowe and his prototype of Shakspeare's finer flesh-and-blood Israelite that we shall not trust our pen in its present narrow limits, but return to the subject next week, when we will also give an account of *Amoroso, King of Little Britain,*⁷ which an accident prevented us from seeing. Those in the meantime who are not acquainted with Marlowe may become so by referring to the Collections of the ancient British Drama, to some separate old plays lately published, and to that excellent work, Lamb's *Specimens of English Dramatic Poets,* where he will find one or two masterly critical paragraphs upon Marlowe's genius.* The possessors also of a new series of publications, entitled *Select Early English Poets,* by Mr. Singer, to which we have long owed the tribute of our approbation, are gratified to find that they are to have the poem of *Hero and Leander,* the united production of Marlowe and Chapman. We shall take opportunity of it to say a few words on this very elegant and desirable publication, especially on the part in it borne by our old, rugged, reverend friend Chapman, who, if he has all the roughness, has also all the oracular majesty of an old oak of Dodona.

May 3, 1818

WE RESUME ⁸ our observations on the *Jew of Malta.* Its performance has been repeated several times to good houses, though, without denying the talent of the author, some think it cannot last as an attraction, some attribute its continuance wholly to Mr. Kean, and, all scarcely know what to think of the principal character, who is generally pronounced as a being en-

---

* Our readers will be glad to hear that the writings of Mr. LAMB, which contain so much profound criticism and sentiment, have been collected for publication by a spirited bookseller, and are now in the press.

tirely out of the pale of human nature. The Jew is certainly a perplexing sort of person, and it requires all the force of his natural intellect to hinder the very greatness and multiplicity of his crimes from tumbling, by their own weight, into the fantastic attitudes of the burlesque. But it appears to us that, with due reference to the times in which the character was conceived, to the principles on which the author intended it to proceed, and to the Anti-Jewish persecution which Shakspeare afterwards made the ground of his nobler work, the perplexity is done away; and the wholesale criminal resumes his station in humanity, not indeed as a specimen of its ordinary or even of its extraordinary offenders, but as a barely possible result, in vehement times and in a warm climate, of the united mistakes of persecution from without, and selfish subtlety from within.[9]

In the time of Shakspeare, the people of Christendom had not left off regarding the Jews with an aversion of which we have no idea in these times. It was horror and loathing. The time was a noble one; but strong prejudices, at least among the middle and lower orders (for the upper and literary classes were thought to be much infected with heresies) had survived its kindlier tastes, and its imaginative character kept them alive. Through the medium of superstition, acted upon by romantic traditions, a Jew was regarded as a wilful and savage opposer of all the best things in the world, a sort of human beast, always ready to plunder and bite, a bearded demon, an old living goblin, haunting the place in which its treasure was buried, or bending and muttering about with a watchful malevolence against every thing innocent, especially children. There was a notion, on which Chaucer has founded his lovely story of the boy who went singing a hymn to the Virgin through Jewry, that they privately sacrificed a little child at Easter with many horrid rites. And not to mention the dress which they wore, and other customs of their own which tended to their exclusiveness from the rest of society, their odium was completed by their money-getting and usurious habits, which were held by our ancestors in particular contempt; though in fact, the very nature of the laws which had long prevailed against the Jews, and still do so in a degree, originally drove them to this only method of maintaining a consequence in society. They had long been objects of extortion all over the world—a remarkable instance of which is to be found in the reign of King John, who drew a tooth from a Jew's head every day till he gave him the sum required. Kings extorted, subjects borrowed; and all hated, so much the more, the men whom they compelled to have this odious advantage over them.

Now Marlowe availed himself of all these civil and religious prejudices which helped to excite a bitter character in the *Jew;* he put him also into a hot and adust climate, upon the irritating chalk of Malta; gave him for country-men and masters the most bigoted Christians, the Maltese and their Knights, who made a vow of warfare against Infidels, and who actually treat him ill; and to complete the subtle and fiery counteraction in the *Jew,* made him a disciple of Machiavel, whose intentions have been such matter of doubt, but who was then regarded, at any rate, as the professor and teacher of all selfish and bloody cunning, a remorseless subjector of means to ends, an incarnation of demoniacal intellect, as void of all human bowels as a clock-case, and only ready, with horrid smile, to thrust his triumphant subtilties into the teeth of simple virtue.

With these lights held up to his shocking old face, Marlowe's *Jew* becomes a very different person from a mere gratuitous destitution of human qualities. He is only an excessive specimen of how they may be devilized by the mistakes above-mentioned; and indeed, with all his enormities, he is scarcely worse than Machiavel's friend, the well-known Caesar Borgia, at least as the latter is represented in history, and partly by the Florentine Secretary himself.

But up rose Shakspeare in the complete wisdom of his humanity; and rescuing the Jew himself from enormities, which with all explanation are still beyond the mark, which were too much for their own subtilty, which overdid the hidden intention of his forerunner, and which our great poet knew to be rather the fancies of stimulated imaginations then possible even to a perverted human being, clothed his dry bones and his vizard face with flesh and blood, gave him passions good and bad in common with those on whom he revenged himself and left only just as much excess in him as was a set-off to the pernicious mistakes of his persecutors. Blessings on thy memory,[10] thou divinest of human beings! who without either vehemence or want of enthusiasm, without either partiality or want of deep affection, without effort, without affectation, without resentment against the most provoking mistakes of what is still human, left us a body of beautiful wisdom, in the spirit of which everything human is done justice to; in which vice is held up neither as inexcusable nor happy; in which the pretensions of happier virtue are made modest and attractive, equally removed from pride towards its fellow-creatures and dust-biting fear towards ill-praised heaven; in which earth is not degraded, nor the justice of futurity committed; in which artificial guilt and innocence are equally deprecated; in which reward is not made a desirable thing for one's mere personal sake, nor punishment threatened us for having been unhappy already; in which no absurdity whatever is explained by another, nor, in impatience of not being able to give one, is converted to threatening; in which, in short, human beings are well-intentioned, mistaken, forgivable, and improvable ones; and which affords genial knowledge enough, if it were attended to, to ripen the long-maturing fruit of human experience, and enable true innocence to realize its old fabled sunshine.

We have seen the new interlude of *Amoroso* and the new afterpiece of the *Mountain Chief*, and after having had our thoughts turned to Shakspeare we may be allowed to say nothing about them, except that one is like an extract from a previous burlesque, and that the other, notwithstanding the natural and various performance of Mrs. Alsop, is a lamentable failure.

[COSI FAN TUTTE]

August 2, 1818   *Italian Opera*

MOZART'S OPERA of *Cosi fan tutte* has been revived here, and most delightfully.[1] It is one of his best, ranking next to *Figaro* and *Don Giovanni;* it is altogether taken up with those subjects and feelings which Mozart played to in so happy a manner—gallantry, arch humour, gracefulness, laughing enjoyment, voluptuousness, and an occasional pathos which is rather the suspension of pleasure than the sufferance of pain.

This opera too has the advantage of being simpler and more obvious in its incidents, of telling its own story better, than any we have ever witnessed. There are six people in it, two pair of whom are the lovers, who vow eternal constancy (Fodor, Cori, Begrez, and Garcia),[2] the fifth an old gentleman (Naldi) who is always laughing at them for it, and the sixth, a servant girl (Mori) who joins with the men in a plot to try the fidelity of the ladies, which the good old gentleman in the first instance warned them against, and which, we must say, is tried with a vengeance. It may have been wrong in the two ladies, whose lovers have apparently taken leave for the army, to listen to the same lovers in disguise, and to feel the courage of their constancy shaken by besiegings, and melancholy implorings, and supposed takings of poison. They ought doubtless to have spared not one kiss of compassion, whatever their notion was of the attachment of the sufferers. They ought, if not to have kicked them into atoms, at least to have let them suffer on as much as they pleased, and drink poison like *eau de vie.* But unfortunately, they were made of too pitiful stuff; and of course the lovers have to regret their success, and to forgive them upon the ground of the "natural viciousness" of the sex. *Cosi fan tutte,* says the play; "It's the way of them all;" and so we must think the worst of it, and then make the best. O wise we!

This is also perhaps the most completely performed opera on the stage. All the singers are at home, with some exception on the part of Miss Cori, who is a good singer but wants spirit as an actress. The fault of Garcia, an excellent singer, is of another sort: he is over-vivacious, if not in his gestures, in his attitudes; and while standing still, as an Irishman would say, keeps writhing and bending himself about like an elephant's trunk. He makes also such doleful mouths, when he is pathetic, that he appears to taste the bitterness of his sorrow literally in his mouth. He seems to want a lump of sugar after it.

What an inexhaustible succession of beautiful airs and harmonies is there in Mozart! One combination after another does not start out with a more sparkling facility in the far-famed Kaleidoscope. The first thing you hear in the present opera is the ardent trio, beginning *La mia Dorabella*, in which the lovers praise their mistresses, and insist that the old gentleman shall give proofs of their possible infidelity; then comes, like a gentler note to the same purpose, the other of *E la fede delle femmine*, the sounds of which absolutely talk and gesticulate; then the happy and polite one of *Una bella serenata*, with that gentlemanly willingness of ascent on the line *Ci Sarete, si signor*, like a bow itself; then the triumphant noises of *Bella vita militar;* then the little sobbing farewell, and entreaty to write every day, *Di scrivermi ogni giorno;* the invocation for gentle winds on the voyage, *Soave sia*, with those delicious risings of the voice, like a siren's from the water; the exquisite laughing trio, *E voi ridete*, with its slippery rhymes, its uncontrollable and increasing breathlessness, and the grave descending notes of the pitying old gentleman in the base; the quiet triumph and lingering enjoyment of *Un aura amorosa;* the nodding and gentle giddiness of *Prendro quel brunettino;* the breathing passion of *Secondate;* the smiling insinuation of *Il core vi dono.* What do we not owe to an art and a master like this, who as it were spoke music as others speak words; and who left his magic imprinted forever in books, for the hand and the voice to call forth, whenever we want solace in trouble, or perfection in enjoyment!

[OTHELLO]

October 4, 1818 *Drury-Lane*

Mr. Kean has returned from his tour to France and Italy—
a very proper relaxation for a man of his talents—and has performed in the course of the week *Richard the Third* and *Othello*.[1]
We saw the latter on Thursday evening; and with all our experience of the stage, and with all our scepticism as to the powers
of the very best actors in characters from Shakspeare, we never
witnessed a performance that struck us so forcibly. It brought
back upon us the earnestness and implicit attention of our
younger days. We have admired Mrs. Siddons, been infinitely
amused with Lewis, been sore with laughing at Munden, been
charmed with Mrs. Jordan; but we never saw anything that so
completely held us suspended and heart-stricken, as Mr. Kean's
Othello.[2] In all parts it is as complete as actor can shew it—in
the previous composure of its dignity, in its soldier-like re-
pression of common impulse, in the deep agitation of its first
jealousy, in the low-voiced and faltering affection of occasional
ease, in the burst of intolerable anguish, in the consciousness
that rage has hurt its dignity and ruined the future completeness
of its character, in the consequent melancholy farewell to its past
joys and greatness, in the desperate savageness of its revenge, in
its half-exhausted reception of the real truth, and lastly, in the
final resumption of a kind of moral attitude and dignity, at the
moment when it uses that fine deliberate artifice and sheathes
the dagger in its breast.

If we might venture to point out any parts the most admirable
in this performance, it would be the low and agitated affectation of quiet discourse, in which he first canvasses the subject
with *Iago*, the mild and tremulous farewell to "the tranquil
mind, the plumed troop," &c. in which his voice occasionally
uttered little tones of endearment, his head shook, and his visage
quivered; and thirdly, those still more awfully mild tones in

which he trembles and halts through those dreadful lines beginning—

Had it pleased heaven
To try me with affliction; had he rained
All kinds of sores and shames on my bare head.[3]

His louder bitterness and his rage were always fine; but such
passages as these, we think, were still finer. You might fancy you
saw the water quivering in his eyes.

And here two things struck us very forcibly; first, how impossible it is for actor and audience to be both as they ought to be
in such large theatres, since Mr. Kean's quietest and noblest
passages could certainly not have been audible in the galleries;
and second, how much an actor's talent must be modified by his
own character off the stage, an observation we may reasonably
make when it leans to the favourable side; for we conjecture
from anecdotes that are before the public, that Mr. Kean's temper is hasty, and his disposition excellent and generous; and it
is of passion and natural generosity that *Othello's* character is
made up. For this reason we can never help being sceptical
about Garrick's excellence in characters of deep and serious interest; since, off the stage, he was little better than a quick-eyed
trifler, full of phrases of gabbling jargon, and coarse-minded
withal.

Of the two new performers—Mrs. West,[4] who repeated *Desdemona*, and Mr. Cleary, who changed from *Othello* to *Iago*—
we have nothing to add to our former observations, except that
the lady performed still better than before.

There is a new afterpiece here, which is below criticism.

Mr. Kean's *Othello* is the masterpiece of the living stage.[5]

[MR. FARREN]

WE WERE PREVENTED from seeing Mr. Farren [1] in *Sir Bashful Constant* on Friday week by the performance of Mr. Kean in *Othello;* but we saw his second appearance in that character on Monday, and his first appearance as *Sir Anthony Absolute* on Thursday; and they have both confirmed us in the opinion which we thought we should entertain of him, when he got out of the comparative disguises of old age.

Mr. Farren's great merit is correctness, and even this is rather on the negative than the positive side. His conception of the author is sensible, but not deep; his manner is quietly strong; his enunciation excellent. He is never out in his part; he rarely does any thing foreign to it; he never commits himself. The chief passages that have told in other hands tell for the most part in his, and a great self-possession gives even to his omissions an air as if they were just what they ought to be, or rather, few people think of them at all. His effect is like that of a man in private life who says little, but seems to think a good deal. He has a staid appearance of thinking himself in the right, or of having made very judicious conclusions whether he thinks so or not; and it is taken for granted.

But all this is a little capital with a great credit. What Mr. Farren wants as an actor is richness and enjoyment. He makes one thought stand for ten; and seems to respect even that more than to relish it. He perceives more than feels; and in matters of genius, this is apt to stop on the surface. It is eye without hands and taste. He sees the part of the ball immediately before him; but what is under it, and about it, and inside of it is comparatively lost. In *Sir Bashful Constant,* for instance, who repeatedly informs us that he is such a good-natured man at bottom, and who is christened after his exceeding modesty, he seems a really angry man in all the angry speeches, and is only abruptly bashful. When he practises a piece of by-play also, it is in too much keeping with *the immediate feeling at the expense of the general character.* Thus, in the same part, when he anxiously tries to find out if anybody overhears him, before he tells his bashful tale and shews what a very good-natured man he is, he goes to the door, and with his two hands and his whole collected force suddenly dashes it back—which might have been half the death of anybody listening.

We are sorry to differ with some of our brother-critics; but the *Anthony Absolute* we cannot but consider as a total failure. Mr. Farren was outrageously Absolute, to be sure; and in one or two scenes, he was sufficiently significant on a gentler subject; but *Sir Anthony* in the hands of his unrivalled representative Dowton has a vein of the genial running through him, which warrants him and his son in referring to the kindlier days of his youth, and makes us fancy that he could have been at that period what the young Captain is at present. Mr. Farren in this character is crabbed and formal, with abrupt starts of the reverse. Peevishness as well as passion seems to be part of him; whereas the inflammable old boy, in the hands of Dowton, is *Anthony* as well as *Absolute,* and always appears to be as agog for a joke as for a quarrel. Besides, Dowton's face, person, and voice are all in better character, and of a higher order of the comic. They are the jolly old knight, who is angry not because he is full of mere irritability, but because he does not want to be disturbed from his ease, and from his infinite stomach for being satisfied. Mr. Farren, with his long person, half shut eyes, crabbed voice, and an aspect at once youthful, dry, and caustic, looks in it like a ready-made old bachelor.

In short, we conceive Mr. Farren upon the whole to be a more than useful actor, but not, as some suppose, an actor of genius. We understand, it is true, that he is young; and he may therefore yet surprise us with more talent than we can at present discover; but neither his faults nor even his merits appear to us to be on the side of youthful promise, which is proverbial for running into exuberance. We are, we confess, in the minority on this occasion; and sincerely hope that Mr. Farren may have all the benefit from that circumstance, which may keep his confidence unimpaired and enable us to find ourselves mistaken if we are in the wrong.

Mr. Charles Kemble again surprised us, in *The Way to Keep Him*,[2] with the new vigour which something or other has given to his comic acting. He has certainly during his late tour got some of the French wines in his head, or been drinking the winy influence of the French Comedy; and there is no knowing how very pleasant a good-natured Englishman becomes with a little grafting from the Southern sprightliness. He did not appear however to so much advantage in the *Rivals*. And what a falling-off was the whole piece from the performance of the same comedy at Drury-Lane. Jones is a pleasant fellow; but to put him into *Sir Lucius O'Trigger* after Johnstone is to make one animal, whether inferior or superior, perform the part of a totally different one—a butterfly, for instance, or a dromedary. Liston is an excellent humourist, but then he is always Liston, and Bannister was *Acres:* and with all our habitual respect for Mrs. Davenport, and her warm-faced industry in digging her comic emphasis, we remember Miss Pope—Miss Pope! Who could come up to her unconscious mistakes and old gentlewomanly resentment in *Mrs. Malaprop?* Comparisons, to be sure, are odious; but so is criticism—is it not, Mr. Farren? Here we have been finding flaws in your clever acting, when for aught we know to the contrary you may be one of the best and pleasantest fellows on the face of the earth. What! You cannot return the compliment?—Well.

[THE RECRUITING OFFICER]

October 25, 1818   *Drury-Lane*

FARQUHAR'S COMEDY of the *Recruiting Officer* [1] was performed here on Tuesday, but produced little effect. The play
itself, though sprightly for the first three Acts, seems as if it began to be tired of its own animal spirits during the two last.
The importance of a conjurer, whose profession is assumed by
Sergeant Kite for the purpose of assisting a lover, is an obsolete
thing now-a-days, at least generally speaking; and the very
sprightliness of the rest of the piece is so intermixed with broad
double meanings that a good deal of it was obliged to be cut
away. Thus, the jovial rakery of the author, which depends
for effect upon its uninterrupted face, was baulked and made
silly; and in fine, as if it was resolved that nothing should contribute to its success, some of the actors were indifferent ones,
the others seemed perplexed with what was left them to say,
the audience were dull, and even Mrs. Mardyn, in her beau's
attire, dropped her voice now and then, and handled her switch
as awkwardly as the text. In a word, the piece was altogether
too broad for the present state of manners and taste, the vices of
which lean towards the sordid and hypocritical rather than the
debauched. The actors themselves felt as much; and it is no
wonder if the audience felt with them. The best part of the
performance was the acting of Munden and Knight in the two
recruits, which was a perfect varying picture of rustic astonishment, doubt, credulity, terror, and vanity. Munden's face is
as potent as ever.

Farquhar was one of those men, who, more sprightly and
witty than deep, and with excellent natural dispositions, just
see far enough into the common-places and hypocrisies of society
to despise them, become hopeless of making them better, and
so, too cheerful to play the weeping philosophers, and too frank
to conceal anything, make a gay compromise with the merrier
and more social-looking vices, and help in fact to continue the

whole error by getting sympathy as bad a name as antipathy.[2] He has the same air also, in his plays, of a conventional townmanliness and a certain young valuing himself upon his intercourse with the sex, which is to be found in those of two greater predecessors, Beaumont and Fletcher, the former of whom died at thirty-two. Farquhar, we believe, died at twenty-nine or thirty, at the very time his *Beaux Stratagem* was going through the first nights of its performance. He was very much beloved, and shewed the fineness of his nature in his behaviour towards a wife who really loved him but who had pretended to be worth money. He realized the love if not the money, and behaved to her with an unabated tenderness, for which she must have adored him. This indeed was making a compromise to some purpose; and if he had not taken at its word a world which he despised, and grown hopeless as well as his inferiors, his love of sympathy, which he degraded in his dramas into mere dissipation, might have opened his eyes to discover "the soul of goodness" in things which he found evil, and which he left so.

This revival was followed by another on Thursday, in which the love of the sexes is equally ill handled but in a very different manner—that of the *Distressed Mother*,[3] translated by Ambrose Philips from Racine. It is French all over, that is to say, dramatically speaking—pompous, frigid, and ranting.[4] Instead of the grand elemental feelings of the Greeks, who half in sublimity and half in superstition talk like the creatures of a newly created and passionate world, sincere and awful, all things, with the usual modesty of the old French system, are brought down to the pitch of the Court of Louis the 14th. The French were too much occupied to go to Nature, and so Nature must come to them; and all the "vasty spirits" of poetry and passion shrink themselves into coals and bag-wigs, as the devils in Milton's Pandaemonium did into pigmies. The persons "Madam" it away, like the ladies in the *Beggar's Opera*.

There was nothing prominent in the performance but the acting of Mrs. West in *Hermione*, and of Kean in *Orestes*; and they were both dreadfully maltreated by their own dialogue, Kean in particular. When he had made some "good hit," as the phrase is, a most frigid common-place with an *Ah* or an *Oh* in it remained for him to speak, and seemed to mock what had gone before. It had just the effect of a man's going to sit down in a dignified manner, and plumping upon a chair too low for him. Mrs. West was very effective in her declamation, and may prove a formidable rival for Miss O'Neil. It was of the very best kind, interspersed with such touches of the natural as would suggest themselves to a woman of taste and feeling in these times of the stage. Her dress was also as correct and classical as her under garments would allow it to appear. Yet the play would perhaps have been damned had it not been for Kean's acting in the mad scene, which turned the doubtful temper of the audience into such a fit of transport that they would not hear any more after his being carried out, and called for him after the dropping of the curtain. A repetition of the piece was given out for Saturday amidst great applause and shouting; but we think it cannot possibly be a favourite.

Covent-Garden

A PIECE of the old mysterious, murdering, Newgate Calendar sort, has been brought out here, which our readers will excuse us from attending to. The plot of it in the daily papers is enough. Its name alone (*Proof Presumptive*) contains a world of criticism. It is said to be a translation by Mr. C. Kemble. We are glad that it is a translation, though sorry that he is the translator.

[THE FAIR ITALIAN IN ALGIERS]

January 31, 1819   *Italian Opera*

THIS THEATRE opened for the season on Tuesday last.¹ The boxes have been newly painted and draperied, but we cannot say, with taste. A fierce struggle of blue, red, and yellow colours, with drab and lead looking on in apathy, is one of the most in-harmonious accompaniments of sight to sound that can well be conceived; and while some of the compartments are painted with bas-relief subjects from the antique (which is very proper), others stare at you with large thick angular patterns, like a border to a Brobdignagian drawing-room. The painting on the ceiling remains as before. The best piece of novelty is a trans-parent shade which has been run round the overpowering bril-liancy of the gas-light chandelier. Smaller chandeliers have in consequence been hung round the lower tier of boxes; and the light altogether is certainly more pleasant and bearable to mortal eyes. To look up at the great burning circle, before, re-minded one of the insufferable mystical ardours which Dante saw in heaven.

The entertainments commenced with an opera new to this country, from the pen of the celebrated living composer Rossini. The reader may remember our account of his *Barbiere di Si-viglia*,² some of the music of which has become familiarized to the public in an afterpiece of Covent-Garden. The merits of *L'Italiana in Algieri* (The Fair Italian in Algiers) are, generally speaking, of a piece with those of *Il Barbiere;* that is to say, there is *more* animal spirit than intellectual, and good compilation than novelty. The author seems to delight in expressing a pre-cipitate and multitudinous mirth; and sometimes works up and ferments a passage, and pours in instrument upon instrument, till orchestra and singers all appear drunk with uproariousness, and ready to die on the spot. He carries this feeling, we think, to a pitch of genius, and even to something exclusive, and peculiar to himself: nor does it hurt perhaps the general effect and character of this species of talent, that nothing seems to come amiss to him, when he gives way to it—old or new, masterly or indifferent. He is like a wit fond of punning and intoxicated with social enjoyment. Old jokes and new, his neighbours and his own, all run merrily through his hands. His good things exalt the occasion; and the occasion, in return, does as much for his bad.

Our memory may reasonably fail us after hearing such music but once; but we remember being particularly amused with passages in the finale of the first Act, with the *terzetto* beginning

Pappataci! che mia sento!

and the *quintett* beginning

Ti presento di mia man
Ser Taddeo Kaimakan,—

in which Ambrogetti's pertinacious repetition of *Crepa* and

Ch'ei starnuti finchè scoppia,

is very ludicrous, and gives us an equal specimen of the humour of the author and the performer.

But the beautiful passages in this opera are not confined to the sprightly ones: and so far from thinking with some of our contemporaries that it is greatly inferior to the *Barbiere di Siviglia,* we are inclined to regard it altogether as containing more originality, though perhaps at the same time more obvious common-place. We agree, however, with the writer in the *Times,* that as the composer approaches the end of the last Act, he gets tired and tiresome. But we were going to speak of the serious passages. We are much mistaken if in these, Signor Rossini has not shewn a greater musical talent, that is to say, a genius for melody, than in any productions of his yet known in England. The *pizzicato* opening of the overture is very striking, and calculated to excite attention; though the overture falls terribly off at last, or rather bursts into mere noise and hubbub. The trio at the beginning of the last scene of the first Act,

Pria di dividerci da voi, Signore,

is full of graceful and cordial expression, suitable to the occasion; and the symphony to thè *cavaliria,*

Languir per una bella,

announced a most beautiful melody, only Signor Garcia, with his superbundant flourishes, would not let it take place. We agree on this last matter with the writer in the *Chronicle,* who says that Garcia's execution of it "operated upon him as a burlesque of the florid or ornamental style of singing." * Every crotchet was literally suffocated with quavers, like the flutterings of so many mosquitoes. It is the greater pity, inasmuch as Signor Garcia has all the powers of a most accomplished singer, and is besides no contemptible actor, especially in comedy. We wish some friend of his would translate the Note below for him, or take some other method of shewing the absurdity of this extravagance, which, carried to such a pitch, is really like nothing better than so much stammering set to music: La-a-a-a-a-a-a-a-a-an—gui-i-i-i-i-i-i-i-ir—per u-u-u-u-u-u-u-u-una be-e-e-e-e-e-e-e-ella. It is as ridiculous as if a Gentleman, in asking a Lady how she did, were to say *How*—and then take a scamper round about the pavement—*do,* and then another scamper—*you* (scamper again)—and so on, to the astonishment of the gathering spectators.

Two new singers made their first appearance in this opera— Madame Bellochi [3] as the heroine, who is a sort of *Roxalana,* and Signor Placci, who is understood to stand in the place of Crivelli.[4] Of the latter, it may be as well perhaps not to speak at present, as an apology was made for him in consequence of

* We take this opportunity of repeating, from a new publication, a joke which we marred in printing a few weeks ago, especially as it is of a kind which cannot afford marring. It was entitled, A Hint to Florid Singers, who were asked "what they would think of a beautiful passage in *Twelfth Night* delivered in the following manner:

If music be the food of—*fally ral de riddle iddle, tum te iddle*—love, play —*tum tum riddle iddle fal de rally*—on.
Give me excess of—*tol lol de riddle fol, liddle toddle*—it; that surfeiting The appetite may sicken, and so—*ti tum de tiddle liddle, tiddle toddle ro —ri tol fal de riddle tum te iddle*—die
But this is nothing to Signor Garcia.

his labouring under a cold. The personal appearance of the lady is not prepossessing. She is not tall enough nor of a good figure; and the expression of her face, when serious, is somewhat tart and scowling. But it is by no means deficient in intelligence; and her smile, though not handsome, lights it up altogether very pleasantly. She is also no mean performer, for a singer, especially in comic passage, which she appears to give with great relish and knowingness; and as a singer, we take her to be a great acquisition. Her voice is powerful, sweet, and of great compass; her articulation clear; her divisions of extraordinary ease and flexibility; her expression distinct and to the purpose, though leaning perhaps rather to the side of force than beauty. She may give a lesson in judgment to Signor Garcia, whom alto-gether however she suits admirably, and not the least in her evident enthusiasm for her art. She seems, in her favourite pas-sages, to nod and look her own relish of them at the audience, and in a manner to become one of themselves, a sort of self-ap-probation and enjoyment which is far from unpleasant, and carries more sincerity than pride with it. Under an appearance of thinking of herself, it shews that she thinks of her art still more. She received very great applause.

We have given but a hint of the story; and the less that is said on that subject the better. It has been well described as an united ill-usage of Marmontel's *Roxalana* and Molière's *Bourgeois Gen-tilhomme;* and this *Bourgeois Gentilhomme,* this cockney who is everyone's butt, is a Bey of Algiers!

Of the new dancers we find it difficult to speak by name, as the characters are not added to the names of these performers in the opera bills. For the most part they seem of a middle kind, between the best dancers already on the stage, and the ordinary ones; and we were much gratified to see, in the new Divertise-ment (*Re-Union Villageoise*) which is very pretty, that there was more grouping and figure-making, and less tee-to-tum spin-ning than usual. The female dancers appear the best. One of them, we cannot tell whether Mademoiselle Le Febre or Ma-demoiselle Goss, a pleasant little brunette, acquits herself in a very sprightly and crisp sort of style, especially in movements that indicate coquetry and skittishness, in which she gives sudden turns and whisks off, that must be as difficult as they are agreeable.

The beautiful ballet of *Zephyr and Flora,* in which Batiste and Milaine perform so well, concluded the first night of the season under auspices the most flattering.

[THE MAGIC FLUTE]

May 30, 1819   *Italian Opera*

THIS HOUSE is the only theatre, now, at which you are sure of hearing something both modern and masterly.[1] There is occasionally something good at the English winter theatres, but the general run of pieces is deplorable, and reminds one of nothing but the stage itself. It is a melancholy round of stage repetitions, as old and dreary as the jog of a mill-horse.

At the Opera, on the other hand, you are almost sure of hearing a work not only masterly, but of the first kind of masterliness in the art of music—some production from the first-rate composers, such as Paesiello, Mozart, Winter, Cimarosa, and Rossini, who, though of various ranks, are as great in their way as the great poets of England or painters of Italy. And it is to be observed that the insurmountable objection to the English winter theatres—their enormous size—does not apply to a large musical house; because singing is naturally of a louder and more distinct utterance than talking; the instrumental accompaniment would fill any place; and if an objection remains as to countenances, an equal variety of distinctness of expression is not demanded of them, nor even wanted, the vocal expression being clear and just, and supplying the feeling to the spectator. We venture to prophesy that at no great distance of time the English winter theatres will either be totally ruined by their size and bad management, or turned into mere places of spectacle; while, on the other hand, the smaller houses will every day grow richer as well as more respectable.[2]

On Tuesday last the Managers, greatly to the credit of their taste and spirit, brought forward another of the masterpieces of Mozart, *Il Flauto Magico* (*The Magic Flute*), better known and long admired in private circles under its German name of the *Zauber Flöte*. We like to mention objections first, as the little boys bite off the hard edges of their tartlets, in order that they may fall unobstructedly on the body of the sweetness within. The opera then, as performed on Tuesday, is justly accused of being a third too long. It was not over, for instance, till nearly 12 o'clock. Now the music is, throughout, excellent; but setting aside other considerations, the most excellent music in the world will not bear a theatrical performance so continued. Its very excellence, unmingled with intervals of other enjoyment as in private society, would tend to overstretch and exhaust attention, just as it strains the faculties to look for hours together at a variety of fine pictures. But when it comes to be considered that this excellent music is divided among a variety of singers, some of them almost inevitably poor and unequal to it, the discrepancy and confusion become perfectly wearisome; and on Tuesday evening for the first time in our lives, and not without some shame, we found ourselves dropping and shutting our eyes in the company of Mozart, not in order to listen with the greater luxury, but to catch a willing unwilling slumber. The remedy of this however is obvious, and we suppose was put in practice on the second night. With regard to the other objections, the new and younger performers whom it was necessary to add to the *Dramatis Personae* are to be treated with tenderness; the most promising young singers may reasonably be allowed to be deficient in giving such compositions their proper effect. We have to find fault however with an agreeable singer, M. Begrez, who whether from negligence or from not having his voice in the best order, gave the sprightly and triumphant air of *Regna Amore in ogni loco* feebly and inefficiently. There is surely, on the other hand, no necessity for the extreme vivacity of the two whirling globes in the scene where the Queen of Night comes down from her throne. They emulated her singing and the orchestra with a noise of which none but tin heads could have been capable.

Such are our objections, all of which are removable. Now to the pleasanter task of approbation. And in the first place, we do not participate in the objection made to the nature of the story, which because it is a fairy tale is thought frivolous. Alas, how frivolous are most of the grave realities of life! We own we have a special liking for a fairy tale; and if we are not greatly mistaken, Mozart himself was of our opinion, and got his wife to read one to him before he sat down to write that divine overture to *Don Giovanni*. Thus his pleasurable and fanciful mind made a fairy tale even a medium of inspiration. And it has a right to be so. It is full of some of the pleasantest associations of one's life. It has "eyes of youth." It is even more; it anticipates for us something of the good, which the human mind, as long as it is worth anything, is so anxious to realize, something of a brighter and more innocent world, in which the good-natured and flowery will is gratified; and the evil spirit, only furnishing a few more anxieties and occupations by the way, is always felt to be the weaker of the two, and sure to be found so at last. But we must take care of our limits. The story of the *Magic Flute* is made up of a mixture of Fairyism and Egyptian mythology. The Queen of Night (Miss Corri), who is a malignant being, has a daughter (Madame Bellochi) who is withdrawn from her by the Priests of Isis (suspicious persons it must be owned), in order to be saved from her influence. A young Prince (Garcia) falls in love with the daughter from having seen her picture, which is put in his way by her mother, and the latter induces him with false representations to try and rescue her out of their hands. A bird-catcher (Ambrogetti), who is a sort of clown to the piece, is made to accompany him as servant. The Prince accordingly gets admittance into the temple of Isis, and makes the due impression on the heart of the lady, who endeavours to escape with him. They are detected, and by degrees brought to have a different opinion of the Priests, who after subjecting them to a variety of trials with that Freemasonry of theirs which was once so celebrated, unite them in marriage. The piece, which, by the way, has the double title of the *Magic Flute; or, The Mysteries of Isis*, receives its first name from a flute given to the Prince, which, upon being played, has the power of averting dangers, and which he makes use of in going through the fiery vaults and other apparent horrors of the said *Mysteries*. *Papageno*, the bird-catcher, is also gifted with a dulcimer, which has the privilege of setting people a-dancing. It is his resort to this charm, when his master and he are about to be seized and made prisoners, that gives rise to the delicious air of *O Cara Armonia*, to which all their assailants suddenly begin treading a delighted measure. We were going to say that the public are intimate with this air, under the name of *Away with Melancholy;* but we should rather say they are on speaking terms with it. The original, with its accompaniments, and with its appendix of another air, is a great deal finer.

And what divine music is there besides? There is, first of all, the finest Overture in the world; then there is bird-like hilarity of *Gente e qui l'uccellatore;* the prophecy about the three youths (*Tre bei Jargon*) who are to descend from heaven on golden wings (the very music comes stepping down, like a ladder from heaven); the magnificent air, *Te guida palma nobile,* which the youths sing when they do descend, and which answers so completely to the character of their mission; all the various and delightful composition, comprising almost every species of emotion, in Scenes 15 and 16 of Act the First; the abundant pomp and solemnity of all the grand melodies and harmonies connected with the Priests and their worship; the placid depth and dignity of *Sarestro's* description of his earthly paradise— *Qui sdegno non s'accende;* and then again, the delicate and tricksome stepping of the return of the Genii, *Gia fan ritorno,* with a quick and dimpled smilingness running throughout it. But the whole opera is one continued and deep river of music, breaking into every possible turn of course and variety of surface, and exhibiting every aspect of the heavens that lie above it. Mozart's genius is here in its most romantic and passionate character, undoubtedly. We can hardly say it is in his best, for nothing can be better than *Figaro;* neither do we conceive it will be so popular as that opera and *Don Giovanni.* It is, we suspect, too poetical to be so—too much referring to indefinable sentiments and sensations out of the pale of common experience; but numberless passages will delight the genuine lovers of music as much perhaps as any in either of those works. It may give a complete idea of what we think of the *Magic Flute* in general, its peculiarities, its chances, &c., when we say, that it is to Mozart's other works what the *Tempest* is to the most popular of

Shakspeare's comedies. We are not sure, for our own parts, that we do not admire it more than any of his operas, if we could candidly rid ourselves of a preconceived notion that Mozart's powers were chiefly confined to the gayer part of enjoyment—a misconception to which all men of various genius seem to have been liable, in return for their bestowing gladness.

We ought not to omit that what Madame Bellocchi has to sing (for it is not much, considering she is the heroine) is sung excellently. Miss Corri also gives some passages *in alto* with so much neatness and truth as to produce an *encore;* but we cannot say we are ever moved by this inexorably frigid performer. We were disappointed, upon the whole, in Ambrogetti. His comedy, perhaps, is naturally of as unpastoral a character as can well be imagined. He looks too beef-eating for a bird-catcher. Angrisani's depth of voice is excellently suited to the part of *Sarestro;* and Garcia, since he has clipped his exuberance, continues to be equally full of power, judgment, and taste. The whole piece is got up with great spirit and magnificence; and when shortened (as we conclude it was, on the second night), will have double the effect.

There is a new ballet here, called *Rose d'Amour,* in which M. and Madame Duport appear with less of the French twirling and a good deal more sentiment. The spectators therefore have reason to enjoy themselves a little, and not merely to stare. They find a little heart in the business, as well as a quantity of legs.

[RICHARD III]

October 31, 1819   *Covent-Garden*

A NEW AND UNEXPECTED CIRCUMSTANCE has taken place here, which promises to rescue the character of the house from the pantomimic degradation into which it was fast falling. Mr. Macready has performed *Richard* twice in the course of the week,[1] with the greatest applause. We must confess we went to see him with no sort of expectations at all commensurate with the greatness of the part. We thought him a man of feeling, but little able to give a natural expression to it, and so taking the usual refuge in declamation. He appeared to us one of the best readers of a part we had seen, according to the received notions of good reading; but with the exception of a character now and then bordering on the melodramatic, like *Rob Roy*—that was all.

We are bound to say that we found our anticipations completely erroneous. A proper sense of the greatness of the part, and of the honorable rank as an actor which he now had to sustain, seems to have roused up all his intelligence to give fit companionship to his sensibility. We expected to find vagueness and generality, and we found truth of detail. We expected to find declamation, and we found thoughts giving a soul to words. We expected to find little more than shewy gestures and a melodious utterance, and we found expression and the substantial *Richard*.

A critic on these particular occasions is forced upon comparisons. However, they sometimes enable him to give his readers a more exact idea of a performance. Compared then with Mr. Kean,[2] we should say that a division of merits usual enough with the performance of such comprehensive characters as Shakspeare's, has taken place in the *Richards* of these two actors. Mr. Kean's *Richard* is the more sombre and perhaps deeper part of him; Mr. Macready's the livelier and more animal part—a very considerable one nevertheless. Mr. Kean's is the more gloomy and reflective villain, rendered so by the united effect of his deformity and subtle-mindedness; Mr. Macready's is the more ardent and bold-faced one, borne up by a temperament naturally high and sanguine, though pulled down by mortification. The one has more of the seriousness of conscious evil in it, the other of the gaiety of meditated success. Mr. Kean's has gone deeper even than the relief of his conscience—he has found melancholy at the bottom of the necessity for that relief; Mr. Macready's is more sustained in his troubled waters by constitutional vigour and buoyancy. In short, Mr. Kean's *Richard* is more like *King Richard*, darkened by the shadow of his very approaching success, and announcing the depth of his desperation when it shall be disputed; Mr. Macready's *Richard* is more like the *Duke of Gloucester*, brother to the gay tyrant *Edward the 4th*, and partaking as much of his character as the contradiction of the family handsomeness in his person would allow.

If these two features in the character of *Richard* could be united by any actor, the performance would be a perfect one: but when did the world ever see a perfect performance of a character of Shakspeare's? When did it ever see the same *Macbeth's* good and ill nature worn truly together, the same *King John* looking mean with his airs of royalty, the same *Hamlet* the model of a court and the victim of melancholy? Mr. Kean's *Othello* is perhaps the most perfect performance on the modern stage; but it is not a perfect *Othello* nevertheless.[3] The union of such a variety of tones of feeling as prevails in the great humanities of Shakspeare seems as impossible to be found in an actor, as the finest musical instrument is insufficient to supply all the effect of a great writer for a band.

At the same time when we thus compare Mr. Macready with Mr. Kean, it is to be recollected that Mr. Kean first gave the living stage that example of a natural style of acting, on which Mr. Macready has founded his new rank in the theatrical world. Nor must we omit that the latter falls into some defects which the former is never betrayed into; and those too of a description inconsistent with the general style of his performance. We allude to some over-soft and pathetic tones towards the conclusion of the part, where *Richard* is undergoing remorse of con-science. *Richard* might lament and even be pathetic; but he would certainly never whine, or deal in anything approaching to the lack-a-daisical. We think both performers occasionally too violent; but this may be partly a stage-necessity. Mr. Mac-ready (and he is evidently quite capable of doing it) should reflect that all depth of feeling in reflecting minds requires a proportionate depth and quietness of expression. It may be as imaginative as he pleases; but it has no taste or leisure for dally-ing with the gentilities of grief.

Upon the whole, Mr. Macready's *Richard* is a very great addi-tion indeed to his reputation, and no small one to the stock of theatrical pleasure. The Covent-Garden stage was thirsty for a little more genius to refresh it; and he has collected all his clouds, and burst down upon it in a sparkling shower. We cer-tainly never saw the gayer part of *Richard* to such advantage. His very step, in the more sanguine scenes, had a princely gaiety of self-possession, and seemed to walk off to the music of his approaching triumph.

Covent-Garden has made another lucky hit in the reproduc-tion of Dryden's altered masque of *King Arthur;* [4] but it would have been luckier had not Garrick's dry and pantomimic abridg-ment hurt the effect of the original. Managers are generally more cunning than wise in these matters; and, finding that dullness cannot do without stage-tailoring, think that genius must be cut and squeezed to it too. Dryden's genius never appeared in so poetical or touching a light as in one character in this piece—that of *Philidel,* the fallen young spirit who is working its way back to heaven with penitence. But his want of sentiment inter-fered even with this; and the whole of the piece is strangely modern-looking and meretricious for a tale of old chivalry and romance. Now the abridgment has kept the meretriciousness, and hurt the nature and the poetry. A good deal of Purcell's fine music too, which though somewhat quaint and crude is full of genius and effect, is unnecessarily missed—as the duet, for in-stance, of *Two Daughters of This Aged Stream* and the wintry singing of the *Frozen Genius.* However, what remains is much

better than usual; and one's national vanity is laudably gratified at hearing those fine old airs of *Britons strike home, Come
if you dare,* and *Fairest isle all isles excelling.* Miss Tree,[5] in
Philidel, has been justly complimented by the *Times* critic (the
profane, not the sacred one) upon her complete execution of
our old English airs.

Drury-Lane

We have not been at Drury-Lane this week; but we see
by the bills, that Comedy is at home, as usual, with her friends
Elliston, Munden, Dowton, Miss Kelly, &c.

[CORIOLANUS]

December 5, 1819   Covent-Garden

MR. MACREADY has appeared twice during the past week in the character of *Coriolanus;* and is to repeat it tomorrow.[1] It is another unquestionable addition to his repute, though not so high a one as his *Richard.*[2] In *Richard,* Mr. Macready seized one particular side of the character—the gayer and more sanguine—and appropriated it to himself. In *Coriolanus* he rather gives additional proof that he deserves to have good parts allotted him in general, than exhibits anything particularly characteristic of the part. Yet it is well worth seeing him in; and this is no mean praise for any performer. In one respect, his *Coriolanus* would have surprised us almost as much as *Richard* did, if we had not seen him in the latter; we mean that the temptation which all such characters hold out to be declamatory did not seduce him back, generally speaking, to that former contentedness of monotonous elocution which we should now perhaps rather conclude to have been discontentedness. Let Mr. Macready take what character he pleases now; we venture to say that since his talents have got an opportunity of shewing themselves, and have been acknowledged, he will never again be found rolling forth that mere melodious declamation which he used to deal out, sentence after sentence, like a machine turning ivory balls.

If Mr. Macready did not touch all the keys of *Coriolanus's* passions truly, he touched them for the most part variously; and often with truth, if not the completest truth. His voice is the finest and most heroical on the stage; not sweeter, we think, occasionally, than Mr. Kean's; which however hoarse in the long run, is as melodious, and finely tempered with passion as any man's in the gentler tones, and before it has been over-exerted; but more according to the old requisites of a hero's utterance, when the general shouted to his army, and the chiefs could be distinguished above the tumult by their respective voices, as they were by their crests and cognizances. As far also as height and figure go, he will have no rival in the part: for though it is curious enough that heroes and great political chiefs have for the most part been short rather than tall (as in the instances of Alexander, Agesilaus, Caesar, Charles the 5th, Frederick the 2nd, and Bonaparte), yet this is not the poetical or sculptural idea of a hero; and the *alta maenia Romae*—the loftiness of Roman domination—has instinctively heightened to our mind's eye the very bodies of the Roman people.

But we doubt whether Mr. Macready's graceful gestures and shapely movements are not somewhat too elegant for *Coriolanus;* perhaps we should say, too softly elegant and swimming. It is true, he holds his head up loftily and looks disdainfully; but even here again we doubt whether there is not a something of ideal grace beyond what Shakspeare intended. *Coriolanus,* though a haughty patrician, was after all a soldier, whose friends found excuses for his unaccommodating temper and style of language in the rudeness of military habits. He could look grand on grand occasions, as in the instance of his sudden and godlike appearance at the hearth of *Aufidius,* but then the circumstance constituted its own grandeur. At other times, especially in his reluctant applications to the people for the consulship, and still more so in the impatience he expressed on that subject to his friends in private, we suspect he was intended to be more short, impatient, and familiar; always haughty indeed, but more plain and soldier-like in his haughtiness, with less of the graceful ungraciousness of the mere patrician.

Again, Mr. Macready would be too loud occasionally even for a hot rude soldier; much more is he so for the elegant personage which he makes him. He is also apt to be too sudden and theatrical in his contrasts, from a loud utterance to a low one; nor must it be concealed that his finest touch of all, where he literally casts in *Aufidius's* teeth the scornful word Boy! was toned and gestured too obviously, however unintentionally, in the manner of Mr. Kean. Still his quarrel with *Aufidius* is altogether a noble scene, and deserved the great applause with which the curtain dropt upon his assassination.

The reader may judge what we think of Mr. Macready's *Coriolanus* with all its drawbacks, when at the same time that we think it worth going to see, we are compelled to say that the rest of the performance of this play is beneath criticism. Miss Foote [3] is a clever as well as handsome actress, and very pleasant to see in such parts as the one in *A Roland for an Oliver;* [4] which we take this opportunity of instancing because we omitted the proper notice of it last Sunday in our comparative list of a week's performances at both houses; but though suitable enough to *Coriolanus's* young wife, with her few unassuming speeches and "those dove's eyes," she cannot be said to give any important addition to the performance. Mr. Blanchard [5] is the only other performer worth noticing; and he is well enough in *Menenius*. Mrs. Faucit belongs to melodrama. A Roman matron did not think it essential to her dignity to step about with her head thrown half a yard back, as if she had a contempt for her own chin.

Drury-Lane

On going to this house from the other on Wednesday evening to see the new after-piece, it was striking to see what we noticed last week—the complete change of fortune in the two theatres with regard to attendance. In Covent-Garden, we again saw half-empty benches at the back of the pit, and a poor account of upper boxes; in Drury-Lane, the house was full. It is true, Mr. Kean had appeared that night in one of his most powerful and appalling characters, *Sir Giles Overreach;* [6] but this, we understand, is the general state of the case. The causes we need not repeat.

The contrast is the more curious, inasmuch as Mr. Elliston, however skilful, liberal, and fortunate he has been in all his other theatrical arrangements, has not been so successful hitherto as the other house with his new pieces; [7] though the posthumous work of Mr. Tobin,[8] with Dowton's and Munden's performance in it, deserved, we think, a better fate. We cannot say so much for the new after-piece called the *Disagreeable Sur-*

prise, which is a string of puns with scarcely anything to hang it upon. We really feel perplexed in attempting to recall anything like a plot to our minds; but there was a young officer in love (Pearman); [9] and a spouting player in an ingenious cocked hat (Harley); and two ladies (Mrs. Edwin and Miss Kelly), who tormented a poor pedantic fellow of a fop (Russell),[10] who happened to be both in love and in a hat at once; for his strange hat was evidently the best joke about him. This unlucky personage, who was made to listen and dance and give up his passion, and do every thing else that he did not wish to do, should have been performed by Liston, for whom perhaps it was originally written. Russell is an excellent actor in what suits him, and can put on a most lackadaisical grin; but the moment he looks grave and angry, he is really so without being foolishly so. His face becomes "no joke."

There were pretty airs from the *Mountaineers* [11] and other well-known sources introduced into the piece; but ill adapted to the words. We ought not to forget that the piece occasionally gave glimpses of something better than its general cast. Some of the sentences were turned with a promise of gentlemanly wit, and some of the puns were very laughable; but the situations were so gratuitous, the persons came in and out so obviously to talk puns at each other, and the puns became at last so engrossing and wilful, that the audience (not being at dinner or supper, to relish those over-peppered devils properly) became tired and hostile.

TWELFTH NIGHT

November 12, 1820   *Covent-Garden*

THE SUCCESSFUL INTRODUCTION of music[1] into the *Comedy of Errors* [2] has given rise to a similar lyrification of this delightful play. It is interspersed with songs, glees, and duets, taken from the German and English masters; and Mr. Bishop,[3] besides adapting these to the scene with his scientific hand, has added some composition, of which though a high, it is no undeserved praise to say that a hearer must be nicely acquainted with the varieties of musical style to distinguish it from the rest. The other modern composers are Mozart, Winter, and Sir John Stevenson; [4] the older ones, Morley, Ravenscroft,[5] and others, who flourished during the golden age of our poetry. Profound in all that was then known of science, which was chiefly occupied in church music, and yet having a people to sing their productions who were much more eager and competent to do so than the contemporaries of their greater successors, the style of their lyrical composition, partly formal and partly tricksome and playful, is like a young chorister anticipating the moment when he shall escape from his surplice and get out among his fields and pastimes.

Mr. Bishop has adapted the songs to the several characters "with difference discreet." *Viola's* are deep and tender; *Olivia's,* like her rank and pride, more vehement, gorgeous, and wilful; those of the others as wilful too, but light, festive, and seasonable. The whole are well executed. Miss Greene, though her acting is suited to nothing but the most passive parts of a character like *Polly,* and is accordingly very unfitted for the haughty *Olivia,* resumed some of the best vocal powers which she exhibited in the *Beggar's Opera.* As to Miss Tree, we never saw or heard her to more advantage in solos. There seemed an analogy in the deep tone of her voice and her affection; and though the former, strictly speaking, is not like a boy's, there is a strength and fullness in the lower notes which, being unusual in a fe-

male, appeared to fall in with the character she had assumed as
a male. Her acting, which is at all times uncommonly good for
a singer, was at its very best in this fortunate part—sincere, unaffected, and graceful. Even her late illness, without diminish-
ing any real strength in the performance, helped to give it a suitable interest; and (as such subjects are eminently critical) we
must be allowed to say that her leg is the very prettiest leg we
ever saw on the stage. It is not at all like the leg which is vulgarly
praised even in a man, and which is doubly misplaced under a
lady—a bit of balustrade turned upside down; a large calf, and
an ankle only small in proportion. It is a right feminine leg,
delicate in foot, trim in ankle, and with a calf at once soft and
well-cut, distinguished and unobtrusive. We are not so intolerant—we should rather say ungrateful and inhuman—on the
subject of legs, as many of our sex, who, without the light of a
good ankle can see nothing else good in a figure. We have a
tender respect for them all, provided they are gentle. But it
is impossible not to be struck, as an Irishman would say, with
a leg like this. It is fit for a statue; still fitter for where it is. It
helped to complete the applicability of the lines which Mr.
Bishop has selected from *Venus and Adonis:*—

> Bid me discourse, I will enchant thine ear;
> Or like a Fairy, trip upon the green;
> Or, like a Nymph, with bright and flowing hair,
> Dance on the sands, and yet no footing seen.[6]

We are sorry we cannot speak so well of the rest of the performance. Such actors as Liston and Emery, performing in a
play of Shakspeare's, cannot be witnessed without *some* amusement; but comparing them with themselves, they are very inferior in *Twelfth Night.* Emery seems to mistake the character of
Sir Toby, who is not so much a surly fellow as a mock-heroic one,
something between the wit of *Falstaff* and the affected pompos-
ity of "mine host of the Garter." Among other instances of want
of relish for his text was his delivery of that memorable moral
question put to *Malvolio.* He gave it thus: "What? Dost thou
think because *thou* art virtuous, there shall be no more cakes and
ale?"[7] But the emphasis should be laid on the word *virtuous.*

Shakspeare, who delights to insinuate these vital philosophies
through the medium of his merry fellows, does not mean to
contrast the mere pretensions of *Malvolio* with the general right
of enjoyment, but the pretensions of affected or mistaken virtue
at large. Thus the wit is more subtle, and the jest in more exquisite taste. "Do you think," says he, "that because your notions
of right and wrong lead you to regard morality in so grave and
formal a light, or because you are *virtuous*, if you please, that
therefore mirth and festivity were made for nothing? Do you
think that because virtue in you is an intolerant coxcomb, it is
to be so in everybody else? Or that nature ought to suppress
wit, mirth, and good fellowship, because you, being virtuous,
are also stupid and unsocial? Or do you hold it incompatible
with the gentility of your virtue to patronize no viands and
drinks that are not of the genteelest description? In short, "dost
thou think, because thou art *virtuous*, there shall be no more
cakes and ale?"

Mr. Liston, in like manner, does not seem up, as the phrase is,
to the character of *Sir Andrew*. He doated well upon the Fool's
jokes; but he did not give the other humours in general with
sufficient prominence of absurdity, sufficient ostentation and
overweeningness. He failed even in that humourous love echo
to *Sir Toby's* mention of *Maria*, which seems quite suited to
him.

Sir And. Before me, she's a good wench.
Sir Toby. She's a beagle, true-bred, and one that adores me. What o'
    that?
Sir And. I was adored once too.[8]

We must except however the duel-scene with *Viola*, which is
ludicrous to perfection. The faintness with which he sinks back
on *Sir Toby's* breast is absolute "dissolution and thaw." [9]

Mr. Farren's *Malvolio*, like most of his performances, is more
good than pleasant, and yet more pleasant in parts than good
as a whole. This may seem paradoxical, but his acting is a para-
dox. It is sometimes not good enough, because it is mistaken;
sometimes not good enough, because it is too good. In short,
Mr. Farren always gives us the idea of a man too much like the

characters he represents; that is to say, too dry and unhumourous in himself. He represents dryness too much as if he could not help it: and this is not pleasant. Animal spirits are pleasant on their own account; but not so the negation of them: not so formality and aridity. The best acting of this kind is to the better sort of performance, what wax-work is to painting or sculpture. It is neither imitation nor reality; but has a certain helpless look of life, too unavoidable to be true. Now upon this score, Mr. Farren's *Malvolio* is perfect. It is dressed in perfect costume; is as like as possible in the whole aspect; its hair is real; but the inward man of it seems as waxen as the outer; and the worst of it is that, when it undertakes to be conscious of itself, it is apt to be as wrong in its apparent identity. For instance, when Mr. Farren ventures to be critical in his part, he is too literal. In the famous soliloquy scene, where he anticipates his dignities as the husband of *Olivia,* and fancies himself about to lecture his "kinsman *Toby,*" *Malvolio* says, "I extend my hand to him thus, quenching my familiar smile with an austere regard of controul." [10] Mr. Farren, in this passage, first acts the familiar smile deliberately over, and then takes up the "austere regard of controul" as he would an extinguisher, and puts it out with it. But the nicety of the picture evidently consists in doing both these things at once; that is to say, in shewing a willingness to smile, as a piece of urbanity natural to him, and at the same time controulling both it and the knight, with a look that warns him against the peril of presuming upon it. Mr. Farren however must be allowed to be a very useful and respectable actor in his way; and we cannot forget that his *Malvolio* has one excellent point. It is where he strains after the hidden meaning of the letters M.O.A.I. He seems repeatedly about to touch the secret of the letter M. which he stretches at, as it were, with the most tip-toe yearning of his mind, rising from guess to guess to a sort of whining apex of eagerness and mumbling, then suddenly he drops his voice into a despairing faintness. The secret has outreached him.

We must except Mr. Fawcett from the list of the imperfect actors of this play. He is a still better representative, we think, than he was, of that obsolete race the witty Court Fool. He has enough of natural gravity to suggest an undertone of conscious smoking and sarcasm, without being at all deficient in the natural humour which is requisite to keep up a character for playfulness. We stopped the play out, on purpose to hear him sing that melancholy-merry song, with its pleasant air,

When that I was and a little tiny boy.[11]

Yet we do not like to think that this was the last song which Shakspeare wrote. It has too much scorn of the world and all that he had seen in it.

But what a good-natured play was not this, altogether, to close his dramas with! for *Twelfth Night* was the last work of Shakspeare.[12] Whatever he might think of the world in general, his last thoughts of it were kind and social. He looked back, and saw nothing on which he would more willingly turn his thoughts than the humours of good fellowship and the young trustingness of love. To sociality, even in its follies, he would not be intolerant; and love, in spite of all he had seen and endured, may be said to have had his last homage as well as last sigh.

The scenery of this piece is beautiful, particularly in the Mask which they have introduced from the *Tempest,* and which reminded us of the times of Inigo Jones and Ben Jonson. After all, we know not whether the managers and their musician have not imposed on us with the help of Shakspeare; and whether we ought not to resent these "pickings and stealings" of him on that very account. But the patchwork added to the play is at least made up from himself, and with a poet or two with whom he has been confounded. *Twelfth Night,* though calculated to be more popular than the *Comedy of Errors,* and quite able to stand alone, must also be allowed to be more fitted for the introduction of songs. In short, with all our criticism and objections, we have been upon the whole much pleased; and if in candour we must mention the one, in gratitude we cannot help confessing the other.

THE PLAY-BILLS

September 17, 1830

THE TATLER in future will contain the play-bills of the evening.[1] They will be printed in an open and distinct manner, to suit all eyes; and, it is hoped may serve as companions to the theatre, like the regular bills that are sold at the doors. The measure has been adopted on the friendly suggestion of a Correspondent, who thinks that the public will not be sorry for this union of a paper with a play-bill; and that by and by, to use his pleasant quotation, *Tatlers* will be "frequent and full" in the pit and boxes. We shall be glad to see them. Nothing will give us greater pleasure than to find ourselves thus visibly multiplied, and to see the ladies bending over us. Happy shall we be, to be pinned to the cushions for their sakes.

Without a play-bill, no true play-goer can be comfortable. If the performers are new to him, he cannot dispense with knowing who they are: if old, there are the names of the characters to learn, and the relationships of the *dramatis personae:* and if he is acquainted with all this, he is not sure that there may not be something else, some new play to be announced, or some new appearance. The advertisements in the papers will not supply him with the information, for they are only abridgments: and he cannot try to be content with a look at the play-bills at the door, for then he would grudge his pence: and he that grudges his pence, cannot be a genuine play-goer. How would he relish a generous sentiment, or presume to admire a pretty face? There is a story, in the tales of chivalry, of a magic seat, which ejected with violence any knight who was not qualified to sit down in it. If the benches at the theatre could be imbued with the noble sentiments that abound on the stage, thus would they eject the man who was too stingy to purchase a play-bill.

But the above are not the only reasons for the purchase. The *Tatler,* for instance, will in future be sold at the play-house doors, as well as by the newsmen. They must be so, or they would not be play-bills. Now the poor people who sell the play-bills deserve all the encouragement that can be given them, for they prefer industry to beggary, and go through a great deal of bad weather and rejection. We may suppose that people who do this, do it for very good reasons. They look as if they did, for they are a care-worn race; they defy rain and mud, and persevere in trying to sell their bills with an importunity that makes the proud angry, and the good-tempered smile. If you look into the face that is pursuing at your elbow, or jogging at the window of your coach, you would often see cause to pity it. However, not to dwell upon this point, or to make a sad article of one that is intended to be merry, on every *Tatler* which these poor people sell, they will get a half-penny. When we consider the stress which great statesmen lay upon pence and pots of beer, in their financial measures, we hope this will not have "a mean sound," except in the ears of the mean passions of pride and avarice. For our parts we affect to despise nothing that represents the food and raiment of mothers and children; though we often wonder how great statesmen can lay so much stress upon the pence they dole out, and so little upon the thousands they receive.—But we shall be stopping too long at the doors.

If a play-goer has a party with him, especially ladies, the purchase of a bill gives him an opportunity of shewing how he consults their pleasure in trifles. If he is alone, it is a companion. He has also the glory of being able to lend it—though with what face anyone can borrow a play-bill, thus proclaiming that he has not had the heart to buy one, is to *us* inconceivable. We grant that it may be done, once or so, out of thoughtlessness, particularly if the borrower has given away his pence for nothing; but *after the present notice,* we expect that nobody will think of making this excuse. It is better to purchase a bill than to give money, even to the sellers; for you thus encourage the sale, give and receive a pleasure, and save the venders from the temptation of begging.

A *Tatler,* we allow, costs two-pence, whereas the common play-bill is a penny. But if the latter be worth what it costs, will it be too great a stretch of modesty to suppose that our new play-bill is worth it also? Our criticisms, we will be sworn, have, at all events, a relish in them: they are larger; and then there is the rest of the matter, in the other pages, to vary the chat between the acts. There will even be found, we presume, in the whole paper, something not unworthy of the humanities taught on the stage. Now as to the bills that are sold at the doors, we have a respect for the common "house-bill," as it is called, that is to say, the old unaffected piece of paper that contains nothing but the usual announcements—the play-bill of old, or "bill o' the play," which has so often rung its pleasing changes in our ears, with the "porter, or cyder, or ginger-beer." Formerly the cry used only to be "porter or cyder": previously to that it was "oranges": and lately we have heard "apples." There is a fellow in the gallery at the English Opera, who half bawls and half screams a regular quick strain, all in one note, as if it were a single word, of "bottled-porter-apples-ginger-beer." It is as if a parrot were shouting it.

This old play-bill is a reverend and sensible bit of paper, pretends to no more than it possesses, and adds to this solid merit an agreeable flimsiness in its tissue. But there are two rogues, anticipators of us respectable interlopers, of whom we must say a word, particularly one who has the face to call himself the *Theatrical Examiner*. This gentleman, not having the fear of our reputation before his eyes, sets out, in his motto, with claiming the privilege of a free speaker. "Let me," says he, quoting Shakspeare, "be privileged by my place and message, to be a speaker free." [2] Accordingly his freedom of speech consists in praising everybody as hard as he can, and filling up one of his four pages with puffs of the exhibitions. The rogue is furthermore of a squalid appearance, "shabby" without being "genteel"; and so is his friend the *Theatrical Observer*. The following is a taste of his quality. The analysis which is given of Mr. Power's [3] style of humour will convey a striking sense of it to the reader: and the praises of the singers are very particular. "Power's *Paddy O'Rafferty*," says he, "was a performance exceedingly rich, and abounded with those exquisite displays of humour which has always characterised his representation of the part.

The piece was throughout well cast, and very well supported. Melrose, as *Captain Coradino*, introduced a song composed by Lee, 'Can I my love resign,' which he sung with great sweetness and effect, and was loudly applauded. Mrs. Chapman, as *Margaritta*, introduced sweetly, 'On the wings of morning,' from Hoffer, which she sung very effectively. Mrs. Weston, of Covent-Garden, made her first appearance as the *Countess*, and gave excellent effect to the character." How judiciously, in this criticism, are our reflections aroused by the emphatic word *those* and how happily are they realized! How full of *effect* also are the remaining six lines! We hope these remarks will not be reckoned invidious. If the hawkers are the critics, we are sorry; but then they should put their names, and the matter would become proper.

We must not forget one thing respecting the "house-bill," which is that, agreeably to its domestic character, it rises in value by being within doors; costing but a penny outside the house, and two-pence in; so that no attention ought to be paid to those insidious decencies of fruit-women, who serious and elderly, dressed in clean linen, and renouncing the evil reputations of their predecessors, charge high for the honour they do you in being virtuous, and will fetch you a glass of water for a shilling. The two-pence of these peoples' play-bills ought to retire before the sincere and jovial superabundance of the *Tatler*, the more virtuous because it does not pretend to be so.

We must add that in our play-bill the names of the *authors* will, we hope, be inserted. The printer also has suggested another refinement, which in this Anglo-Gallic age we hope will be duly appreciated; to wit, the precedence now for the first time given to the ladies.

PERFORMANCES FOR THIS EVENING [1]

THEATRE ROYAL, DRURY-LANE

THIS EVENING, the Tragic Play of *Pizarro* (by Mr. Sheridan)

Cora, Miss Phillips
Ataliba, Mr. Younge
Sentinel, Mr. Salter
Elvira, Mrs. Faucit
Rolla, Mr. Wallack

Orozembo, Mr. J. Vining
Alonzo, Mr. Cooper
Pizarro, Mr. H. Wallack
Las Casas, Mr. Thompson

In Act II, The Temple of the Sun: *High Priest*, Mr. Horn; *Priests, Virgins, Matrons, &c.,* Misses Byfield, S. Phillips, Russell, Bruce, Crawford, Mrs. Bedford, Mrs. Newcombe; Messrs. Bedford, Bland, and Yarnold

PREVIOUS TO THE PLAY, Spontini's Overture to "Ferdinand Cortez"

TO CONCLUDE with, the New Splendid Christmas Comic Pantomime, called *Davy Jones; or, Harlequin and Mother Carey's Chickens* (by Mr. W. Barrymore)

The Overture and Music by Mr. R. Hughes

Columbines, Misses Barnett and Baseke

Harlequin, Mr. Howell   *Pantaloon*, Mr. T. Blanchard

Clowns, Messrs. Southby and E. J. Parslowe

The Order of the Scenery: Scene I, The North Foreland, with Light House. II, Mother Carey's Refectory, and Coral Cave in the Deep, Deep Sea. III, Quarter-Deck of the Spanker. IV, Susan's Cottage, by Moonlight. V, The Bilboes. VI, The Sun's Watery Bed. VII, Farm-House, Sunrise. VIII, Ruins of the Argyle Rooms the Night after the Fire. IX, Belle Vue Cottage and surrounding Neighbourhood. X, The Brighton Archway, Erected in Honour of their Majesties' Visit to Brighton, August 30th, 1830; with a New Nautical Ballet. XI, Commercial Dock Canal. XII, Nursery for Pet Children. XIII, Outside of Upholsterers. XIV, The Diorama. XV, Grand Hydraulic Temple, Illustrative of the Union of the Waters.

Diorama, Designed and Painted by Mr. Stanfield. The Various Views will Display the Stupendous and Extraordinary Military Pass of the Simplon. Town of Sion (on the Valois).—Valley of the Rhone.—Brieg.—The Simplon.—The Schalbet, by Moonlight.—Village of the Simplon.—Gallery of Algaby (with the Effects of a Storm).—The Grand Gallery! cut through a solid rock 596 ft. long.—Crevola.—Domo D'Ossola.—Fariolo.—Lago Magiore, with the Boromean Islands.

TOMORROW, *The School for Scandal*, and the Pantomime

THEATRE ROYAL, COVENT-GARDEN

THIS EVENING, the Tragedy of *Romeo and Juliet* (by W. Shakespeare)

Lady Capulet, Mrs. Lovell	*Juliet*, Miss Fanny Kemble
Prince Escalus, Mr. Henry	*Romeo*, Mr. Abbott
Montague, Mr. Turnour	*Paris*, Mr. Duruset
Benvolio, Mr. Baker	*Capulet*, Mr. Egerton
Mercutio, Mr. C. Kemble	*Tybalt*, Mr. Diddear
Friar John, Mr. Mears	*Friar Lawrence*, Mr. Warde
Page, Miss Fortescue	*Apothecary*, Mr. Meadows
Abram, Mr. Heath	*Balthazar*, Mr. Irwin
Gregory, Mr. Norris	*Samson*, Mr. Atkins
Nurse, Mrs. Gibbs	*Peter*, Mr. Keeley

PREVIOUS TO THE TRAGEDY, Mozart's Overture to "Die Zauberflöte."

TO CONCLUDE with the New Grand and Comic Pantomime, called *Harlequin Fat, and Harlequin Bat* (by Mr. Farley) The Overture and Music, by Mr. G. Stansbury, with a Speaking Opening by Mr. Peake. Characters by Mr. Baker and Mr. Keeley

Columbine, Miss Louisa John-	*Harlequin*, Mr. Ellar
stone	*Pantaloon*, Mr. Barnes

Clown, Mr. Paulo
The Order of the Scenery: Scene I, The Giant's Causeway, by Moonlight. II, The Boyne Water. III, Exterior of King O'Roirk's Castle. IV, The Grand Banqueting Hall. V, The Banshee's Ravine. VI, McMurragh's Keep. VII, Extensive View of the Lake of Killarney. VIII, The Custom-House and Quay (Dublin). IX, The New Bridge over the Menai. X, The Pool, Tower, and St. Katherine's Docks. XI, The Globe Hotel and Cutler's Shop. XII, A Market. XIII, Windsor Park and Castle. XIV, Portsmouth Harbour. The Royal Yacht passing along the Coast, till she arrives off Brighton, and the Illumination. XV, The Triumphal Arch, Erected in honor of the Arrival of their Majesties at the Royal Pavilion, on August 30, 1830. XVI, Frog Farm and Kitchen. XVII, Ludgate Hill and St. Paul's, as it was intended to be on the 9th of November, 1830. XVIII, Lost in a Fog. XIX, Guildhall as fitted up for the Lord Mayor's Festival. XX and last, The Fairy Grove and Magic Palace.

TOMORROW, *Cinderella,* and *Harlequin Fat or Harlequin Bat*

French Plays

Theatre Royal, Haymarket

THIS EVENING, on commencera à Sept Heures et demie par *L'Heritière*, Vaudeville, en Un Acte, de M. Scribe
Madame de Melval (jeune Veuve), Mademoiselle Herminie
M. de Gourville, M. Behier St. Aubert
Gustaves (son Neveu), M. Paulin

SUIVI DE *Jean!* Pièce en Quatre Parties Mêlée de Chant, par MM. Taeaulon et Alphonse Signol
Madame de Ligny, Mademoiselle Florval
Madame de Sirval (Parente de Madame de Ligny), Mademoiselle Eliza
La Marquise d'Olban (amie de Madame de Ligny), Madame Paulin
Madame veuve Chopin (Limonadière), Madame Préval
Adelaide (sa Fille), Mademoiselle St. Ange
Louise (Femme de Chambre), Madame Gamard
M. Derval remplira le Rôle de *Jean*
Rigolard (Maître de Danse, et Parrain de Jean), M. Laporte
M. de Walbruck et M. D'Offtenn (Attachés à l'Ambassade), M. Paulin et M. Guenée
Un Garçon (d'estaminet), M. Arnaud
Un Valet, M. Grannille

ON FINIRA par *Le Bouffe et le Tailleur,* Petit Opéra, en Un Acte Musique de Gaveau
Celestine (sa Fille), Mademoiselle Florval
Cavatini (Chanteur Italien), M. Alfred
Benini (son Homme de confiance), M. Gamard
Barbeau, Maître Tailleur, aimant passionnément la Musique), M. Preval

Theatre Royal, Adelphi

THIS EVENING, a Domestic Burletta, in two Acts, called *The Wreck Ashore*

Act I: Winter

Alice, Mrs. Yates
Dame Barnard, Mr. Daly
Miles Barnard, Mr. Yates
Captain Grampus, Mr. O. Smith
Bella, Mrs. Fitzwilliam

Jemmy Starling, Mr. Buckstone
Walter Barnard, Mr. Hemmings
Marmaduke Magog, Mr. J. Reeve

(A lapse of Five Years is supposed to occur between each Act.)

Act II: Summer

Alice, Mrs. Yates

Grampus, Mr. O. Smith

Jemmy Starling, Mr. Buckstone

Bella, Mrs. Fitzwilliam

Miles Bertram, Mr. Yates

Blackadder, Mr. S. Smith

Marmaduke Magog, Mr. J. Reeve

Walter, Mr. Hemmings

TO WHICH WILL BE ADDED, a New Comic Burletta, called *Was I to Blame?*

Julia, Mrs. Yates

Lord Charles Everard, Mr. Hemmings

Melville, Mr. Yates

Mathew Multiply, Mr. Bayne

AFTER WHICH, the Comic Burletta, called *A Dead Shot*

Louisa Lovetrick, Mrs. Fitzwilliam, in which character she will introduce her celebrated Description of "A Sunday Concert"

Chatter, Miss Daly

Mr. Hector Timid, Mr. Buckstone

Charles, Mr. V. Webster

Captain Cannon, Mr. Bayne

Mr. Wiseman, Mr. S. Smith

TO CONCLUDE with a New Grand and Comic Christmas Pantomime, called *Grimalkin, the Great* (by Mr. Buckstone)

The Overture and Music by G. H. Rodwell

Columbine, Miss Stallard

Clown, Mr. Sanders

Harlequin, Mr. Gibson

Pantaloon, Mr. King

ROYAL OLYMPIC THEATRE

THIS EVENING, an entirely New Historical Burletta, called *Mary Queen of Scots*

Mary Stuart (Queen of Scots), Miss Foote

Lady Douglas, Mrs. Knight

Lady Fleming, Miss King

Moggy, Miss Langley

Lord George Douglas, Mr. Fredericks

Sir Robert Melville, Mr. Worrel

Roland, Mr. Raymond

Sandy, Mr. J. Knight

Catherine Seyton, Miss Pincott

Mattie, Miss Kibrey

Jenny, Miss Slater

Lord Lindsay, Mr. Brougham

Lord Ruthven, Mr. Beckwith

Drysdale, Mr. Newcombe

TO WHICH WILL BE ADDED, a Grand Allegorical Burletta, in One Act, entitled *Olympic Revels* (by Mr. Planché)
Pandora, Madame Vestris
Prometheus (an eminent Manufacturer), Mr. J. Cooper
Swiss Boy (a great Anachronism), Mr. Beckwith
Immortals—Olympic Revellers: Ganymede, Miss Greener; *Minerva*, Mrs. Thomas; *Juno*, Miss Stuart; *Hope*, Miss Langley; *Jupiter*, Mr. J. Knight; *Neptune*, Mr. W. Young; *Hercules*, Mr. Worrel; *Plutus*, Mr. Paget; *Vulcan*, Mr. Brown; *Apollo*, Miss Melbourne; *Bacchus*, Mr. W. Vining; *Momus*, Mr. D. Smith; *Esculapius*, Mr. Coates; *Somnus*, Mr. James; *Mars*, Mr. Brougham; *Cupid*, Miss Josephine; *Mercury*, Mr. Newcombe

TO BE FOLLOWED by a Comic Burletta, called *The Little Jockey*
Ariette, Miss Foote, in which she will sing, "Why pretty Maiden," and "The Boy in yellow wins the day"

Clotilda, Miss Nursey	*Maude*, Miss Kibrey
The Baron D'Acourt, Mr. W. Vining	*De Limburg*, Mr. Paget
	Jocose, Mr. Collier
Floriville, by a Gentleman	*Pierre*, Mr. Brown
Denis, Mr. Young	

THE WHOLE TO CONCLUDE with a Comic Burletta, called *Clarissa Harlowe*

Clarissa Harlowe, Mrs. Glover	*Mrs. Harlowe*, Miss Fitzwalter
Clerimont, Mr. Raymond	*Mr. Harlowe*, Mr. Paget
Captain Cape, Mr. W. Vining	

SURREY THEATRE

THIS EVENING, an entirely new Drama, entitled *Nancy of Portsmouth*

Nancy Bloomfield, Miss Somerville	*The Widow Crabjuice*, Mad. Simon
Constantia, Miss Jordan	*Kitty Bustle*, Mrs. Vale
Old Margery, Mrs. Rogers	*Becky Sims*, Miss Rummens
Sir Edward Gayton, Mr. Gough	*Frederick Gayton*, Mr. Edwin
Captain Splashaway, Mr. Hicks	*Fiery Ned*, Mr. D. Pitt
Joe Barton, Mr. C. Hill	*Bounce*, Mr. Rogers
Tim Tipple, Mr. Vale	*Tapwell*, Mr. Hobbs
Capt. Friendly, Mr. Lee	*Long Bill*, Mr. Almar
Jemmy Gonimble, Madlle. Rosier	*Short Bill*, Mr. Webb

AFTER WHICH, a new Drama, entitled *Baron Trenck* (by Mr. Osbaldiston)

Countess of Hulsdorff, Madame Simon

Victorine, Miss Somerville

François Bassentrompdorf (with an entirely new Comic Song), Mr. C. Hill

Countess of Lewemberg, Miss Rumens

The Count of Linsdonn, Mr. Gough

Mayor Muffledorf, Mr. D. Pitt

Baron de Trenck, Mr. Osbaldiston

Augustus, Mr. Edwin

Boltzheim, Mr. Almar

TO CONCLUDE with, a New splendid Comic Christmas Pantomime, entitled *The New Year's Gift* (by Mr. W. Barrymore)
The Overture and Music by Mr. Blewitt

Columbine, Mademoiselle Rosier

Harlequin, Mr. Honor

Pantaloon, Mr. Asbury

Clown, Mr. T. Hill

Zany, Mr. Grammer

TOMORROW, *Nancy of Portsmouth; "PS, Come to Dinner";* and the Pantomime

CODURG THEATRE

The Hut of the Red Mountain.—The Banks of the Hudson.— Harlequin Silver Penny

SADLER'S WELLS THEATRE

Skimmer of the Seas.—Harlequin and Mother Goose

Published by J. Onwhyn, 4 Catherine Street, Strand (to whom all books, parcels, and communications for the Editor are to be addressed). Sold by J. Chappel, 98 Royal Exchange; A. Hays, 165 Regent Street; J. Field, 16 Air Street, Piccadilly; Marsh, 145 Oxford Street, next door to Fladong's Hotel; at Eber's Library, Old Bond Street; and by all Booksellers and Newsmen
C. and W. Reynell, Printers, Broad Street, Golden Square

[MISS PATON]

MISS PATON had a brilliant reception last night.[1] The audience were so glad of the prospect of seeing her that they gave each of her precursors a double welcome; and when she made her appearance in the balcony the shout was enormous. The people rose in the pit, waving their hats, and absolutely roaring with delight. We heard no notes of objection. If there were any, they were drowned in the tumult of applause; but we do not believe there were. The pit, in the front and centre, rolled with the black hats like a billow.

It was curious to see the fastidiousness or affected indifference of the boxes, and how little it signified. We observed some handkerchiefs waving from the upper boxes over the stage, and here and there was a solitary clapping of hands in the lower circle: but for the most part, the representatives of the aristocracy (or those who would be taken for such) sat still and expressionless. The pit (to compare small things with great) heeded them as little as the French Chamber of Deputies did the Peers: they settled matters their own way, and the others acquiesced. Throughout the piece, the same cordiality was exhibited. Opportunities were taken, though of the most obvious passages only, to shew that the applauders considered her unjustly treated *in the first instance,* and therefore to be charitably regarded afterwards; and we believe, notwithstanding the timidity of the boxes (for their seeming indifference was nothing else) that this was the general, and we must add the proper feeling of the house. It is said to be a wholesome thing in politics to recur now and then to first principles, and give a brush to the pool of conventional corruption, to the sordid pretences that overgrow principle, and become confounded with it; and we believe, as the world at this time of day believes, that similar recurrences are not without their use in morals. These are the days of first principles: and it is not likely that, when so many are remembered, any one of them will be forgotten.

We availed ourselves of this opportunity of paying more attention to Miss Paton's claims as a singer than we had done before, not having resumed our visits to the theatre when she first appeared, and seeing her very little afterwards. The part she performed was *Rosina* in *The Barber of Seville*, which was followed by that of *Clari*.

Miss Paton is a fine singer of a certain order, but not, we think, of the finest; and she is a better actress than we had supposed her, but entirely of the artificial kind. Her acting seems to have been taught her and she has learnt it well; but the "system" is displayed at every turn: she is obvious and declamatory; loud or low, indignant or patient, as the surface of the feeling suggests, her face being all the while singularly devoid of expression. In short, she is a very good self-possessed actress, for a singer; and shows how little real feeling of a character is required to attain the conventional style of performance.

As a singer, Miss Paton exhibits great compass and execution; has rich tones in the lower notes, delicate ones in the upper, is beautifully articulate, and in a word, a fine specimen of the musical-instrument order of singers. If she ever appears anything more, it is in certain little womanly insinuations of archness, which may be taught; and these are repeated on system. The song which she sings to her own accompaniment on the piano-forte, with her sleepy guardian on one side of her, and her inamorato on the other (*An old man would be wooing*) shows her, both as an actress and a singer, to her greatest advantage. She displays the powers of her voice; she is loud and soft; she goes winding her notes about, not in a very new, but in a very easy style; takes a long circuit before she comes to the shake, shakes admirably, and even surprised us with an arch repetition of a *sforzando* shake, as if she did it to "twit" the old sleeper with her powers: and yet, except in that instance (which must unquestionably have been put in her head) she did not touch the feelings either on this or on any other occasion. We listened, and heard a beautiful instrument, and were delighted to hear it; but hearing was all.

We cannot help thinking that Miss Paton's face, and her
manner while singing, answer to this opinion of her merits. She
is a fine-looking young woman, is said to have very beautiful
hair and skin (as may be easily imagined) and she carries herself well, and like a gentlewoman; but her countenance wants
expression: the features are not hard, and yet there is a sort
of neutral harshness in the look; and when she sings, the thought
of the singing-book so much predominates with her over the
sentiment that she makes absolute grimaces, looks sometimes
as if she were masticating her notes, and now and then plunges
at them with a sort of fury, as if she would get through them
tooth and nail. What is even more offensive to us than this, she
cares as little, that is to say she knows as little, about the demands of a beautiful melody, full of expression, as the most
common-place executionists of the day. The music in the *Barber
of Seville* is made up from Paesiello, Rossini, and others. The
first thing she sings is a part of that divine air of Paesiello's, *Io
sono Lindoro*, well-known to the public as *For tenderness form'd*.
It would have been literally *impossible*, for a person not acquainted with this air to make anything of it, she cut it up so
into bits and flourishes of her own. Now this, to us, is high
treason against the divinity of music: and when we add that she
did nearly as much evil to the pathetic air of *Home Sweet Home*
in the afterpiece, the reader will pardon us for coming away at
the end of it, and for thinking that this celebrated vocalist,
whom we heartily sympathize with as a woman, is a much finer
and more powerful singer than a feeling one.

[THE BALLET]

October 30, 1830   *Drury-Lane*

WE INDULGE OURSELVES, by way of variety, with a notice of the ballet which we saw last night [1] at this theatre, called the *Romantic Amoureux*. The plots of ballets are seldom painfully clear; the violence of their nods of the head and other explanatory gestures is apt to be lost upon us: we wish extremely to comprehend the old father who tries to thump the mystery into us with his stick, and the youth or his mistress who comes delicately bending to the front of the stage, with a sidelong eye and the aforesaid nods, to illustrate all which the father has left obscure; but our endeavours are seldom repaid. We only get a general impression that there is love going on, that the old gentleman does not like it, and that the young people do.

However, in the present instance, the plot appeared more than usually intelligible. We are unable, for want of help in the play-bills, to distribute the characters to the names of the persons to whom they belong; so we must content ourselves with stating that there is a party of gallant young sailors, come home from the sea, who appear, the moment they land, to be joined by all the pretty girls of the place; and of course fall a-dancing with all their might. An old gentleman issues from a house and detaches two or three of these damsels, at the same time driving the men away. A fantastic lover then makes his appearance, with a huge neck-cloth, who is patronized by the father, but rejected by all the young ladies. He dances however with one of them, his dance being parodied all the while behind him by the favourite sailor. The other sailors return, of course with their damsels, all dancing as hard as they can drive; the *Romantic Amoureux* is hustled about, and whirled from one to the other; and the goddess of his idolatry completes his mortification by sealing his eyes, not with a kiss, but with a handful of flour. In fine, the true lovers prevail; a collateral lady and gentleman, who are always good-natured enough to join dancing parties uninvited, and to put everybody else in the back-ground, make their appearance, and perform the requisite quantity of saltation; and then there is a pell-mell dance, and the curtain falls.

This is a clever ballet, cleverly performed. We have never seen a better mock-dance than the one performed by Monsieur Simon (we believe), the author. It was awkward and ludicrously stiff in the joints, without being overdone. A young lady near us laughed all the while this personage was on the stage, with a genuine glee that did us good to hear it. Mons. Gilbert (if such is the name of the main collateral dancer above mentioned) was also very clever, vaulting hither and thither with elegance, and sometimes appearing almost to lie along the air. And two principal damsels twirl about to the music in good crisp and easy style, particularly one of them, who has a latitude of leg we have seldom seen equalled. She seemed about to step into one stage box, while she shook hands with the other.

The appearance of the sailors at the commencement reminded us of the episode of the Isle of Love, in the *Lusiad*.[2] They are very delicate sailors, not more genuine than becomes them; only we wish they would not look so very grave in the face while their lower extremities are being so lively. The last scene, where [with] alternate [bows] . . . the men and women part sideways from each other, is very pleasing.

It is a pretty fantastic world this, of dancing, to live in for half an hour. We have only to fancy a planet in which the people dance to music instead of walk, and gesticulate instead of talk, and all the rest follows as reasonably as need be. You are approached in a trip, and avoided with a twirl. You bow to a bass-note; spin round like a top, in order to express a satisfaction; make love with *ballet* (instead of *billet*) *doux;* and if the lady gives you any encouragement, you have a right to stretch out your leg as far as possible behind you, holding her at the same time delicately by the waist; while she stretches her leg with equal remoteness the other way, and looks fondly at the air. If you have any love in you, you then dance a good while by yourself, spinning, vaulting, and caressing, till you think fit, in the

most elaborate manner, to make a present of your leg to the
side scenery. The lady does the same on her part, first making a
kind of inverted cup of her petticoats, as she spins, and showing
us how fat are the legs of fair dancers. And so, with a trip or
two more together, and another presentation of her by the
waist to Heaven knows whom, the lovers make a sudden hop
into the shades, and the mystery concludes.

We are inclined to like everything French at present; but our
illustrious neighbours have now left some of their old celebrities
far behind, and they can afford to be told that the best French
dancing (on the stage) is, after all, not to be compared with
the best Italian or Spanish. Those who have not seen De Martins
of Italy, the very antelope of dancers (as a Persian might call
her) have not seen what grace and activity can do conjoined;
and a single Spanish bolero, with its fervid excess of life and the
very soul of motion beating time to its grace and energy, is worth
a dozen evenings of the ostentation of twirls and tee-totums.

[THE RIVALS]

Performances of Last Night
DRURY-LANE: *The Rivals; A Divertisement; The Brigand*
COVENT-GARDEN: *The Stranger; Clari*

December 2, 1830   *Drury-Lane*

THE LAUGHABLE COMEDY of the *Rivals* was performed here last night,[1] but did not excite half the laughter we have known it. Dowton in his old character, Sir Anthony Absolute, is not to be surpassed. He looks stuffed with good living and provocation, and has a pair of calves to support his rage; and well does his genius second his physical power. Whether he is pleased or provoked, he expresses the feeling from top to toe. The mere expansion of his hand on the top of his walking-stick, when he stretches his fingers to and fro, which have been grasping it and are about to do so again, looks as if he relished the property of thumping which resides in the stick. His utterance of the word "Jack," is as good as a dash of the ferrule on the ground. And his love-making is as passionate as the rest. When he says he has "a good mind to marry the girl himself," we are hardly sure that his son is not at a positive disadvantage with his pretensions.

Mrs. Glover's we think a very good *Mrs. Malaprop*, even though we have seen Miss Pope in the character. It is not of so high an order of comedy as that lady's; it wants her perfection of old gentlewomanly staidness, and so far wants the highest relish of contrast in its *malapropism;* but for a picture of a broader sort, fine and flower-gowned and powdered, it is very good indeed. If Miss Pope looked as though she kept the jellies and preserves, Mrs. Glover looked as if she ate them.

But Harley, though an amusing *Acres*, does not remind us sufficiently of the clods from which he takes his name. He is not heavy enough in his bustle. He is more like the village hairdresser come to town, than the squire. Bannister's words used to drag, in the midst of their liveliness; there was a swing and a weight in them, like a clown's shoulders. And his fight in the duel scene was at once more lumpish and quivering than Harley's, so that the terror was more comic and characteristic. Harley looks too deplorably frightened—too ghastly. We remember a pleasant action of Bannister's in this scene, which we do not find copied by the present performers. He used to let his hat fall, and push it about on the ground with his trembling fingers before he could pick it up.

Wallack's *Captain Absolute* has some lively passages. His resolution of keeping the miniature, when about to restore it, is particularly well given. But what are any *Captain Absolutes* now-a-days after Elliston? And how deplorably are we reminded, whenever a comedy is performed, that there really is no true gentleman comedian on the stage! Those who attempt the parts belong to tragedy, to melodrame, to country theatres—to anything but the class of the Ellistons and the Lewises.[2]

But if we cannot eulogize Mr. Wallack's gentlemen, what are we to say to Mr. H. Wallack's [3] Irishmen? They cannot even speak the brogue. Their *meads* are the *meads* of England, not *maids;* their *Delias* have vowels like any other woman. An aspirate now and then tips their tongue, that is all. And they have no unction besides. They do not repose on their sentences with a comic luxury, nor look lack-a-daisical in their energy, nor send everything trippingly off their tongue, blithe and breathless as if it had terminated a sup of whiskey. We do not remember seeing Mr. H. Wallack before, and he may be good in other parts; but it is lamentable to see him in this, and recollect Irish Johnstone.

Mr. Cooper's [4] *Falkland* wants that delicate mixture of a comic sense of the character's failings which constitutes the value of its performance. He does not know how to put them entertainingly forward. This character too used sometimes to be acted by Elliston, and acted excellently well. A grave insinuation of the ludicrous was never lost with him.

Miss Chester's *Lydia Languish* is a handsome easy woman, but not *Lydia Languish.* It is not young nor slender enough;

not sufficiently girlish. A lady of Miss Chester's appearance would be too well-informed to make *Lydia's* childish mistakes, or be angry at the facilities offered her for a good sensible marriage. She would not put up a romantic lip at the idea of "consent of friends"; nor doubt the truth of the *Captain's* assertion that "a little wealth and comfort may be endured after all."

We did not see the footman and maid-servant in this piece; so that we cannot speak as to *Mr. Fag's* philosophy, or *Mrs. Lucy's* bustling service about her languid mistress.

One of the pleasant things in being present at this comedy is to see how *Mrs. Malaprop's* blunders are hailed by the persons around you. It furnishes a curious insight into the respective amounts of their reading and education.

[ENJOYMENTS OF THE THEATRE]

Performances of Saturday Night
DRURY-LANE: *The Hypocrite; The Jenkinses; Turning the Tables*
COVENT-GARDEN: *The Carnival at Naples; The Omnibus; Black-Eyed Susan*

December 13, 1830

THERE WAS NOTHING at the great theatres on Saturday that we have not already noticed.[1] To-morrow we shall report the proceedings of Mr. Matthews at the Adelphi. To-day we must content ourselves with looking back upon our criticisms, and seeing if we have anything to add or to alter. We can remember nothing but omitting to speak of Mr. Wrench [2] when enumerating the comic performances at Covent-Garden, and furthermore leaving him out of our notice of the *Recruiting Officer*.[3] He acted the part of *Sergeant Kite*, and did it very pleasantly. His domestic, quick-speaking manner is hardly on a scale powerful enough for these large theatres; but he is very agreeable. He is one of those actors whom, without any personal knowledge of them, we conclude to be pleasant fellows; chaps for a Christmas fire, with good humour for all the circle, and no objection to the pudding.

We confess it is no mean satisfaction to us when we see the name of an actor like this in the play-bills. Of all sights in the world, we value none so much as that of human enjoyment. It never comes amiss to us. We know what it is to like a gloomy day, much as we in general would wish to bask in fine ones; there is sometimes a smile upon the face of inanimate nature, which, however unwarrantable, the fancy converts at the moment into an aspect of want of feeling; but in the human countenance, knowing how much we can all suffer, and how precious to us is the possession of pleasure, we are so far from desiring the presence of gloom, in our most painful moments, that we never, at any time, so much desire the reverse. We speak not of such as cannot help sharing our sufferings, but of the faces of strangers, and of all those in which circumstances do not render it unnatural or ungraceful to retain their cheerfulness. On this account, the sight of the pleasant actors and the pleased audience in a theatre is never discordant to us, even though we should sit isolated in the little darkness of our own griefs as in a closet, and be unable to feel the warmth and light that we behold. The tears on its windows are from within, and not from without. We see that happiness is still going on. We seem to represent the few, while the audience are the many; and at all events, there do we see a large assemblage of human beings, certainly not come to be displeased but the reverse, and enjoying for hours a common sense of pleasure, the nature of which encourages and refines their humanity. There the rich learn that the poor are still of account; and the poor, that the rich learn it; there high and low, rich and poor, one with another, smile at the same pleasure, and feel their eyes dimmed with the same sympathy; and we breathe the exalted air of poetry and rejoice to find it proper to us; and all faces are bent at the same time on one object (as they might, and we believe, will be, in the greater world); and brutality, if it come in, is put down by the common voice; and generous sentiments are hailed with shouts, as if they were prosperous gentlemen; and we behold heaps of faces, aye even the hardest, looking for the moment full of faith and interest; and ingenuous youth; and amiable and beautiful women; and strangers who are old friends (the actors); and the poor girls, who bloom out their short lives in the borders and vindicate their common humanity between disgrace and daring; and brilliant light; and art; and architecture; and scenery, by means of which all our town eyes look suddenly into a solitude or a distant region; and between the acts run beautiful strains of music, that allow not a crevice of deficiency in the whole amusement, but fill up the pauses of thought with a golden sweetness.[4]

You may be certain that an audience at a theatre does not consist of the least intelligent or the least social portion of the town. There is pretty strong evidence, in their love of the entertainment, to shew that they belong to a different class. To know therefore that every evening there are large houses, some enormous ones, containing masses of human beings of this sort, is to feel that you have a pleasure at hand of the most social kind, whenever you are able to enjoy it, and that it exists at all events, whether you can relish it or not sufficiently at the moment.

[CHRISTMAS AND THE THEATRE]

December 25, 1830

As THE THEATRES ARE CLOSED for two nights, we have no play to criticise for two whole days,[1] an extraordinary event for this journal: nay, we shall be at home for two whole evenings; shall have no mud at six, shall not be living for hours together with our eyes fixed upon people we never spoke to, nor breathe a yard of cold air before us on our return home, nor see the saloup-men [2] dancing and hugging the tips of their fingers under their arms, nor eternally mystify the watchman, who wonders what can induce us to be out "at that time of night every morning," and unquestionably takes us for a spy, or a coiner, or a lover, or a "French foreigner," or the man that sets fire to the ricks in Norfolk, or somebody who is "shown" and so cannot walk by day, or a Jesuit, or the "gentleman that's missing," or one whose cloak knows more of lace than it appears to do, or some miserly proprietor going to see that his men are up, or a poet (meaning a man avoiding bailiffs), or "some actor-man," or a tavern-keeper, or the old bachelor who always keeps them up at the Southampton Arms, or "Mr. Smith," or somebody who has something to do with some curious business, or lastly (now he has it, and draws himself up respectfully) the commissioner of police, who goes about to see that the men do their duty.

Watchman. Good morning, Sir.
The Mystery. Good morning. Terribly cold!
Watchman. Terrible, indeed, Sir. (Aside.) It can't be the Commissioner. He wants dignity, like. He's too civil-spoken.

The performers cannot know the pleasure of a holiday, as we daily critics do. They have intervals—repeated gaps; and besides, they can be ill. But the scene-shifter must enter into our comforts. To have two whole evenings to himself, not Sunday ones, must be a novelty to him. Suddenly meditative in the midst of his children's gaiety, he thinks how pleasant it is to be sitting there by the fire, instead of thrusting cold summer-bowers upon the stage, or running with one half of a house at his shoulder, to meet Jenkins with the other. The candle-snuffer too must be glad not to enlighten the stage. And the musicians, who nightly warm the feelings of the audience with their charming passages and cold fingers, they too must feel with the critic in this matter, especially if he likes an orchestra as we do, and loves to be near it.

Then there are the poor people who sell fruit out of doors, and the play-bills. They work so hard, and get buffeted by such cruel bleak winds that they must surely look to have their solace on Christmas night. We asked one of them the other evening, who was standing against a corner of the theatre hopping on either foot and wrapping a bit of a cloak about her, whether she was not cold. "Sir," said she looking us earnestly in the face, "I am *downright* cold." Her manner said as much as her simple words. She felt too much to exaggerate. How these people stand it, we can hardly think, but especially the old watchmen, who must feel the cold pierce their bones through and through. They must get into bed (when they do get) like withered bits of ice. And Christmas night, to them, is no Christmas! [3] Thaw them, dear readers, with a cup of your best.

PATENT THEATRES AND
MR. ARNOLD

January 27, 1831

THE FURTHER CONSIDERATION of this question before the Lord Chancellor is postponed till Monday.¹ Meanwhile it has been once more resumed, but we find nothing new in the arguments. The most ingenious thing in the whole discussion is the eschewal of the real spirit of the question. His Lordship in vain endeavours now and then to bring it a little into play.

The Lord Chancellor: In a book published by the late Lord Carlisle—a person of no mean authority in theatrical opinions and affairs—it was stated that the largeness of the theatres was inimical to the development of the expression of the actors' faces, &c. which, accordingly, prevented the representation of any fine comedies. This was an argument used by many persons, and he only wished, for his own information, to know whether such was the case or not.

Mr. Adam said it certainly was not the case in either of the theatres. Not only old pieces, but new were represented—amongst which was *The Chancery Suit*, a piece of five acts, and one which bade fair to be a stock-piece. For the sake of the many eminent persons who had written the comedies, he wished their Lordships to be informed that the drama had not decreased in such a way as might appear from the discussion on the preceding evening.

The use of the word "any" in the Lord Chancellor's speech (if the report be correct) here enabled the learned Counsel to answer truly, as far as regards the letter of the question: but the spirit of it is always evaded. The largeness of the theatres has certainly not prevented the representation of every fine play; but as certainly, it is inimical to the habit of representing fine plays. A few of the best pieces produced in later times, such as the *School for Scandal* and the *Rivals*, Goldsmith's comedy of *She Stoops to Conquer*, and some of the pieces of O'Keefe, are kept alive by the inheritance of certain favourite parts from one popular actor to another. These actors, when they make their debut, try their strength in them, in order to prove their claims to be considered successors to the others; and a certain small round of good plays are repeated in consequence, as long as these principal performers can render them attractive. But the rest of the pieces, with the exception of one of Otway's [2] and a few of Shakspeare's, which are, for the most part, ill performed, and which struggle on between the marvellous force of their appeals to nature and the appearance of a single good actor or so in one of the characters, are generally of a mediocre description. There are the plays of Morton, for instance, of Murphy, of Tom Dibdin, of Colman, &c., and a world of melodramas and other feeble monsters, which generally die soon after they are born; but how often is it that we hear of Congreve, Wycherley, and Farquhar? and what a mine is there of precious dramatists of the old time, including Beaumont and Fletcher, which, if it depended for fame on the theatres, would almost remain unknown? The managers tell us that the productions of these writers, however beautiful, would not attract audiences. True; not in immense theatres where they cannot be heard, and with bad actors who exist there upon the strength of their faces being invisible. What would be the use of being invited upon one side of Salisbury Plain to hear Handel performed on the other, or to see one of the paintings of Raphael? The plays of Shakspeare, of Massinger, of Beaumont and Fletcher, of Decker, Webster, and others, came out in small theatres, not bigger sometimes than those yards of inns from which they were in fact copied, and of which our present pit and boxes are imitations. The very best actors only draw occasionally and for short periods; and when they do, only half the house can hear and see them properly; which is the reason why they are not more attractive. Now and then some new debutante attracts the public curiosity, generally to no lasting purpose, and with injury to the very powers evinced, because of the temptation to rant. The most genuine satisfaction is caused by singing and spectacle, because in those cases the appeals to hearing and eyesight are on a large scale, and the new stars pierce the remote regions of the upper boxes. Acting, too, is not expected of singers, partly because they have been accustomed to do without it. As to melodrama, nobody looks for expression in the whiskered cheeks and Tamerlane gestures of a bandit: an elephant can dispense with delicacy of inspection; and storms, murders, Newgate-Calendar plots, shipwrecks, crashes of music, dogs, horses, real water, anything, in short, but real plays, are at length not only tolerated but desired by the public, out of an instinctive sense that they are the best things which the houses are fit for. For our parts, we have no objection to a spectacle when it is good of its kind, still less if it is founded on one of those fairy or Eastern tales, which are not less full of genius and delight because they are the delight of children. But the success of these upon the stages most fit for them ought not to hinder the creation of other stages fitter for the performance of tragedy and comedy. The counsel for the patentees the other night mentioned, as a curious fact illustrative of this question, that the same dramas which had attracted full houses in the large theatres, were performed by the same actors in the Haymarket Theatre to halfpenny benches. Name! Name! as they cry in parliament. We know not how truly this gentleman may have been informed nor does he mention how often the fact occurred, or under what circumstances; but we will venture to affirm either that the dramas must have been bad ones, or of such an inferior nature as to demand a large house, or else that it was wholly owing to the difference of season and the emptiness of the town. On the other hand, if our memory does not greatly deceive us, the same dramas which attract full houses at the Haymarket, have been acted to half-empty benches in the great theatres, though we cannot say whether or not in the same hands. At all events, the argument nullifies itself; for, as the Solicitor-General observed, if little theatres cannot draw full houses, and great ones can, why do the latter fear them? and if it is not desirable to see and hear in the very best manner, why are good actors requisite at all? and how is it that the great theatres do not get rich? Sir Charles Wetherell,[3] who appeared for Mr. Morris during the last mooting of the question, said that Mr. Arnold, instead of producing musical dramatic entertainments and ballets of action, had done little but emulate the "spurious performances" of Sadler's Wells and the Olympic; while he gave us to understand that no such performances were represented at what he called the "three regular theatres." The truth is that the Haymarket is the most regular theatre at present existing, if by that term we are to understand a theatre devoted to regular plays, farces and opera; and, accordingly, with the help of its being a small theatre, it is in general well filled, in spite of its performing during the summer months only. We may venture on this occasion to observe, as speaking from critical experience and a love of the stage, that it is on that account, solely, our own favourite play-house, and that we have often expressed our pleasure at sitting there and coming as it were into social contact with the dramatis personae. Nor has this opinion been expressed by ourselves only. People have been in the habit of observing how well the Haymarket fills, in spite of the heat of summer time, and of adding that it must be owing to the facilities afforded for seeing and hearing. We do not think, we confess, that the heat of the summer is so great an objection as people suppose it, the greater amount of animal spirits during that season being perhaps more than an equivalent for any inconvenience occasioned by the smallness of the accommodation. But not to lose sight of Sir Charles Wetherell, the two great theatres notoriously partake to a great extent in the spurious performances which he attributes exclusively to Sadler's Wells and the Olympic. The Adelphi complains that they deprive it of its nautical after-pieces. Their condescension to show and spectacle, to dogs and horses, have been repeatedly burlesqued by the minors; and in brigands and bandits, and Old Bailey plots, they absolutely strive hard to outdo Sadler's Wells and the Coburg. The very best pieces they have produced for a long time are such as those which the Olympic, the Adelphi, Mr. Arnold's theatre, and Mr. Morris's have been producing every day, namely, light little pieces from the French: the only other good novelties, with the exception of the appearance of Miss Inverarity [4] (and we speak with the utmost deliberation, and from the experience of nightly attendance), have been the beautiful series of landscape scenery in the present pantomime at Drury-Lane, and the custom introduced in the orchestras of playing the finest pieces of Mozart and others. Even the two pantomimes now running at the great theatres, notwithstanding the means possessed of giving them the greatest effect, are in the universal opinion of the town inferior to the pantomime at the Adelphi. The Adelphi is constantly producing new pieces that do it great credit; the Olympic, in its light way, promises to do as much; the Haymarket has always maintained its reputation; and from what we hear of the Coburg and the Surrey, and have seen of a variety of printed dramas which have been sent us, performed at those theatres and written by Mr. Jerrold,[5] they have been making the most praiseworthy exertions for informing as well as amusing the important multitudes that visit them; a circumstance, we may venture to say, which is not unworthy the serious consideration of the Lord Chancellor, as serving to shew him the importance of exciting intellectual emulation among a variety of play-houses. Sir Charles Wetherell has given it as his opinion that a multiplicity of theatres is injurious to good morals, and he says that this opinion was *confirmed*, many years ago, by a speech which he heard at Oxford from the lips of the present Archbishop of Canterbury. What the Archbishop said, or how this confirmation of ancient date has withstood all the precious accumulation and vigorous coherency of Sir Charles's ideas in the interval, we are not told; neither do we think it necessary to repeat anything on the point. Liberal knowledge must advance in a liberal manner, and in a just confidence that real morals and intellectual freedom will flourish together. The more the world knows, the more they will know wisely; and the more good-naturedly they are taught the knowledge, the sooner it will come.

There was one thing we were very sorry to see in the report of these later arguments. It was the appearance of a gentleman on the behalf of the Duke of Bedford, who joins the patentees in opposing the extension of Mr. Arnold's license, in consequence of his being the ground landlord of Covent-Garden. His Grace, we presume, who has the reputation of being a good-natured man, has condescended to come forward for the benefit of others. We are sorry for it, because he is very rich, and might have afforded to let the question take its most liberal course.

[THE MESSIAH]

Performances of Last Night

COVENT-GARDEN: Oratorio, *The Messiah*

February 24, 1831   *Covent-Garden*

THE PERFORMANCE of the *Messiah* last night,[1] at this theatre, though we are great admirers of Handel, did not please us
so much as the *Selection of Music* at Drury-Lane; [2] doubtless
because the effect upon the whole was more sombre and un-
varied, and the mind occupied with a succession of thoughts
more painful than befits an evening's music. Music is a pleasurable art, even in its melancholy, and should not deal with many
continuous thoughts more painful than amount to pensiveness.
The more we feel it, the less we like to have it rendered the
medium of repeating to us all the sorrows and agonies of the
divine heart, which this Oratorio records, however invested as
it may be with unearthly grandeur, exalted with trumpets, or
deified with choral shouts. Handel is, to be sure, a prodigious
musician. "He strikes you, whenever he chooses," said Mozart,
"with a thunderbolt." We could like a selection of his thunder-
bolts very well: the very finest pieces of his *Messiah* brought
together, and none else, we should not complain of, as a burden
of solemn beauty. But even Handel has his comparatively common matter, not only of an old fashion, but of a heavy weight;
and there is something too much of this in a whole oratorio devoted to one subject. In short, the *Oratorio* was upon us too
much last night, in its old shape and shadow. The audience
looked as melancholy as they went in and out; and the orchestra,
mounted above one another on their benches, presented the
old melancholy, middle-aged, solemn, and somewhat stiff-look-
ing hierarchy in black coats, whose bows and viols cut rather a
different figure from those of the Saint Cecilias in the pictures of
the Correggios and Domenichinos.

When Handel, however, is at his finest, there is no desiring
anything better. Music has no greater

Pomp and threatening harmony [3]

than his (to speak in the noble language of Mr. Wordsworth):
nor did sorrow ever receive a sweeter and more affecting pity.
The blasts of his trumpets upon the word *Wonderful* ("His name
shall be called Wonderful") naturally make us repeat the epithet, in delighted astonishment. They issue immediately from
the preceding notes, and from a level with them, as if the trumpets blew directly at us, and we beheld their mighty mouths.
(Roubiliac [4] seems to have been inspired by one of these passages, when he placed the mouth of the trumpet right before
us by the side of Handel's statue—a fine stroke of genius, and
a singular union of letter with spirit.) Then what a truly pastoral
simplicity there is in the Recitative, "There were shepherds abid-
ing in the fields!" What a pure tenderness in "He shall feed his
flock," with its caressing accompaniment! And what an excess
of pity in "He was despised and rejected of men"!—"Thy rebuke
hath broken his heart" is of the same perfect class of the pathetic,
and was admirably sung by Mr. Braham, who seemed resolved
last night to show how pure and masterly could be his style.
We must confess that we do not think his expression could have
been mended. His tones had a trembling tenderness, without
hurting their manhood. Miss Paton was in greater force than
on the preceding night; but did not strike us altogether as having to sing airs so well suited to her. However, we did not hear
them all. Miss Russell does not throw out her voice enough; but
she sang "He was despised" better than we had looked for; and
here the lowness of tones was less objectionable. Miss Bruce
obtained considerable applause in "He shall feed his flock": and
we must not forget that we never heard Mr. Phillips [5] to such
advantage, in our opinion, as in "The people that walked in darkness." His voice seemed to be less in his throat than usual, and
he gave excellent expression to the words that speak of the
"great light." The singers in these oratorios would do well in
general to put a little more of the dramatic spirit into their performances, as Mr. Phillips and Mr. Braham do. They turn their

music-books over, for the most part, with an air of grave nothing-ness, and pretend to read them, in order to have something to do with their hands and eyes. It would be better to think of the meaning of what they are singing, and do their utmost to express it.

Between the first two acts, Mr. Nicholson [6] performed, with great applause, a Fantasia on the flute. This gentleman is an example of the difference between a clever and a fine player. He is a very clever player on the instrument, but he does not apprehend the spirit of music. He is all for the letter, and tosses about his alphabet marvellously, but he never gets really beyond the gamut. All his *sforzandos,* and *crescendos,* and *appogiaturas,* do not get at the soul of what he is about. His is not the art

Dead things with inbreath'd *sense* able to pierce.

He fetches out of his flute all that mere breath and skill can do, but he puts no heart and mind in it: he excites no feeling but that of a sense of his cleverness. If Sir Thomas Urquhart,[7] the translator of Rabelais, could have heard him, he would have described him as one who trills, intonates, tips, tongues, tootletoos, plunges, pifferates, peck-o'-peppers, gamutifies, whiffles, and wambles his flute, "now careering it, and now caracoling it," and all marvellously; but for the music, it is as if a man should say, "Let us shew how we can do without it."

[BONNETS AT THE THEATRE]

Performances of Last Night

DRURY-LANE: *Henri Quatre; High Ways and By Ways;* And *The Illustrious Stranger*
COVENT-GARDEN: *Cinderella; Saint Patrick's Day;* And *Teddy the Tiler*

March 23, 1831

IN DEFAULT of having anything better to write about in our present number,[1] we beg leave to remonstrate with certain bonnets, and other enormities, with which the ladies put out our eye-sight in the theatres. The bonnet is the worst. If you sit right behind it, it shall swallow up the whole scene. It makes nothing of a regiment of soldiers, or a mountain, or a forest, or a rising sun; much less of a hero, or of so insignificant a thing as a cottage, and a peasant's family. You may sit at the theatre a whole evening, and not see the leading performer. Liston's face is a glory obscured. The persons in your neighborhood, provided they have no bonneted ladies before them, shall revel in the jocose looks of Farren or Dowton, and provokingly reflect the merriment in their own countenances, while you sit and rage in the shade. If you endeavour to strain a point, and peep by the side of it, ten to one (since Fate notoriously interferes in little things, and delights in being "contrary," as the young ladies say)—ten to one but the bonnet seizes that very opportunity of jerking sideways, and cutting off your resources. We have seen an enthusiastic play-goer settle himself in his seat, and evidently congratulate himself at the evening he was about to enjoy, when, a party of ladies swimming into the seats before him, one of them has been the ruin of all his prospects. Even a head-dress, without the bonnet, shall force you to play at bo-peep with the stage half the evening; now extinguishing the face of some favorite actress, and now abolishing a general or a murder. The other night, at the Queen's Theatre, we sometimes found ourselves obliged to peep at the Freemasons in a very symbolical manner, through the loops of a lady's bows. But the bonnet is the enormity. And we are sorry to say that the fair occupants who sit inside them, like the lady in the lobster, too often shew a want of gallantry in refusing to take them off, for, as we have said more than once, we hold gallantry, like all the other virtues, to be a thing mutual, and of no sex; and that a lady shews as much want of gallantry in taking advantage of the delicacies observed towards her by the gentleman as a man does who presumes upon the gentleness of a lady. We felt, the other night, all the reforming spirit of our illustrious predecessors of the *Tatler* and *Spectator* roused within us and in the same exact proportion to our regard for the sex, upon witnessing the following prodigious fact: A lady who came with a party into one of the boxes at Covent-Garden, joined very heartily in expressing her disapprobation of some person in a seat below her, who was dilatory in taking off his hat. It chanced that this lady got into the very seat that he had occupied, and her bonnet turning out to be a much greater blind than the hat, what was the astonishment and the merriment of the complainants, upon finding that she was still less accommodating than the gentleman? Nothing could induce her to perform the very same piece of justice which she had joined in demanding from the other.

We are aware that in modern, as in ancient theatres, ladies come to be seen as well as to see:

Spectatum veniunt, veniunt spectentur ut ipsae.[2]

But we are desirous that they should not pay themselves so ill a compliment as to confound their dresses with themselves; it is the bonnets that are seen, in these cases, and not the ladies. When seen themselves, they make a part of the spectacle, but who cares to look upon these great lumps of gauze and silk? Something we grant, is to be allowed to fashion, but the wearers might be content with showing that their heads could be as absurd as other people's, and then lay aside the absurdity, and show that they understood the better part of being reasonable. They urge, when requested to take their bonnets off, that they "cannot" do it; meaning, we suppose, besides the will not, which cannot so often signifies, that their heads are not prepared to be seen—that their hair is not dressed in the proper manner; but it would be easy to come with it so dressed; the bonnet is not the only head-dress in fashion; and above all, it would be a graceful and a sensible thing in them to remember that, in coming to a place where the object is to enjoy pleasure, their own capability of pleasure is interested in considering that of others. We never feel angry with a woman, except when she persists in doing something to diminish the delight we take in complimenting the sex.

[MADAME PASTA]

Performances of Last Night

KING'S THEATRE: *Medea; La Nayade*
DRURY-LANE: *Alfred the Great; The Illustrious
Stranger; Turning the Tables*
COVENT-GARDEN: *Azor and Zemira; The £100 Note*

May 13, 1831   *King's Theatre*

MADAME PASTA was received last night [1] in the manner to
be expected.[2] Milton speaks of "raining influence." [3] The moment she was recognized, the clapping of hands came down in
a perfect *hail*-storm of approbation: and she stood bending in
her graceful fashion under the shower. We looked with some
anxiety to know whether our love was to be put to the test by
her having grown fatter; but she is not at all so. We think she has
altered in that respect for the better.

The part she appeared in was *Medea*,[4] which is reckoned her
finest. We know not how that may be, for we have seen her but
in few of her characters; but that it is one of the finest things on
the stage, we can bear testimony. (By the way, the subject
and conduct of this Italian opera of *Medea*, its altars and hymns,
and its choruses of spectators, who bring victorious or agitating
news, give as good an idea of the Greek drama as is likely to be
had in modern times; [5] and perhaps a better one than we should
suppose from its being all set to music; for there was a great deal
of music in the Greek tragedies; nor is the Italian recitative
unlikely to have borne a much nearer resemblance to the reci-
tation of their actors, than the style of our northern speech
might lead us to conceive. Recitative is nearer to the speech of
the modern Italians than most people imagine.)

The charm of Madame Pasta's style consists in the wonderful
truth of it, invested with moral beauty; that is to say, she never
minces what she feels, or goes aside of it, or affects anything as
superior to it, or has any doubt about it; but is as full of faith

as a child, and being child-like in her faith, she is rewarded by having as much grace in her exposition of it as a child has in its movements. We do not mean that she is as unconscious as a child. The stage itself, as well as her knowledge, would prevent that; nor would it be natural, if she were. What we mean is, that grace in her is always subordinate to the truth, and moulded by it. She knows as truly the best attitudes in which she can put herself, as she knows what passion she is to express, and she knows the one because of the other. The tree bends with the fruit. She carries so much beauty and truth in her that she must carry it in the most beautiful manner.

This is the reason why a little superfluity of person never stood in the way of the effect produced by this divine actress—at least with those who had any perception of the morally beautiful themselves. And for the same reason, her voice, which though excellent, is not of the very finest order, does not stand in the way of what it expresses. It is the vehicle, as all voices should be, of emotion. Those who value no singer except their voice or execution be perfect, and are contented if it is, mistake the means for the end. Madame Pasta's execution can be extraordinary when she pleases; but in general she restrains it, agreeably to what nature requires. In every respect, the means with her are subordinate to the end; and hence it is that, with less means than some, there is no singer or actress upon the stage who attains her end so perfectly.

Madame Pasta's style is epic. She hits the great points and leaves you to feel the rest. Her gestures are voluminous; the tender ones are full of the last soul of love, her threatening or calamitous ones, appalling; there is catastrophe in them, the certainty of doom. Thus when *Jason* tells her she is to look for his love no longer, and she feels the first dim movements in her soul of all that is about to happen, she walks away, *laying her hands over her eyes,* as if she did not dare to look upon the mournful and dreadful things that must happen. Afterwards, when she threatens *Jason,* she holds out to him a hand, trembling as if it held misery for both of them; and when she is to express a passionate resolution, by suddenly leaping to a high note, she dares, with a noble confidence, to make almost a shriek of it.

It is as if a Pythian priestess were crying from her tripod. Her classical dresses and attitudes are known to everybody. They are fine, not merely because they are classical, but because the ancients, in the height and purity of their perceptions, hit upon the finest attitudes, and she and the ancients think in this matter alike. In only one point could we conceive that Euripides would have desired a finer *Medea* than she (supposing that he had the luck to have so good a one); and that is when she relents a while from her murderous impulses against her children and fondles them with love. We think (with submission) that Madame Pasta is somewhat *too* much absorbed in the love, and that it makes her look a little too happy. We would have had her look at them as if there were tears in her eyes.

We have not time to say more, or to speak of Taglioni,[6] whom we must notice at a future opportunity. We can only add that the music of this opera, by Mayer, though you do not carry any passages away from it, is good and expressive; that Lablache,[7] in *Creonte*, looked like a king of the old heroic times, when kings were great stalwart fellows, a head and shoulders taller than their subjects; that his voice was worthy of such a royalty, and as easy as it was powerful; that Miss Fanny Ayton,[8] though weak in her voice for this stage, and not always in tune, is a clever little *opera* person, who has more feeling than she appears to have from her ambitious theatrical style, and might reasonably get a little more applause now and then: that the merit of Curioni [9] is perhaps just upon a par with Mr. Meyer's *Jason;* and that Signor Rubini [10] is spoiled by his execution, much about in the same manner, and with the same amount of wit, as some men are by a good set of teeth. He is always for shewing it. He is one of your greatest mistakers of the means for the end; and all the mistaken people in the house applaud him; which is a pity, for with a voice at once powerful and sweet, he ought to do better. But we are afraid he errs for want of ideas. He seems to think at present, that there are but three things in the world: to be full of demisemiquavers, to be loud, and to be soft. He thunders on one half of a bar, and languishes through the rest. He snaps a pistol at your head, and then falls to scratching it.

[PAGANINI]

Performances of Last Night

COVENT-GARDEN: *The Maid of Judah; Napoleon Buonaparte*

HAYMARKET: *The Happiest Day of My Life; Secrets Worth Knowing; The Widow Bewitched; A Roland for an Oliver*

FRENCH PLAYS: *Antoine; Le Tailleur de Jean Jacques Rousseau; Les Anglaises pour Rire*

June 23, 1831   *King's Theatre*

SIGNOR PAGANINI favoured the public with his "fifth and last concert at this theatre," last night,[1] but not, it seems, with his fifth and last appearance; for he is to play this evening for the benefit of Lablache,[2] besides the four other performances, we suppose, which he is to be prevailed upon to bestow upon us, and the forty elsewhere. Well: the public are accustomed to these managerial tricks, and ought to be prepared for them; which does not seem to have been the case with some persons last night, by their hissing at the commencement of the benefit. Besides, Paganini is fine enough to make the public wish to hear him again and again, at some little expence to the perfection of his *morale*. Whether he would not be finer still if his proceedings were as straight-forward as his bow is a question of refinement, which it may be hard to urge in a matter of violin-playing.

Let us not belie the effect however which this extraordinary player had upon us last night. To begin with the beginning, he had a magnificent house. We thought at first we were literally going to *hear* him, without seeing his face; for the house was crammed at so early an hour that, on entering it, we found ourselves fixed on the lowest of the pit stairs. It was amusing to see the persons who came in after us. Some, as they cast up their eyes, gaped amazement at the huge mass of faces presented in all quarters of the house; others looked angry; others ashamed and cast a glance around them to see what was thought of them; some gallantly smiled, and resolved to make the best of it. One man exclaimed, with unsophisticated astonishment, "Christ Jesus!" and an Italian whispered in a half-execrating tone, "Oh, Dio!"

Meantime we heard some interesting conversation around us. We had been told, as a striking instance of the effect that Paganini has produced upon the English musical world, that one eminent musician declared he could not sleep the first night of his performance for thinking of him, but that he got up and walked about his room. A gentleman present last night was telling his friends that another celebrated player swore that he would have given a thousand guineas to keep the Italian out of the country, he had put everybody at such an immeasurable distance. These candid confessions, it seems, are made in perfect good-humour, and therefore do honour to the gentlemen concerned. The truth is, as a late writer observed, that men of real pretensions are not apt to grudge higher pretensions in others, if they are of a very genuine surpassing nature. Envy is lost in admiration.

The performances commenced with Haydn's beautiful symphony, No. 9, the fine, touching exordium of which, full of a kind of hushing meaning, appeared admirably adapted to be the harbinger of the evening's wonder. A duet between Santini and Curioni [3] followed; and then, after a due interval, came in Signor Paganini, and "brought the house down" with applause.

As it was the first time we had seen the great player, except in the criticisms of our musical friends, which had rendered us doubly curious, we looked up with interest at him from our abysm in the pit. A lucky interval between a gentleman's head and a lady's bonnet favoured our endeavour, and there we beheld the long, pale face of the musical marvel, hung, as it were, in the light, and looking as strange as need be. He made divers uncouth obeisances, and then put himself in a masterly attitude for his work, his manner being as firm and full of conscious power when he puts the bow to the instrument as it is otherwise when he is not playing. We thought he did not look so old as he is said to be; [4] but he is long-faced and haggard, with strongly-marked prominent features, wears his black hair flowing on his neck like an enthusiast, has a coat of ancient cut which astonishes Fop's Alley; in short, is very like the picture of him in the shops. He is like a great old boy, who has done nothing but play the violin all his life, and knows as much about that as he does little of conventional manners. His face at the same time has much less expression than might be looked for. At first it seemed little better than a mask; with a fastidious, dreary expression, as if inclined to despise his music and go to sleep. And such was his countenance for a great part of the evening. His fervour was in his hands and bow. Towards the close of the performances, he waxed more enthusiastic in appearance, gave way to some uncouth bodily movement from side to side, and seemed to be getting into his violin. Occasionally also he put back his hair. When he makes his acknowledgments, he bows like a camel, and grins like a goblin or a mountain-goat.

His playing is indeed marvellous. What other players can do well, he does a hundred times better. We never heard such playing before; nor had we imagined it. His bow perfectly talks. It remonstrates, supplicates, answers, holds a dialogue. It would be the easiest thing in the world to put words to his music. We heard an enthusiastic violin player assert once, in the heat of argument with a painter, that it would be as possible to call for a chop at a tavern by playing, as by painting it. Last night we almost began to think that this hyperbole was hardly a fiction. We are sure that with a given subject, or even without it, Paganini's best playing could be construed into discourse by any imaginative person.

Last night he began a composition of his own (very good, by the way)—an *Allegro Maestoso* movement (majestically cheerful) with singular force and precision. Precision is not the proper word; it was a sort of peremptoriness and dash. He did not put his bow to the strings, nor lay it upon them; he struck them, as you might imagine a Greek to have done when he used his plectrum, and "smote the sounding shell." He then fell into a tender strain, till the strings, when he touched them, appeared to shiver with pleasure. Then he gave us a sort of minute warbling, as if half a dozen humming birds were singing at the tops of their voices, the highest notes sometimes leaping off and shivering like sprinkles of water; then he descended with wonderful force and gravity into the bass; then he would commence a strain of earnest feeling or entreaty, with notes of the greatest solidity, yet full of trembling emotion; and then again he would leap to a height beyond all height, with notes of desperate minuteness, then flash down in a set of headlong harmonies, sharp and brilliant as the edges of swords; then warble again with inconceivable beauty and remoteness, as if he was a ventriloquizing-bird; and finally, besides his usual wonderful staccatos in ordinary, he would suddenly throw handfuls, as it were, of staccatoed notes, in distinct and repeated showers over his violin, small and pungent as the tips of pins.

In a word, we never heard anything like *any* part of his performance, much less the least marvel we have been speaking of. The people sit astonished, venting themselves in whispers of "Wonderful!"—"Good God!"—and other unusual symptoms of English amazement; and when the applause comes, some of them take an opportunity of laughing, out of pure inability to express their feelings otherwise.

But we have come to the end of our room, and must have another article upon him to-morrow.

June 25, 1831

OUR WIZARD's *Allegro Maestoso* [5] was succeeded by an "*Adagio Flebile con Sentimento*"—a composition with a very "particular fellow" of a title, by which we are to understand a strain of pathos amounting to the lachrymose, and disclosing a deep perception of the delicacy of that matter. If we are inclined to doubt the perfection of Signor Paganini's playing it would be upon this point. He has a great deal more feeling than is usually shewn by players of extreme execution: his supplication in particular is admirable; he is fervent and imploring; you would think his violin *was on its knees;* the very first note he draws, in movements of this character, is the fullest, the gravest, the most forcible, and the most impassioned we ever heard; it is wonderfully in earnest. And yet, though there is a feeling of this kind throughout, and we never heard notes so touching accompanied with such admirable execution, we cannot help thinking that we miss, both in the style and the composition, that perfection of simplicity, and of unconsciousness of everything but the object of its passion or admiration, which is perhaps incompatible with these exhibitions of art. It is difficult to avoid speaking of ultra-refinements of playing, like those of Paganini, except in terms of ultra-refinement. What we mean to say is that, with all his feeling, we think that science and force are still the predominant qualities of his playing, and that his "sentiment" is of a less profound cast than he takes it for. It is evident enough that he supplicates; it is evident that he implores; it is plain that he holds a long and fervent argument, extremely to the purpose; but supposing, for the sake of a ground to go upon, that he is entreating a mistress, or remonstrating with fate for depriving him of some friend, he sets about it, we should say, still more obviously than deeply, or at all events endangers the simplicity and truth of the sentiment by the literality of the address. If he is to be supposed making love, we should say that he did it with more fervour of the senses than entireness of heart. In short, it is easier to doubt the perfection of his sensibility than of his skill. His *Andantino Gaio,* that followed, might be reckoned, in a similar spirit of comparison, defective of *gaiety.* There was gaiety in it, but by no means in proportion to the skill and the quaintness. In the quaint and fantastic, his mastery is equal to his execution. His performances the other night concluded with a *Dance of Witches;* and here he left nothing to desire. The author of the music in *Macbeth* would have hugged him for it. Levity, gravity, the homely, the supernatural, the odd, the graceful, figured in strange combination; and every now and then a voice was heard as of some fearful old beldam venting herself in a strain of feeble mystery, at once humorous and alarming. You imagined a pale old woman, dancing and whining, with a sort of ghastly affectation of the ridiculous.

Signor Paganini's exploits on the "single string" have been already described. Suffice it to say, that it was as marvellous the other night as ever, and that his single string beats other men's whole instrument. It has been said, that some portions of the phenomenon are not without *trick;* that is to say, that all which he does is not done by legitimate bowing. It is thought he must use some legerdemain. We have only to say this, that if he does so, a man of his consummate skill has a right to do it, if he increases the effect; because we are to suppose it done, not out of his own poverty, but the instrument's. At least, doing what he does do, the rest may be allowed him as a privilege. It was a trick in Rembrandt to lay a positive *relief* of paint on some of his pictures—as in the crust of jewellery over the altar-piece, in the picture of the "Woman taken in Adultery"—but Rembrandt is allowed to do what we should have refused to a lesser man, because his conceptions (if anything could) warranted the indulgence.

Upon the whole, our experience of the playing of this wonderful person has not only added to our stock of extraordinary and delightful recollections, but it has done our memories another great good, in opening afresh the world of ancient Greek music and convincing us of the truth of all that is said of its marvellous effects. To hear Paganini, and to see him playing on that bit of wood with a bit of catgut, is to convince us that the Greeks might really have done the wonders attributed to them with their shells and their quills. We always thought it unaccountable that Plato, and Plutarch, and others could have written the extraordinary things they have done respecting the mysteries of the musical art, and the transports occasioned by the lyrical feats of their countrymen, and that the Greeks all the while should have been the infants in music which the self-love of modern art has been too willing to suppose. Scriblerus's performance in the balcony is still a good joke; but from this moment our faith is confirmed in the wonders recorded of Aeolic and Doric modulations; and we owe gratitude to Paganini, if only for confirming it, and doubling the pleasure with which we read of the Timotheuses [6] and Terpanders.[7] What if he is but a poor player to the least of them? For now that we see what such instruments can do, there is no knowing how much they can do beyond it.

But even after what we have heard, how are we to endure hereafter our old violins and their players? How can we consent to hear them? How crude they will sound, how uninformed, how like a cheat! When the Italian goes away, violin-playing goes with him, unless some disciple of his should arise among us and detain a semblance of his instrument. As it is, the most masterly performers, hitherto so accounted, must consent to begin again, and be little boys in his school.

[FURTHER REMARKS ON PAGANINI]

Performances of Saturday Night
KING'S THEATRE: *L'Italiana in Algieri; La Prova d'Un Opera Seria; A Favorite Ballet*
COVENT-GARDEN: *Fazio; Napoleon Buonaparte*
HAYMARKET: *The Widow Bewitched; The Road to Ruin; The Review; Monsieur Tonsen*

June 27, 1831   *King's Theatre*

A CELEBRATED COMPOSER has published a piece of music entitled "Recollections of Paganini." We do not wonder that those who have heard this wonderful performer try to recall him to their minds, both for their own sakes and those of their friends. We find ourselves repeatedly called upon to say something about him, and every time seem to recollect something new. These reminiscences have induced us to add a word or two to our former articles.[1]

Singular and complicated as the compositions of Paganini are, he sometimes plays from memory; perhaps always, when the composition is one that he repeats often. For the music-book before him proves nothing. There is nothing very extraordinary in this: but it is curious to observe with what masterly precision he gives the cue to the orchestra, how exact to the time his memory is, and with what instantaneous and easy nicety he takes up, as it were, the whole of the weight of the accompaniments on the tip of his bow, and hangs it on the right peg. The official conductor at the piano-forte seems to sit staring in pure wonder; and the people that crowd behind the musicians on either side the stage turn around to one another with lifted hands and smiles of astonishment. All the orchestra appear mechanical, and he the soul standing in front.

When the transports of the audience have produced a dead silence, Paganini seems to take advantage of it to introduce his marvels of delicate execution, and passages *sui generis*. It is then that he treats us with his distant warblings of birds, and those singular showers of little distinct notes, as if he sprinkled one's ears in play. However, there is no playfulness in his face. He looks so grave that we begin to see nothing but grave mystery in his performance; a fancy which is increased by his own little intervals of silence, as if he were preparing his charm like a sorcerer. Now he comes down with his flashing harmonies— and then is silent. He then gives us some of his showers—and is again silent. Then, when the listening is at its height, and everybody is sitting in breathless expectation, he touches the minutest of notes *in alto,* and comes rapidly *whispering* to us all down his violin in the most extraordinary of chromatic passages, as if some wonderful nightingale were making experiments upon its voice, and knew that the neighborhood were enchanted.

He seems to have few of the affected gestures and attitudes of other players. His position, when he begins, is admired as being highly *comme il faut,* and like a man who knows how to plant himself to his violin; but his manner is generally simple. He now and then indulges his conscious mastery, at the termination of a favourite passage, by thrusting his bow beyond the instrument, and chucking the note, as it were, up into the air; as though he had delivered something worthy of its reception.

But as an instance of what we doubted respecting the profundity of his "sentiment," we may observe, that the *tender* mode in which he thought fit to play the German "God save the King," ("God preserve the Emperor Francis") appeared to us altogether a mistake. This composition of Haydn's is surely a point of severe and simple playing, and not a subject for whining and chromatics. The style in which Paganini gave it the other night was rather what we should have expected from some unthinking shower-off than a great master. It should have been affectionate, but only in such a way as to be compatible with a Hymn, and with the modesty of a religious petition—fervent, cathedral, deferential, yet at the same time self-collected; conscious of a presence, before which there is to be no unseemly weakness or overweeningness. Yet to those who were aware of the nature of the subject, and recollected the words, Paganini's chromatical,

fond, and effeminate manner of playing it resembled a caricature of some morbid loyalist, who had got maudlin with the
Emperor's wine, and must needs go sighing and dying through
the National Hymn. Here was a deficiency in that judgment
which implies the very deepest taste, or the perfection of the
sense of truth.

[LATE HOURS AT THE THEATRE]

Performances of Last Night

HAYMARKET: *Clari; A Friend at Court; A Day After the Wedding; High Life below Stairs*
ENGLISH OPERA: *The Feudal Lady; "Wanted a Governess"; Middle Temple*

July 7, 1831

IT WAS OUR INTENTION [1] to see Mr. Reeve [2] in the character of *Brutus Hairbrain* last night, in the farce of the *Middle Temple*,[3] which was announced in the first instance to be performed between the play and another after-piece; but as it was afterwards put last, we thought proper to waive the entertainment. It turns out that theatrical readers are not the best patrons of this paper; and we decline killing ourselves with late hours, even for the honour of dying in the service.

Everybody complains of the late hours to which theatrical performances are protracted. The weekly papers complain, the daily papers complain; yet the managers go on, heaping one piece upon another, and sometimes, as in the present instance, keeping the best for the last, as if to bribe people to stay. We are to open our mouths, *and shut our eyes,* and see what twelve o'clock will send us. It is like keeping a child up at a late visit, by thrusting another bit of cake into its hand.

What is the reason for this passion for heaping one's plate, whether we desire it or not; this loading us, like pretty dears, with five apples to the penny, and a grin of complacency to see how we carry them? We do not complain of Mr. Arnold, though we suppose he means to load us like the rest, by his saying nothing to the contrary. It was his putting his best attraction last that led us to speak on the subject; and this is the next bad thing to his giving us four pieces for three. Three pieces are often a whole one too many. The Haymarket and other theatres are sometimes not over now-a-days till a good bit past midnight.

There is a first piece, "after which" comes another, "to which will be added" another, and "to conclude" with a fourth. The linking phrases are varied with all the ingenuity of experience. By and by, we suppose, we shall have "to be further concluded" by a fifth, "subsequent to which" a sixth, "to be followed" by a seventh, and "the whole to be wound up" with an eighth. "N.B.: Night-caps and breakfast in the lobbies."

This dire advantage, or supposed advantage, taken of the English propensity to have enough for their money, originated, there is reason to believe, in the practice that came up at the Haymarket, of giving us three of their small farces for the old stock play and after-piece. The practice was followed by other minor theatres, in order that they might not be outdone in the show of abundance; and at length it increased to its present overwhelming pitch. Each shop was afraid of being out-bid by the others, if it did not clap a fresh piece of cheese on its pennyworth.

Madame Vestris,[4] with the shrewd tact of a woman, was the first to innovate on this custom. She knew that three or four hours of good sprightly entertainment, with the eyes open, was better than pretending to pleasure, half asleep. She announced that her theatre would close at a reasonable hour. It did so; and it is understood that she had a remarkably successful season. We are persuaded that if the other theatres would do as much the result would be the same. The young and the old alike, both of whom were play-goers twenty years ago, are almost equally shut out from the theatres, when they are so late. The late hours frighten mothers and grandmothers. It is not pleasant to take children away before the entertainments are over, and it is impossible to keep them up till one or two o'clock.

There is a notion perhaps with managers that, because hours in general are thrust forward, and people dine so much later than formerly, they like to find as much for their money when they arrive at the theatres as they used when they dined sooner. But if you look round at theatrical audiences now-a-days, it will be pretty evident that they do not consist of very fashionable people. The lateness of modern hours has indeed been injurious to theatres: and this brings us to another question, upon which we shall say a few words—the supposed decline of a taste for the drama.[5]

We call the decline a supposed one because we cannot think that the taste is less than it was, numerically speaking, though we grant it has shifted quarters. To those who talk of the diminished number of play-goers, it is enough surely to point to the increased number of theatres. We lay little stress upon the causes usually assigned for the decline of play-going, where it has declined—such as high prices, bad plays, bad acting, &c., and, least of all, the immoral state of the lobbies. High prices are not considered by people of fashion; the plays and the acting are both good enough, considering what was tolerated, and even liked, twenty years back; and as to the sights in the lobbies, fashionable eyes are not so squeamish as people fancy them. They would have to differ too often with their own looking-glasses.

The whole secret of the matter we take to be this: first, that the richer classes, besides the drawback of late hours and the diminution of tavern habits on the part of the gentry, have so abounded of late years in the luxuries of new books, music, and visiting, that they have outgrown a disposition to go to the theatre; and second, that the diffusion of knowledge has been bringing up the uneducated classes to the point where the others left off, and giving them an increase in all sorts of intellectual pleasures, previous to their having anything like a critical knowledge of them, or care for criticism. Ten years hence, perhaps, the trade of a theatrical critic will be better than it is now, and over the water, in preference to the once witty neighbourhood of Covent-Garden. The best thing said by a manager in his play-bills, for many years, is what Mr. Davidge of the Coburg has said, relative to the classical ground of Southwark, the scene of the triumphs of Shakspeare and Ben Jonson, where Mr. Kean is now performing. And this reminds us, that if Mr. Davidge will send us tickets, we will go to see his theatre, and give a report of the renewed honours of the neighbourhood.

[ROMEO AND JULIET]

Performances of Last Night

HAYMARKET: *Romeo and Juliet; Spring and Autumn;*
  Peeping Tom
ENGLISH OPERA: *Irish Girl; Wanted, a Governess;*
  The Spring Lock

July 12, 1831   *Haymarket*

WE SAW Miss Taylor's *Juliet* [1] last night.[2] It is not Shakspeare's; but it may compete with Miss Kemble's.[3] Shakspeare's women are not to be had every day; and the worst of it is that when they are to be had, or something that resembles them, the likenesses will not let themselves alone. They must still be adding something to please their looking-glasses. Here is Miss Taylor, a sensitive, intelligent girl (to judge by her face) who might have done anything with a lively character, had her friends, or teachers, or applauders known how to develop her own; but some twist or other in her education has prevented her from having a proper faith; she thinks she must be still adding some conscious grace; she will not give herself up to a passion, and let it act for her; in which case it would supply all the graces which she fancies she gives it: she must needs bolt her head, and pant, and keep a lachrymose and ever-trembling voice, and hurry a little bit, and stop short, and kick her train aside as if it was biting her—in short, adopt all the little received tricks to which she ought to be superior; and the consequence is, that instead of the *Juliet* she ought to be, she is clever, artificial Miss Taylor, and little more.

We think however that she abated her mannerism a little last night; and we congratulate her upon it. What would we not have given, had one half of her *Rosalind* been as good as the other; had the details been as good as the general conception! and *Juliet*—why could she not have given us the cordial, passionate, natural, romantic girl at once, fresh born out of child-

hood's school into love's, instead of the full-dressed consciousness and misgiving art of the *Juliet* theatrical? However, the
truth is, there is no *Juliet* on the stage, nor will there ever be till
some new Mrs. Jordan arises, who has all her nature and high
gentility besides! When shall we see such a phenomenon? The
modern *Juliets* are not in a room of their own; they are not in
their own thoughts, not in a dream of love and grief, no more
thinking of their faces than of their new shoes; they are always
on a stage. We wish, by the by, that some substitute could be
discovered of equal grandeur and less inconvenience for stage
heroines than their long trains. They make a most impertinent
interference with the legs of ladies in distress, and the latter
seem to think so, by the manner in which they kick and whisk
them about.

Miss Taylor's *Juliet* is not so sustained an effort of art as Miss
Kemble's. It wants the breadth and thorough confidence of the
other's family training, and would not tell so well in a large
theatre; but it has points which we think preferable to any in
Miss Kemble's, because of this very imperfection. When *Juliet*
is to be perplexed, Miss Taylor seems more really so: there is
not so mechanical a grandeur and wound-up theatrical tone
in the declamatory parts; and occasionally there was a gentle
natural sentence, a bit of failing voice, a little feminine cry of
mixed patience and urgency, which Miss Kemble never gave
us. There was a robustness throughout in Miss Kemble's *Juliet*
which did not argue the sensibility of the other. Miss Taylor's
best and worst points were shewn in the scene with her father.
What we have just spoken of was in those. Her worst passage was
where she plays the artifice upon him and pretends that she
has made up her mind to the marriage. She did this in too earnest and sincere a tone. She ought to have shrunk more from the
duplicity, like an honest girl, and affected as low and quiet a
tone as possible. The major part of the performance was of the
regular theatrical cast; and the general delivery disfigured by
too regular a tremble of the voice, which, by reason of its great
beauty on occasion, becomes offensive and a trick when used
always. *Juliet* should often speak in a perfectly natural and

simple tone; but with Miss Kemble she is always wound up to *concert pitch;* and with Miss Taylor she is a great deal too much so. The new *Juliet,* however, met with considerable applause, though she had not a full house.

Mr. Cooper, we fear, is the best *Romeo* on the stage, now that Charles Kemble has ceased to perform the character! For Mr. Wallack is never anything but a *Mazzaroni,* let him act what he may. But though Cooper is a clever actor, and there is something about him that we like to praise, it is hardly necessary to add that his *Romeo* is no *Romeo.* It is merely a sufferable piece of stage cleverness, for want of a better. We will venture to say he never once feels a piece of his author's love of poetry, from beginning to end of the character; but is always Mr. Cooper doing his best to look young and to shift his attitudes.

Mr. Vining [4] is a very miniature *Mercutio:* and Mrs. Gibbs,[5] with all her talent, will not do the *Nurse* at all. She has too much invincible life in that buxom person of hers and those round relishing tones, and cannot contrive to be broken down.

We thought to have added something to our yesterday's article upon Elliston; but must defer it till to-morrow.

[HENRY VIII]

Performances of Last Night
DRURY-LANE: *King John; Hyder Ali*
COVENT-GARDEN: *Henry the Eighth; A Genius
Wanted*

October 25, 1831   *Covent-Garden*

IT HAS ALWAYS STRUCK US as a curious thing in the play of
Henry the Eighth, which was performed here last night,[1] that
Shakspeare should have drawn so plain and uncompromising
a portrait of that bullying tyrant, that he should have exhibited
him not only in all the plenitude of his will, but in what may be
styled the corpulence of his whole character (for his mind was
as bloated as his body) and in all the vulgar homeliness of his
personal manners, down to the very familiarity of his huffing
phrases. What the poet meant to insinuate to a few choice spirits,
it is impossible to say; but we are not to suppose that he thought
of making the character ridiculous to the many. It only shews
us to what a late period the best constructions would be put
upon the worst actions of royalty, and how popular with our
bluff and not very thinking ancestors was the bluff King Harry.
In that matter "their legs were both of a thickness." What was
a thump to a yeoman's wife, they thought might reasonably be
decapitation to an offending queen. Certainly it is difficult for
us of the nineteenth century, who have the benefit of our ancestors' experience, and of all the Kings who have since flourished,
to look upon a scene like that in the play before us where one
of the greatest blackguards in the universe has all England at
his feet, with bowing lords and bishops making a divinity of him,
and not wonder how he could have been endured for a week
together. But a little reflection will make us value ourselves
rather upon the results and good fortune of that experience than
upon any superiority of our own; especially when we consider

that we still have such things as game-laws, and pluralities, and judges' wigs, and huffing hereditary fools, and Bishops who beard Ministers, and a hundred and ninety-nine men who can say to the whole people of England, "You shall have no more justice than we choose to allow you."

Mr. Charles Kemble, who performed *Henry the Eighth* for the first time, did it excellently well. The increase of his person helps the truth of the likeness; and none of the bluffness was lost in voice or manner. He was loud, insolent, sudden, restless, a proper victim to his will; making victims of others. Some might have thought the likeness a caricature; but it was not so. *Henry* was himself a caricature, an exaggeration of will and power; and so have many other Kings been; nay, it is lucky for any King to escape being one in some respects, inasmuch as he is a man not amenable to ordinary rules, and in some measure absurd by office.

Our heresy with regard to Miss Kemble we have too often had occasion to speak of, and we do not find ourselves bound to re-cant it on the present. She is very clever, and made a very clever *Queen Katharine;* and, as usual, gave the more sarcastic pas-sages with good effect; but she wants dignity and natural power for the character. We remember Mrs. Siddons, and whenever we see her niece in the characters that she performed we can-not help thinking her an inferior likeness of her, cut down and artificialized.

Young's *Wolsey* is natural and touching. We confess he sur-prised us with the old, quiet, churchman-like tone in which he contrived to keep down (and yet not the less but the more to insinuate) the *Cardinal's* ambition; for this is the style in which a priest might be expected to shew it, at any rate one who had been used to it so long, and who, therefore wore it as a habit, not like the new lawn sleeves of Dr. Philpotts.[2] We think there was hardly *pause* enough in *Wolsey's* manner, when he *first* be-comes sensible of the change in his fortunes, and begins to make melancholy speeches; but the general performance of the part was a rare union of the simple and effective; and the speech,

"Had I served my God," &c., was admirably given. We have not seen Mr. Young a long time, and should hardly have known him, he contrived to look so old and so clerical.

Miss Ellen Tree [3] makes, of course, a good *Anne Bullen,* but the part is only worthy of her inasmuch as it is kept so long before the audience and rendered important as a part of the spectacle. The coronation-scene is made the most of, we suppose in reference to a late spectacle on a greater stage. All the pomps of royalty and of Catholic worship are heaped upon it, and all the town, we suppose, will go and see it. The scenery throughout is beautiful, and true to the period. The apartments are encrusted with Gothic sculpture; and there is a magnificent view of old London, seen over the Thames, as it existed in the age of the Tudors, with old St. Paul's and its spire, and the houses built in that card-like fashion, one story projecting over the other, such as we see them still in a few instances in the Strand and other places.

The house was crowded; nor must we omit to observe, that Miss Kemble, as well as her father and Mr. Young, received great applause.

APPENDIX

WHAT A MASTERLY piece of character is this *Shylock!* and what a noble, an elegant, and wise composition is the whole play! We cannot help quoting here a passage respecting it from the work which has just appeared from the pen of Mr. Hazlitt, and of which it is the least of all its praises to say that it must inevitably supersede the dogmatical and half-informed criticisms of Johnson.

This is a play [says Mr. Hazlitt] that in spite of the change of manners and of prejudices still holds undisputed possession of the stage. Shakespear's malignant has outlived Mr. Cumberland's benevolent Jew. In proportion as *Shylock* has ceased to be a popular bug-bear, "baited with the rabble's curse," he becomes a half-favorite with the philosophical part of the audience, who are disposed to think that *Jewish revenge is at least as good as Christian injuries. Shylock* is *a good hater;* "a man no less sinned against than sinning." If he carries his revenge too far, yet he has strong grounds for "the lodged hate he bears *Anthonio,*" which he explains with equal force of eloquence and reason. He seems the depositary of the vengeance of his race; and though the long habit of brooding over daily insults and injuries has crusted over his temper with inveterate misanthropy, and hardened him against the contempt of mankind, this adds but little to the triumphant pretensions of his enemies. There is a strong, quick, and deep sense of justice mixed up with the gall and bitterness of his resentment. The constant apprehension of being burnt alive, plundered, banished, reviled, and trampled on, might be supposed to sour the most forbearing nature, and to take something from that "milk of human kindness," with which his persecutors contemplated his indignities. The desire of revenge is almost inseparable from the sense of wrong; and we can hardly help sympathizing with the proud spirit hid beneath his "Jewish gaberdin," stung to madness by repeated undeserved provocations, and labouring to throw off the load of obloquy and oppression, heaped upon him and all his tribe, by one desperate act of "lawful" revenge; till the ferociousness of the means by which he is to execute his purpose, and the pertinacity with which he adheres to it, turn us against him; but even at last, when disappointed of the sanguinary revenge with which he had glutted his hopes, and exposed to beggary and contempt by the letter of the law on which he had insisted with so little remorse, we pity him, and think him hardly dealt with by his judges. In all his answers and retorts upon his adversaries, he has the best, not only of the argument, but of the question, reasoning on their own principles and practice. They are so far from allowing of any measure of equal dealing, of common justice or humanity, between themselves and the Jew, that even when they come to ask a favour of him, and *Shylock* reminds them that "on such a day they spit upon him, another spurned him, another called him dog, and for these curtesies request he'll lend them so much monies," *Anthonio*, his old enemy, instead of any acknowledgement of the shrewdness and justice of his remonstrance, which would have been preposterous in a respectable Catholic merchant in those times, threatens him with a repetition of the same treatment—

> I am as like to call thee so again,
> To spit on thee again, to spurn thee too.

After this, the appeal to the Jew's mercy, as if there were any common principle of right and wrong between them, is the rankest hypocrisy, or blindest prejudice; and the Jew's answer to one of *Anthonio's* friends, who asks him what his pound of forfeit flesh is good for, is irresistible:—

"To bait fish withal; if it will feed nothing else, it will feed my revenge. He hath disgraced me, and hindered me of half a million; laughed at my losses, mocked at my gains, scorned my nation, thwarted my bargains, cool'd my friends, heated mine enemies; and what's his reason? I am a Jew. Hath not a Jew eyes; hath not a Jew hands, organs, dimensions, senses, affections, passions; fed with the same food, hurt with the same weapons, subject to the same diseases, healed by the same means, warmed and cooled by the same winters and summers that a Christian is? If you prick us, do we not bleed? If you tickle us do we not laugh? If you poison us, do we not die? And if you wrong us, shall we not revenge? If we are like you in the rest, we will resemble you in that. If a Jew wrong a Christian, what is his humility? revenge. If a Christian wrong a Jew, what should his sufferance be by Christian example? why, revenge. The villainy you teach me I will execute; and it shall go hard but I will better the instruction."

If we could add any thing to these and the remaining observations, it might perhaps be this: that the great and wise poet who could find "a soul of goodness in things evil" has, after all, given virtues both to his Christians and his Jew; though we suspect that the main feeling he had in writing the play was to give a kindly lecture to the egotism of sects and opinions. He has indeed spoken of certain things and persons in a manner which might startle a Christian assembly, if what he said did not come in the midst of such a heap of humane wisdom, as takes the vain as well as charitable part of us unawares, and anticipates objection by making it seem ignorant and brutal. In truth, the whole audience at this play are a set of involuntary philosophers, and with one accord forget their prejudices for the sake of their feelings. But how humane is the poet throughout! The conduct of the Christians to the Jew is infamous and hard-hearted; and that of the Jew in return would seem still more so, if it had not been so outrageously provoked; yet he contrives to shew us, in the former instance, that the hard-heartedness arises not from want of feeling but from prejudice; and in the latter, that the love of revenge is of a social rather than a personal and selfish nature, *Shylock*, as Mr. Hazlitt observes, seeming "the depositary of the vengeance of his race." Thus the Jew loves his tribe, and his daughter; and sets a special value on his ring because it was given him by his wife Leah; and on the same principle of humanity, the Christians, who are shocking persecutors, afford examples nevertheless of gallant and excellent friends; and though they have the shameful indecency to claim a mercy which they do not show, are full of charity out of the pale of their faith. The more this immortal poet is considered the more he will be found superior to all times and circumstances, and the more we shall feel inclined to echo the words of the German critic, who, with the exception of a few scattered criticisms from Mr. Lamb, had hitherto been the only writer who seemed truly to *understand* as well as feel him. "In strength a demigod," says Schlegel, "in profundity of view a prophet, in all-seeing wisdom a protecting spirit of a higher order, he lowers himself to mortals, as if unconscious of his superiority; and is as open and unassuming as a child."

What particularly charms us in the *Merchant of Venice* is the *friendship*—a virtue, of which Shakespeare appears to have had an intense feeling. It is not affected with him, nor interested, nor formal, nor at the mercy of circumstances of any sort. We could imagine Shakespeare to be left by a friend, because we can easily imagine persons ambitious to be his friends, and unable from vain or bad qualities of their own to remain so; but we cannot imagine him leaving one himself, or not clinging to him as long as the other desired it, or as long as he had need of it, and was not an absolute traitor: nay, we can fancy his clinging even then, at least in his pity and his silence, and revering to the last the spirit of what he thought *had* been. For our parts, we boast somewhat to our own minds of our enthusiasm for this quality, though perhaps our feeling of it is as inferior to his, as all our other qualities are; but we believe that we possess two or three friends that would have been worthy of him; one, at any rate, we have proved with all good proof; and we could not hear the noble conclusion of the first scene of the first act, without feeling, in our eyes, unaccustomed but far from unhappy tears. *Esto perpetua.*
—"Theatrical Examiner," *Examiner* (July 20, 1817), pp. 457–458.

NOTES

1. "Theatrical Examiner," No. 1, *Examiner* (Jan. 3, 1808), pp. 11–13. The following passage from Steele at first appeared below the "Theatrical Examiner" heading:

It is with me a matter of the highest consideration what parts are well or ill performed, what passions or sentiments are indulged or cultivated, and consequently what manners and customs are transfused from the Stage to the world, which reciprocally imitate each other.—Spectator. No. 370.

In the *Examiner* of Nov. 12, 1809 (p. 728), Hunt again reviewed *Much Ado*, adding "one fresh remark" to his previous comments:

Dr. Johnson objects to the similarity of contrivances practised on the two wits of the piece; and Mr. Steevens, too, wishes "that some other method had been found to entrap *Beatrice*, than that very one which before had been successfully practised on *Benedick.*" The uniformity of the case however appears to me to be a great beauty. The same tempers are naturally caught in the same way, and two lovers must be gratified to find that the same sort of appeal was thought requisite to both their feelings. There is an equalization in the artifice, that seems to regard them as persons made for each other.

Hunt's opinion recalls A. W. Schlegel's, expressed in his twenty-fourth lecture at Vienna, 1808; published 1811, and reprinted in *Lectures on Dramatic Art and Literature.* tr. John Black, 2d ed. rev. by Rev. A. J. W. Morrison (London: Geo. Bell & Sons, 1904), p. 386.

Some one or other, not over-stocked with penetration, has objected to the same artifice being twice used in entrapping them [Benedick and Beatrice]; the drollery, however, lies in the very symmetry of the deception. Their friends attribute the whole effect to their own device; but the exclusive direction of their raillery against each other is in itself a proof of a growing inclination.

(Future references to Schlegel's dramatic criticism will be to this edition.)

Coleridge, discussing the "Characteristics of Shakespeare," remarked that the use of the same stratagem in Benedick and Beatrice was justified, and that the interest of the play depended on the characters, not the plot. Cf. *Coleridge's Shakespearean Criticism*, ed. T. M. Raysor (Cambridge, Mass.: Harvard University Press, 1930), I,

226. (Future references to Coleridge's Shakespeare criticism will be to this edition.)

2. This could be either Charles Dibdin, the younger (1768–1833), or his brother Thomas John Dibdin (1771–1841), both prolific playwrights. Hunt probably meant the latter, whom he had attacked earlier in the *News*. See the introduction to *Dramatic Essays. Leigh Hunt,* ed. W. Archer and R. W. Lowe (London: Walter Scott, Ltd., 1894), pp. xxvii–xxix. (This book will be referred to hereafter as Archer and Lowe.) Another attack on Tom Dibdin followed in the "Theatrical Examiner" for April 10, 1808.

3. A theme developed by Schlegel in his twenty-third lecture at Vienna, 1808 (*op. cit.,* pp. 374–376).

4. Inexactly quoted from Johnson's life of Congreve. Cf. Samuel Johnson, *Lives of the English Poets,* ed. Geo. Birkbeck Hill (Oxford· Clarendon Press, 1905), II, 228.

5. The actors referred to in this paragraph—William Thomas Lewis (1748?–1811), Robert William Elliston (1774–1831), and John Fawcett (1768–1837)—are characterized by Hunt in his *Critical Essays on the Performers of the London Theatres* (dated 1807; actually published at the beginning of 1808). The articles on Lewis and Elliston are reprinted by Archer and Lowe.

6. Mrs. Henry Erskine Johnston (1782–?).

7. Mrs. Dorothy or Dorothea Jordan (1762–1816) was one of the most successful actresses of comedy in her day; for a long time she was the mistress of the Duke of Clarence, later William IV, to whom she bore ten children. Hunt describes her in the *Critical Essays* (1807), reprinted in Archer and Lowe.

8. Maria Rebecca Duncan, later Mrs. James Davison (1780?–1858). Hunt praises her Beatrice in the "Theatrical Examiner" for Nov. 12, 1809; see also his *Critical Essays* (1807).

9. John Philip Kemble (1757–1823), the famous Shakespearian actor, manager of Covent Garden.

10. See Hunt's articles on pantomime, pp. 140–145, below.

11. See Ambrosius Theodosius Macrobius, *Saturnaliorum Conviviorum Librii VII,* ii, 7.

MR. T. DIBDIN'S MOCK-MELODRAMA

1. "Theatrical Examiner," No. 15, *Examiner* (April 10, 1808), pp. 234–235. Thomas John Dibdin (1771–1841), prolific writer of farces and melodramas, was a favorite target for Hunt's scorn.

2. For an account of the melodramas of this period, see Allardyce Nicoll, *A History of Early Nineteenth Century Drama, 1800–1850*

(New York: The Macmillan Co.; Cambridge, England: Cambridge University Press, 1930), I, 100–120. As Mr. Nicoll points out, the early nineteenth century theatres were "the home *par excellence* of spectacularism and of melodramatic effect," I, 100.

3. Boileau's famous mock-epic, of which the first part appeared in 1674, and the whole after the poet's death in 1711.

4. Henry Fielding's satiric drama *The Tragedy of Tragedies; or, The Life and Death of Tom Thumb the Great,* first performed in 1730.

5. John Philips' *The Splendid Shilling, an Imitation of Milton,* 1705.

"KING LEAR" REVIVED

1. "Theatrical Examiner," No. 18, *Examiner* (May 22, 1808), 331–333. This review is historically significant in romantic Shakespeare criticism. It appeared in the same spring that Schlegel was lecturing on Shakespeare in Vienna, and Coleridge on Shakespeare at the Royal Institution. Hunt's sympathy with the romantic point of view is apparent here in his attack on Dr. Johnson and the neo-classical objection to Shakespeare's disregard of poetic justice. Shakespeare made *King Lear* end unhappily, asserts Hunt, because real nature requires such a tragedy. Through this review and certain of his later articles on the drama, Hunt added impetus to the English romantic movement by his adoption of romantic criteria in an influential newspaper which gave his ideas a wide dissemination, that is, in the *Examiner*. This contribution of Hunt's to romanticism has not, to our knowledge, been pointed out.

2. Nahum Tate (1652–1715); George Colman, the elder (1732–1794). Hunt constantly protested against the alteration of Shakespeare. Ten years later, he condemned the addition to *Romeo and Juliet* of a passage in which Romeo survived the poison long enough to talk to Juliet. (Cf. *Examiner,* April 5, 1818, p. 219.) To Hunt, such an addition was not only an irreverence to Shakespeare, but an overloading of tragedy which the great dramatist would never have effected.

3. Hunt's belief that the Fool is out of date and could well be omitted from the play differs strikingly from the opinion of Coleridge: ". . . the contrast of the Fool wonderfully heightens the colouring of some of the most painful situations. . . ." (1811 lecture, *Coleridge's Shakespearean Criticism,* ed. T. M. Raysor, II, 73); he is "unlike all the other fools of Shakespeare, and one of the profoundest and most astonishing of his characters" (1812 lecture, *ibid.,* II, 245); "With Shakespeare his comic constantly re-acted on his tragic char-

acters. Lear, wandering amidst the tempest, had all his feelings of distress increased by the overflowings of the wild wit of the Fool . . . ; thus even his comic humour tends to the development of tragic passion" (1813 lecture, *ibid.*, II, 266).

4. Hunt's comments on the conclusion of *Lear* should be compared with those of Schlegel, expressed in this same year. Cordelia's death, said Schlegel,

has been thought too cruel; and in England the piece is in acting so far altered that she remains victorious and happy. I must own, I cannot conceive what ideas of art and dramatic connexion those persons have who suppose that we can at pleasure tack a double conclusion to a tragedy; a melancholy one for hard-hearted spectators, and a happy one for souls of a softer mould. After surviving so many sufferings, Lear can only die; and what more truly tragic end for him than to die from grief for the death of Cordelia? and if he is also to be saved and to pass the remainder of his days in happiness, the whole loses its signification. According to Shakspeare's plan the guilty, it is true, are all punished, for wickedness destroys itself; but the virtues that would bring help and succour are everywhere too late, or overmatched by the cunning activity of malice. The persons of this drama have only such a faint belief in Providence as heathens may be supposed to have; and the poet here wishes to show us that this belief requires a wider range than the dark pilgrimage on earth to be established in full extent.—*Op. cit.*, p. 405.

The portion of Schlegel's lectures which covered Shakespeare was published in 1811, in German. Hunt said that he did not read German. See L. A. Brewer, *My Leigh Hunt Library: the Holograph Letters* (Iowa City: University of Iowa Press, 1938), p. 300; and "Specimens of Celebrated Authors: Goethe," *Leigh Hunt's London Journal* (July 30, 1834), I, 142. Nevertheless, he was familiar with Schlegel, probably through the translation of John Black (1815), and declared that prior to Hazlitt, Schlegel "with the exception of a few scattered criticisms from Mr. Lamb" was "the only writer who seemed truly to *understand* as well as feel" Shakespeare (*Examiner*, July 20, 1817, p. 458).

Charles Lamb similarly protested against Tate's alteration of *King Lear*, in his essay "On the Tragedies of Shakespeare . . . ," published in the *Reflector*, No. IV (1812).

5. See Dr. Johnson's notes in his edition of Shakespeare, 1765. *Johnson on Shakespeare*, ed. Walter Raleigh, (London: Oxford University Press, 1931 [c. 1908]), pp. 161–162.

6. William Richardson, professor of humanity at the University of Glasgow, in 1783 published *Essays on Shakespeare's Dramatic Characters of Richard III, King Lear, and Timon of Athens, with an Essay on the Faults of Shakespeare.*

7. Rowe's text.

8. ". . . o'er bog and quagmire. . . ."

9. ". . . could I have him now,—and there,—and there again, and there."

10. *King Lear*, III, iv, 46–66, 69–73.

11. Dryden, *Absalom and Achitophel*, ll. 163–164. Line 163: "Great wits are sure to madness near allied." Cf. *The Works of John Dryden*, ed. Sir Walter Scott, revised by George Saintsbury (Edinburgh: Wm. Paterson, 1882–1893), IX (1884), 239.

12. *King Lear*, V, iii, 271–273.

13. *Ibid.*, V, iii, 305–311.

14. With this criticism of John Philip Kemble as Lear, cf. Hunt's later review of Edmund Kean in the part:

We must confess indeed (to resume the style royal of criticism) that since we have witnessed Mr. Kean's performance of *Lear,* we are the less unwilling to cut short the theatrical part of our subjects: for we are unfortunate enough to differ with our brother critics upon its scale of merit. We say unfortunate, not because it is our business to lament a mere difference of opinion in general or upon all points; but because there are some writers with whom we like to agree as we do with pleasant company; and because we would rather fall in at all times with the general opinion, where it is on the side of approbation and enthusiasm. Mr. Kean's performance of *Lear* is undoubtedly better than any other actor's is likely to be, with whom we are acquainted. There are even some touches in it, in the more familiar and domestic parts at the end, which are masterly and complete. It is consequently worth going to see by all who are not frightened away by the visible anatomizing of a tortured old heart, or by Mr. Tate's endeavours to patch it up again, and make it "live happy after." But we are exceedingly sceptical as to the power of any actor to represent such a mind as *Lear's,* just as we are in the case of *Hamlet.* The acting faculty is a thing not intellectual or sensitive enough: and if it were, it would defeat itself; it would sink under such a wear and tear of the union of thought and passion with the physical representation of it. Still, to confess the truth, we had higher expectations of Mr. Kean's *Lear* than we found realized. We were afraid that, though not good enough, he would be too good a representative of the maddened old father. The obstinacy of the character, we thought, would be a suitable substratum for him to work on; and we knew he could be pathetic, for he is highly so in *Othello.* But *Othello* is a common every-day person to *Lear*—we mean in the cast of his intellect. The latter is all imagination as well as passion; and here it was, we think, that Mr. Kean found himself baffled; for however appearances may have been since, we shrewdly suspect that on the first night, neither he nor his audience well knew what to make of the business. All the imaginative parts—the whole scene of the storm for instance—fell as flat as the actor's voice. His favourite piece of abruptness, the one sudden drop of his voice, would not do here. It was not enough by a hundred. *Lear* should have been all abruptness and *distraction*, a mind torn a hundred ways; not one, nor fifty. Mr. Kean fairly seemed to *read* most of the passages. His best touches consisted in looking stedfastly, and moving his hands about. But he should have looked a hundred ways and things; he should have varied his voice as often: he should have been loud, and low, and monotonous, and tossing about, and loud again, "like the vexed sea," and quaint, and fantastic, and full of a sort of mockery of his own dignity without altogether losing it, and silent by fits, and shifting from place to place, and making fantastic postures on the ground, and even hanging his hands idiotically, and running helplessly about, shaking his old impotent gray locks. But then how could all this have been borne? An actor who performs *Lear* truly, should so terrify and shake the town, as to be requested never to perform the part again. If he does this, he does it well. If not, he does not do it at all. There is no medium, in a scene which we are to witness with our *eyes*, between an unbearable *Lear*, and no *Lear*. In Shakespeare's time, the scenery, dresses, &c. were so unlike any thing real, and the public came so much more to hear the *writing* of the thing than to see the acting of it, that it was comparatively another matter; but now that the real man is before us, with his white beard, and the storm howling about him, we ought not to be able to endure the sight, any more than that of a mad old father in the public street. And indeed we are little able to do so, as it is.—*Examiner* (April 30, 1820), pp. 278–279.

Hazlitt, like Hunt, was unfavorably impressed by Kean's performance. For the general reception in 1820 of Kean's Lear, see H. N. Hillebrand, *Edmund Kean* (New York: Columbia University Press, 1933), p. 191.

15. Charles Kemble (1775–1854), youngest of the three Kemble brothers, and father of Fanny Kemble. Hunt characterizes him in the *Critical Essays* (1807), reprinted in Archer and Lowe.

MR. YOUNG'S MERITS CONSIDERED

1. "Theatrical Examiner," No. 39, *Examiner* (Jan. 15, 1809), pp. 43–45.

2. Charles Mayne Young (1777–1856) first played in London on June 22, 1807. Joseph Knight says of him that he "became accepted as the leading English tragedian, until his supremacy was challenged, first by Kean [1814] and subsequently by Macready. . . . Young was perhaps the most distinguished member of the Kemble school. He had to undergo formidable comparisons with Kemble first, then with Kean and Macready, held his place creditably, and had a small world which believed him superior to all competitors."—J. Knight, "Charles Mayne Young," *Dictionary of National Biography* (1937), XXI, 1281–1282.

3. Edward Moore's play, first produced in 1753.

4. John Henderson (1747–1785), a rival of David Garrick (1717–1779), and considered to have ranked next to him.

5. Richard Burbage (1567?–1619), Shakespeare's famous contemporary and a member of his company. Thomas Betterton (1635?–1710), one of the great Shakespearian actors.

6. James Quin (1693–1766); Henry Mossop (1729?–1774?); Barton Booth (1681–1733); Spranger Barry (1719–1777); John Mills (d. 1736).

7. *Macbeth*, II, i, 38–39.

8. *Ibid.*, II, i, 49–50.

9. Mrs. Sarah Siddons (1755–1831), the great Shakespearian actress; sister to John Philip, Stephen, and Charles Kemble. See Hunt's earlier appraisal of her in the *Critical Essays* (1807), reprinted in Archer and Lowe.

10. *Macbeth*, III, iv, 106–107.

11. Henry Siddons (1774–1815), son of Mrs. Sarah Siddons. Hunt speaks disparagingly of him in the *Critical Essays* (1807).

[COVENT-GARDEN REDECORATED; O.P. RIOT]

1. "Theatrical Examiner," No. 52, *Examiner* (Sept. 24, 1809), pp. 618–620. Hunt describes here the first of the O.P. (Old Price) riots, occasioned by public resentment at the increased prices charged at the Covent Garden Theatre when it reopened on Sept. 18, 1809. The old building had been destroyed by fire. John Philip Kemble, as manager, finally compromised with the leaders of the rioters on Dec. 14, 1809, but he and all the Kembles were temporarily unpopular during the disturbances.

2. George Colman, the Younger (1762–1836), dramatist and manager of the Haymarket Theatre; Richard Brinsley Sheridan (1751–1816), the famous dramatist, statesman, and manager of Drury Lane Theatre; Thomas Harris (d. 1820), proprietor and stage-manager of Covent Garden Theatre.

3. Angelica Catalani (1780–1849), Italian dramatic soprano, who first sang in London in 1806.

4. According to Joseph Knight: "An influential committee, consisting of the solicitor-general, Sir Thomas Plumer, the recorder of the city of London, John Silvester, Alderman Sir Charles Price, bart., M.P., John Whitmore, governor of the Bank of England, and John Julius Angerstein, drew up a report in favour of the management, but this, like other efforts, proved futile."—"John Philip Kemble," *Dictionary of National Biography* (1937), X, 1264.

[THE O.P. RIOTS AND COVENT-GARDEN]

1. "Theatrical Examiner," No. 58, *Examiner* (Nov. 19, 1809), pp. 744–745. See the preceding article for an account of the first riots. The retainers mentioned here were men hired by the management to suppress the rioters who objected to the increased price of admission.

2. Lumley St. George Skeffington (1771–1850), a great dandy and inconsequential playwright, who set the fashions for the young men of his day. Byron has a sneering passage on him in the *English Bards and Scotch Reviewers*, ll. 590–604. In 1835, however, Hunt speaks of him as

the most good-natured of men. We remember him thirty years ago, gracing the theatre with his bland and well-dressed presence, and diffusing urbanity in the boxes around him, to the shame (had they been wise enough to feel any) of the petulant young critics of those days; and there is he still, the immortal *beau garçon*, adorning the same places, leading the same pleasant life, and encouraging the same talents of the young and fair. *Leigh Hunt's London Journal* (Dec. 5, 1835), II, 426.

[THE CONSCIOUS LOVERS]

1. "Theatrical Examiner," No. 63, *Examiner* (Jan. 21, 1810), pp. 40–41. Steele's last comedy, produced at Drury Lane, November, 1722. Genest in *Some Account of the English Stage* records that the *Conscious Lovers* was performed on Jan. 16, 1810, at Covent Garden, and on April 25, 1818, at Bath. Many years later, Hunt wrote: "I must own that I prefer open-hearted Steele with all his faults, to Addison with all his essays."—(*The Autobiography of Leigh Hunt*, ed. Edmund Blunden (Oxford University Press, 1928), pp. 56–57. The present article is Hunt's only one on Steele.

2. Thomas Dibdin (1771–1841); Frederic Reynolds (1764–1841); James Cobb (1756–1818).

3. Charles Kemble (1775–1854). Hunt characterized him in the *Critical Essays* (1807), reprinted in Archer and Lowe.

4. Maria Theresa Kemble, Mrs. Charles Kemble (1774–1838).

5. Richard Jones (1779–1851), a popular comedian commonly known as "Gentleman Jones."

[KING JOHN]

1. "Theatrical Examiner," No. 70, *Examiner* (June 3, 1810), p. 344.

2. From the notes to Dr. Johnson's edition of Shakespeare, 1765. Cf. *Johnson on Shakespeare*, ed. Walter Raleigh, p. 109.

3. The romantic idolatry of Shakespeare, characteristic of this period, is suggested by Hunt's defense of the inferiority of the play: If *King John* is poorer than some of Shakespeare's other plays, nevertheless Shakespeare is not at fault, but his subject, which has failed to draw forth his utmost powers.

4. This praise of Kemble is infrequent with Hunt, who more often objected to Kemble's manner of acting. The dignified part of King John, however, was well suited to Kemble's style. The preceding year Hunt had written of him: ". . . whatever may be his defects in parts of more nature [than Cato], [he] is unrivalled in characters of studious and dignified severity."—*Examiner* (Feb. 5, 1809), p. 95. Cf. also Hunt's long characterization of Kemble in the *Critical Essays* (1807), reprinted in Archer and Lowe.

In 1831, Hunt reviewed a performance of James Prescott Warde (1792–1840), in *King John* at Covent Garden:

King John is the best character that we remember to have seen this player perform; yet we cannot congratulate him on his having the right notion of it. It is indeed a high difficulty for any actor to attain to the right performance of one of Shakspeare's characters; and Mr. Warde, like many a one before him, is to seek in the whole matter. He takes any stage King for Shakspeare's. He does not ventriloquise with the King in the play. He does not throw himself into it, and become part of it; he crowns himself, Warde, takes a sceptre into his hand, or an additional elevation into his head, and thinks that the tip-top of Mr. Warde's manner is the perfection of the poet's design. Oh let him not believe it. The best *King John* we ever saw was Macready's. There was more of the weakness and vacillation of the real historical character in it than in any other; and the very hair was so dressed as to resemble the King's upon the coin. What it wanted was the poetry: we do not mean the mouthing and the declamation, but the imaginative grace—not the consciousness of the wording, but the rich and varied consciousness of the thoughts. The late Mr. Kemble's *King John* was the *beau ideal* of the King theatrical; very clever too, and not unimpressive in parts, but *too* conscious, and putting the manner before the matter. Mr. Warde's *King John* is Mr. Kemble's with the ideal taken out of it and a coarse grain put in. John Kemble, though he always gave you the idea of an actor, gave you that of an actor who had something of the romantic or elevated in his own personal character: Mr. Warde succeeds only in giving you that of something peremptory and assuming.—*Tatler* (April 14, 1831), II, 763.

[TWELFTH NIGHT]

1. "Theatrical Examiner," No. 88, *Examiner* (March 3, 1811), pp. 140–141. Cf. Hunt's review of *Twelfth Night* in the *Examiner* (Nov. 12, 1820), pp. 227–231, below.

2. From the notes to Dr. Johnson's edition of Shakespeare, 1765. Cf. *Johnson on Shakespeare*, ed. Walter Raleigh, p. 93.

3. *Twelfth Night*, V, i, 230–231.

4. Sarah Booth (1793–1867).

5. William Blanchard (1769–1835). Hunt characterizes him in the *Critical Essays* (1807).

6. In a letter, watermarked 1813, Mrs. Kemble requested Hunt to publish certain critiques in the *Examiner*. "The London Journals," she asserted, "are the only dependable vehicles for such information and *The Examiner* of all other papers the most read and best credited. . . ."—Luther A. Brewer, *My Leigh Hunt Library, The Holograph Letters* (Iowa City: University of Iowa Press, 1938), p. 97.

7. John Emery (1777–1822). Hunt characterizes him in the *Critical Essays* (1807), reprinted in Archer and Lowe.

8. William Barrymore, a minor dramatist who was also an actor.

9. Daniel Egerton (1772–1835).

[BLUE BEARD]

1. "Theatrical Examiner," No. 90, *Examiner* (March 24, 1811), pp. 186–188.

2. *Blue Beard; or, Female Curiosity*, by George Colman, the Younger (1762–1836), was a musical entertainment first acted in 1798. Hunt contributed an essay on Colman to the *Edinburgh Review* (July, 1841), which is reprinted in *Leigh Hunt as Poet and Essayist*, ed. Charles Kent (London, New York: Frederick Warne & Co., 1889).

3. For a contemporary reaction to these horses, cf. the "Theatrical Examiner" (July 21, 1811), pp. 50–51, below.

4. Cf. Scene 9 of Fielding's *The Tragedy of Tragedies; or, The Life and Death of Tom Thumb the Great.*

[QUADRUPEDS]

1. "Theatrical Examiner," No. 97, *Examiner* (July 21, 1811), pp. 470–471. See the preceding review of *Blue Beard* for Hunt's objections to the use of quadrupeds.

2. The Covent Garden Theatre was destroyed by fire in September, 1808, rebuilt, and opened to the public in September, 1809.

3. A mock-tragedy first presented at the Haymarket Theatre, July 2, 1767, with Samuel Foote (1720–1777) in the part of Francisco. According to Genest, the author's name is unknown. Hunt later said

of the *Quadrupeds,* "This most lofty of tragedies is the best written burlesque next to *Tom Thumb,* though with a long interval."—"Play-Goer," *Tatler* (Nov. 10, 1830), I, 231. The 1830 version was an amplified one.

4. William Lovegrove (1778–1816).

[M.P.; OR, THE BLUE STOCKING]

1. "Theatrical Examiner," No. 99, *Examiner* (Sept. 15, 1811), pp. 593–596. This review is believed to have brought about the acquaintance of Moore and Hunt. For Moore's letters to Hunt concerning *The Blue Stocking,* see Hunt's long article on Moore in the *Tatler* (Jan. 11, 1831), II, 442, and see also Hunt's *Examiner* review of the *Irish Melodies* (Jan. 3 and 17, 1819).

2. Thomas Shadwell (1642?–1692); Thomas D'Urfey (1653–1723).

3. Moore's comic opera *The Gipsy Prince* was first performed at the Haymarket, July 24, 1801, and was given about ten times. Genest (*op. cit.,* VII, 522) quotes the Dramatic Censor as saying "it was a very poor piece." Moore also wrote, in 1804, a tragedy entitled *Montbar; or, The Buccaneers.* Neither Genest nor Professor Allardyce Nicoll record any performance of it.

4. An allusion to the licentiousness of Moore's early verse.

5. William Oxberry (1784–1824).

6. Charles Edward Horn (1786–1849), singer and composer.

7. Mrs. Rosoman Mountain (1768?–1841).

8. Thomas Philipps (1774–1841), vocalist and composer.

9. Frances Maria Kelly (1790–1882), the actress whom Charles Lamb loved.

10. Andrew Cherry (1762–1812), actor and dramatist.

11. Isaac Pocock (1782–1835), painter and dramatist.

12. Pope's *Dunciad,* II, 295–298.

[ORATORIO]

1. "Theatrical Examiner," No. 108, *Examiner* (Feb. 20, 1812), pp. 74–75.

2. St. Hugh of Avalon (1135?–1200), Bishop of Lincoln.

3. Feast of Charles I, Martyr.

4. Probably two brothers: Charles Ashley (c. 1770–1818), a violinist who played Viotti concertos for the violin with the composer Viotti himself; and Charles Jane Ashley (1773–1843), an accomplished cellist and accompanist.

5. Mrs. Maria Theresa Bland (1769–1838), operatic soprano and ballad singer.

6. Mrs. Maria Dickons (1770–1833), English operatic singer.

7. John Stafford Smith (1750–1836), music antiquary, tenor, organist, and composer. The melody for the *Star Spangled Banner* was taken from Smith's *Anacreon in Heaven.*

8. motions] motion. Cf. *The Works of John Milton,* ed. Frank A. Patterson and others (New York: Columbia University Press, 1931–1938), I (1931), p. 28. (Hereafter referred to as The Columbia *Milton.*)

[JULIUS CAESAR]

1. "Theatrical Examiner," No. 112, published in two parts in the *Examiner* (March 29, and April 5, 1812), pp. 204, 217–218.

2. With Dr. Johnson's opinion, contrast that expressed by Coleridge in his marginal notes: "The power of interesting never was more strongly manifested than in these plays [*Julius Caesar* and *Antony and Cleopatra*]. Why, they really are flesh and blood individuals. More true pathos in Brutus and Cassius' quarrel."—*Coleridge's Shakespearean Criticism,* ed. T. M. Raysor, I, 13. Cf. also Coleridge's note: "I know no part of Shakespeare that more impresses on me the belief of his genius being superhuman than this scene [IV, iii. The quarrel of Brutus and Cassius]"—*Ibid.,* I, 18.

3. From the notes to Dr. Johnson's edition of Shakespeare, 1765. Cf. *Johnson on Shakespeare,* ed. Walter Raleigh, p. 179.

4. Hunt at this time did not know the work of Schlegel. Observe, however, Hunt's statement in 1817, that prior to Hazlitt and "with the exception of a few scattered criticisms from Mr. Lamb," A. W. Schlegel was "the only writer who seemed truly to *understand* as well as feel" Shakespeare.—*Examiner* (July 20, 1817), p. 458.

5. Charles Gildon (1665–1724).

6. Beginning of the second part of the review, "Theatrical Examiner," No. 113 (April 5, 1812).

7. Daniel Egerton (1772–1835).

[MRS. SIDDONS' FAREWELL PERFORMANCE]

1. "Theatrical Examiner," No. 119, *Examiner* (July 5, 1812), pp. 428–429.

2. Daniel Terry (1780?–1829).

3. William Dowton (1764–1851), earlier characterized by Hunt in his *Critical Essays* (1807), reprinted in Archer and Lowe.

4. Horace Twiss (1787–1849), nephew of Mrs. Siddons.

5. Queen Katharine in *Henry VIII*, and Constance in *King John.* Hunt's description of Mrs. Siddons should be compared with that in his *Critical Essays* (1807), reprinted in Archer and Lowe.

6. In Otway's *Venice Preserved.*

7. As a tribute to Mrs. Siddons, Reynolds signed his name on this portrait on the hem of her garment. For an account of the painting, see Yvonne Ffrench, *Mrs. Siddons: Tragic Actress* (London: Cobden-Sanderson, 1936), pp. 108–110.

[THE BEGGAR'S OPERA]

1. "Theatrical Examiner," No. 122, *Examiner* (Sept. 13, 1812), pp. 589–590.

2. One of Hunt's favorite plays. For example, he reviewed Miss Greene in the part of Polly for the *Examiner* (Sept. 24, 1820), but the whole article discussed certain actresses rather than the play itself. Another review appeared in the *Tatler* (Dec. 27, 1831).

3. Charles Incledon (1763–1826), a popular tenor who first sang in London in 1790, and who won his best success as a ballad singer. In the *Critical Essays* (1807), Hunt wrote of him, Incledon "has really a finer voice than any English singer on the stage, ever succeeds in descriptions of his former [naval] life, but when he attempts a love-song or any other more refined part of his science, . . . cannot help reminding us of the sailor. . . ."—*Dramatic Essays. Leigh Hunt,* ed. Archer and Lowe, p. 53.

NOTE UPON DESDEMONA

1. *Examiner* (Aug. 14, 1814), pp. 525–526. An article by William Hazlitt "On Mr. Kean's Iago" had been published in two parts in the *Examiner* for July 24 and Aug. 7, 1814. The passage which Hunt quotes here had appeared as a footnote to Hazlitt's article for Aug. 7, and was probably added by Thomas Barnes, then the theatrical critic for the *Examiner* and later well known as the editor of the *Times.* The footnote is not reprinted in the standard editions of Hazlitt's works as a part of his article. On Sept. 4, Barnes replied to Hazlitt in the "Theatrical Examiner," and a week later Hazlitt responded with a letter to the *Examiner.* The dispute over Kean's Iago was terminated by Barnes on Sept. 18, with a reply to Hazlitt in the "Theatrical Examiner." Hunt's contribution was written from the Surrey Gaol.

2. Cf. Schlegel's interpretation (1808) of Desdemona:

She is not, it is true, a high ideal representation of sweetness and enthusiastic passion like Juliet; full of simplicity, softness, and humility, and so innocent, that she can hardly form to herself an idea of the possibility of infidelity, she seems calculated to make the most yielding and tenderest of wives. The female propensity wholly to resign itself to a foreign destiny has led her into the only fault of her life, that of marrying without her father's consent. Her choice seems wrong; and yet she has been gained over to Othello by that which induces the female to honour in man her protector and guide,—admiration of his determined heroism, and compassion for the sufferings which he had undergone.—*Lectures on Dramatic Art and Literature,* p. 403.

On Feb. 21, 1831, Hunt reviewed *Othello* for the *Tatler,* concluding with a characterization of Desdemona:

This character of Desdemona is one of the loveliest ever conceived. She has the heart of a child with all the feelings of a woman. She is generous, painstaking, patient, pleasurable, unwitting of ill. Her ruin comes of her goodness. Some gross commentators have delighted, by Iago's help, to discover that she was more sensitive than she need be, or at least not less so than the liveliest of her sex. Why should she be, if she was good and warm-hearted? She fell in love with Othello for his mind and soul first, and for all which he had gone through. True sympathy was the ground of her passion. If upon this, all the rest of her being followed, and we are to suppose that her love was a world of pleasure as well as pride to her, it only shows that she was in every respect the woman she ought to have been—as perfect in body as in heart. Grossness is when there is no heart at all, and no just passion.—"Edmund Kean as Othello," *Dramatic Essays, Leigh Hunt,* ed. W. Archer and R. W. Lowe, pp. 208–209.

3. Artificer of fraud; and was the first
   That practisd falshood under saintly shew.—*Paradise Lost,* IV,
   121–122 (Columbia *Milton,* II, 110).

ON RESUMING OUR THEATRICAL CRITICISM

1. "Theatrical Examiner," No. 186, *Examiner* (Jan. 1, 1815), p. 11; written while Hunt was in prison. He and his brother were released on Feb. 2, 1815.

2. Hunt was a theatrical critic for the *News,* 1805–1807. Prior to that he had published poetry and about 1804 had contributed some articles (now lost) to the *Traveller,* entitled "Mr. Town, Critic and Censor General."

3. Eliza O'Neil, later Lady Becher (1791–1872). From 1814 to 1819, she was one of the most successful actresses on the English stage in both comedy and tragedy.

THE COMIC ACTRESSES

1. "Theatrical Examiner," No. 187, *Examiner* (Jan. 8, 1815), pp. 25–26: "Sketches of the Performers."

2. Elizabeth Farren, Countess of Derby (1759?–1829), was reputed to have been skillful in the parts of fine ladies. She last appeared on the stage in 1797.

3. Jane Pope (1742–1818), an excellent actress who played Mrs. Candour in the first performance of *The School for Scandal*, 1777. Retired in 1808. Characterized in Hunt's *Critical Essays* (1807), reprinted in Archer and Lowe.

4. Arthur Murphy's play *The Citizen* was first performed at Drury Lane, Feb. 7, 1761.

5. Elizabeth Rebecca Edwin (1771?–1854).

6. Maria Theresa Kemble (1774–1838).

7. Mary Ann Davenport (1765?–1843).

8. Sarah Harlowe (1765–1852).

9. Mary Ann Orger (1788–1849).

THE TRAGIC ACTRESSES

1. "Theatrical Examiner," No. 188, *Examiner* (Jan. 15, 1815), pp. 38–39: "Sketches of the Performers."

2. Mrs. Sarah Bartley (1783–1850).

3. Mrs. Siddons had retired from the stage in 1812.

4. William Enfield's *The Speaker: or, Miscellaneous Pieces, Selected from the Best English Writers, and Disposed under Proper Heads, with a View to Facilitate the Improvement of Youth in Reading and Speaking; to Which Is Prefixed an Essay on Elocution* (London: Jos. Johnson, 1774). Often reprinted.

5. Mrs. Julia Glover (1779–1850).

6. Mrs. Renaud (d. 1831).

7. Mrs. Henry Erskine Johnston (1782–?).

THE COMIC ACTORS

1. "Theatrical Examiner," No. 189, published in two parts in the *Examiner* (Jan. 22 and 29, 1815), pp. 54–55, 73–74.

2. Richard Tarleton or Tarlton (d. 1588).

3. Joseph Shepherd Munden (1758–1832), earlier characterized by Hunt in the *Critical Essays* (1807), reprinted in Archer and Lowe;

Joseph Grimaldi (1779–1837), whose memoirs were edited by Dickens in 1838.

4. James Nokes (d. 1692?); Colley Cibber (1671–1757); Charles Macklin (1697?–1797).

5. James William Dodd (1740?–1796); Thomas King (1730–1805).

6. Alexander Pope (1763–1835), characterized by Hunt in the *Critical Essays* (1807), reprinted in Archer and Lowe.

7. John Liston (1776?–1846) and John Bannister (1760–1836) are both described in Hunt's *Critical Essays* (1807), reprinted in Archer and Lowe.

8. John Tobin's *Honey Moon*, first performed at Drury Lane, Jan. 1805.

9. James Kenney's *Matrimony*, first performed at Drury Lane, Nov., 1804. Mrs. Jordan played Clara, and Elliston played Delaval. Cf. Mrs. Inchbald's *Collection of Farces and Other Afterpieces* (London: Longman, Hurst, Rees, Orme, and Brown, 1815), I, 150.

10. Isaac Bickerstaffe's *Hypocrite*, first performed at Drury Lane, 1768.

11. "Theatrical Examiner," No. 190.

12. Charles Mathews (1776–1835); characterized in Hunt's *Critical Essays* (1807), reprinted in Archer and Lowe.

13. *John Bull*, by George Colman, the Younger, was first performed at Covent Garden, March 5, 1803.

14. The point in Thomas Morton's play at which the servant Walter returns home after having lost the children in the wood and "drops with a stare of mute anguish into a seat." *Dramatic Essays. Leigh Hunt*, ed. Archer and Lowe, p. 39. *The Children in the Wood* was first performed at the Haymarket on Oct. 1, 1793.

15. A character in two plays by Mrs. Centlivre: *The Busie Body*, first performed at Drury Lane, May, 1709; and *Mar-Plot*, first performed at Drury Lane, Dec., 1710.

16. Mrs. Centlivre's *A Bold Stroke for a Wife*, first performed at Lincoln's Inn Fields Theatre, Feb. 3, 1718.

17. A character in Miss Sophia Lee's *Chapter of Accidents*, first performed at the Haymarket on Aug. 5, 1780.

18. Henry Fielding's play, 1730.

19. John Emery (1777–1822); characterized in Hunt's *Critical Essays* (1807), reprinted in Archer and Lowe.

20. A character in *The Mountaineers*, by George Colman, the Younger, first performed at the Haymarket, Aug. 3, 1793.

21. Hunt probably refers to the conclusion of Act II of Tom Morton's *School of Reform*, first given at Covent Garden, Jan. 15, 1805. The character mentioned is Tyke.

22. A character in *The Critic,* by Sheridan, first produced at Drury Lane, Oct. 29, 1779.

23. Thomas Dibdin's *The English Fleet, in 1342,* first performed at Covent Garden, Dec. 13, 1803.

24. Probably Thomas Knight's musical farce, first performed at Covent Garden, Nov. 14, 1799.

25. George Colman, the Younger's play, first performed at the Haymarket, July 15, 1797.

26. *The Review; or, The Wags of Windsor,* by George Colman, the Younger, first performed at the Haymarket, Sept. 2, 1800.

THE TRAGIC ACTORS

1. "Theatrical Examiner," No. 191, *Examiner* (Feb. 5, 1815), pp. 89–90: "Sketches of the Performers."

2. Mrs. Siddons retired in 1812, although she made occasional appearances thereafter; Edmund Kean first played in London on Jan. 26, 1814.

3. Richard Cumberland's *Wheel of Fortune* was first performed at Drury Lane, Feb. 28, 1795.

4. Hunt was still in jail and had not seen Kean perform.

5. Probably William Barrymore, a minor dramatist, who acted in his own play, *The Forest of Bondy,* Sept. 30, 1814, at Covent Garden.

6. Hunt had earlier written:

the countenance of Mr. RAYMOND in scenes of interest can flash into expressions peculiar to the man of feeling and genius. He is not however a tragedian of the highest class, since his chief excellence is in the vehement passions; but in these he is always natural: . . . those who have seen him in the character of *Macduff* have seen a picture of the strong pathetic that cannot be surpassed. Everybody can clench his fist, can sob, and can strike his bosom every other minute; but to change the voice and the countenance into all the transitions from desperate to languid sorrow, or from resentment of wrongs to piteous complaint, and gradually to become vehement or gentle, powerful or powerless, as the passion fluctuates, belongs to a master only.—*Critical Essays on the Performers of the London Theatres* . . . (London: John Hunt, 1807), pp. 30–31.

SINGERS, &C.

1. "Theatrical Examiner," No. 192, *Examiner* (Feb. 12, 1815), pp. 105–107: "Sketches of the Performers."

2. John Braham (1774?–1856).

3. Mrs. Rosoman Mountain (1768?–1841).

4. The first wife of the composer Sir Henry Rowley Bishop; she made her debut as a singer at Drury Lane, 1807.

5. Mrs. John Liston (d. 1854).

6. Charles Smith (1786–1856).

7. John Sinclair (1791–1857).

8. James Bartleman (1769–1821).

9. Edward Knight (1774–1826).

10. William Oxberry (1784–1824).

11. John Henry Johnstone (1749–1828); praised briefly in Hunt's *Critical Essays* (1807), pp. 118–121.

12. Perhaps John Lake, author of the play *House of Morville*, 1812.

[RICHARD III]

1. "Theatrical Examiner," No. 193, *Examiner* (Feb. 26, 1815), p. 140. This performance of *Richard III* is not listed by Genest. Hunt's criticism of Kean as Richard III should be compared with Hazlitt's numerous passages on the same subject. Later, in the *Tatler* (Feb. 2, 1831), Hunt had occasion to quote Hazlitt's review in the *Morning Chronicle* of Kean's first appearance as Richard, and described Hazlitt's criticisms as "masterly."

2. Kean's sensational first appearance in London occurred on Jan. 26, 1814.

SOME ACCOUNT OF THE ORIGIN AND NATURE OF MASKS

1. This essay was prefatory to Hunt's *The Descent of Liberty, a Mask*, published in March, 1815, and is another instance of the many occasions on which Hunt fostered the romantic interest in the Elizabethans. The present text is from the edition of 1816 (London: Gale and Fenner), pp. xix–lv. The mask itself is reprinted in the Oxford edition (1923) of Hunt's poems, pp. 283–313. Many years later, Hunt wrote:

I have spoken of a masque on the downfall of Napoleon, called the *Descent of Liberty*, which I wrote while in prison. Liberty descends in it from heaven, to free the earth from the burden of an evil magician. It was a compliment to the Allies, which they deserved well enough, inasmuch as it was a failure; otherwise they did not deserve it at all; for it was founded on a belief in promises which they never kept. There was a vein of something true in the *Descent of Liberty*, particularly in passages where the domestic affections were touched upon; but the poetry was too much on the surface. Fancy (encouraged by the allegorical nature of the masque) played her part too entirely in it at the expense of imagination.

I had not yet got rid of the self-sufficiency caused by my editorial position, or by the credit, better deserved, which political courage had obtained for me. I had yet to learn in what the subtler spirit of poetry consisted. —*Autobiography*, ed. E. Blunden, (1928), pp. 308–309.

2. Davenant's *Salmacida Spolia*, presented in 1640, "was the last masque performed at the English Court for many years. With the fall of the Stuart monarchy the social conditions which made the masque possible came to an end, and the few masques which were performed after this date are merely belated examples of a form of art that had long lost its *raison d'etrê*." Enid Welsford, *The Court Masque* (Cambridge: University Press, 1927), p. 242.

3. Thomas Warton, *History of English Poetry*, ed. W. C. Hazlitt (London: Reeves & Turner, 1871), III, 317.

4. Cf. the definition of *mask* in Johnson's Dictionary.

5. For an account of the origin of the masque, see E. Welsford, *op. cit.*, pp. 3–18.

6. *The Tempest*, IV, 42–49.

7. Warburton's note on *Romeo and Juliet*, I, iv, 3: "That is, *masks* are now out of fashion. That Sh. was an enemy to these fooleries, appears from his writing none; and that his plays discredited them is more than probable."—*Romeo and Juliet*, A New Variorum edition, ed. H. H. Furness, 14th ed. (Philadelphia: J. B. Lippincott, 1913), p. 53.

8. Describing the masques at court, Warton opined that Anne, queen consort of James I, "was the first of our queens that appeared personally in this most elegant and rational amusement of a court." —*Op. cit.*, III, 320.

9. Probably a reference to a passage in the *Eikonoklastes*. Cf. Columbia *Milton*, V, 263.

10. Thomas Warton, *op. cit.*, III, 321. On Browne's *Inner Temple Mask* as a source of *Comus*, see *The Poetical Works of John Milton*, ed. David Masson (London, New York: The Macmillan Co., 1890), III, 212–213; and John Milton, *Comus*, ed. A. W. Verity (Cambridge, England: Cambridge University Press, 1927 [c. 1909]), p. xxxii.

11. For a more scholarly text of this "Argument" and the first passages of the masque, see *The Works of Francis Beaumont and John Fletcher*, ed. A. R. Waller (Cambridge, England: Cambridge University Press, 1912), X, 379–80.

12. *Ibid.*, p. 380.

13. "Upon whose stocks fair blooming virtues flourish."—*Poems of Thomas Carew*, ed. Arthur Vincent (London: Geo. Routledge & Sons, Ltd.; New York: E. P. Dutton & Co., 1899), p. 215.

[TIMON OF ATHENS]

1. "Theatrical Examiner," No. 258, *Examiner* (Nov. 4, 1816), pp. 699–700.

2. According to Genest, the performance of *Timon* preceding that of 1816 was one given in 1786 (Hull's alteration).

3. "The season of 1816–17, save for one notable event, was the dullest that Kean had thus far endured. . . . None of the new parts won anything but an indifferent success. *Timon of Athens* (October 28) was given seven times running and then dropped forever."— Harold N. Hillebrand, *Edmund Kean* (New York: Columbia University Press, 1933), p. 164.

4. Is Hunt thinking of Byron? Note his defense of Byron a few months previous at the time of the poet's separation from his wife, *Examiner* (April 21 and 28, 1816).

5. From the notes to Dr. Johnson's edition of Shakespeare, 1765. Cf. *Johnson on Shakespeare*, ed. Walter Raleigh, pp. 165–166.

6. William Richardson, *Essays on Some of Shakespeare's Dramatic Characters* . . . , 5th ed. (London: J. Murray & S. Highley, 1798), p. 313.

7. Cf. Schlegel: "Timon was a fool in his generosity; in his discontent he is a madman: he is every where wanting in the wisdom which enables a man in all things to observe the due measure."— A. W. Schlegel, *op. cit.*, p. 417.

8. George Lamb, the adapter, attempted here "to restore Shakspeare to the stage, with no other omissions than such as the refinement of manners has rendered necessary. . . ."—[John Genest], *Some Account of the English Stage, from the Restoration in 1660 to 1830* (Bath: Printed by H. E. Carrington; Sold by Thos. Rodd, London, 1832), VIII, 584. Genest describes the adaptation.

[ON PANTOMIME]

1. "Theatrical Examiner," No. 266, *Examiner* (Jan. 5, 1817), p. 7.

2. Underlings.

3. Richard Savage, "The Bastard's Lot," l. 8.

4. John Rich (1682?–1761).

5. See the essay immediately following. In 1831, Hunt reviewed at great length a performance of *Hop o' my Thumb and His little Brothers,* with the following prefatory remarks:

It is agreed on all hands that Pantomimes are not what they were. The story with which they used to set out, and which used to form merely a brief excuse for putting the Harlequinade in motion, now forms a considerable part of the performance; an innovation which we should hail with pleasure if it were always in such good taste as in some instances, but which is rarely apt to be so, and is followed by a set of tricks and transformations equally stinted and wanting in fancy, and a total departure from the old and genuine Harlequin plot, which consisted in the run-away vivacities of a couple of lovers full of youth and spirits, the eternal hobbling after them of the decrepid Pantaloon, and the broad gluttony, selfishness, and mischief of his servant the Clown, all tending to one point. The Clown retains something of his character still, but the rest has become a mere mass of gratuitous absurdity without object. There is no real action going on. Sometimes none at all. Columbine takes her rest; Harlequin dances at his leisure; the parties, instead of pursuing one another, often join with one accord in a mysterious truce; and Pantaloon, though at Covent-Garden he has fallen into the hands of one who ought to represent him best, has become as active as Harlequin, and without any shadow of pretence for not overtaking him. The Clown talks too much, without saying anything to the purpose. At least he says very little to the purpose. He does not enter into the true humour of the Clown, which is to be merely sensual and selfish in ordinary, and never to speak, except at some rich and rare interval, when an overwhelming sensation forces the words out of his mouth;—better if one word, or a monosyllable. When Grimaldi used to say, "Don't!" to some fellow putting him to a horrible torture; or "Nice!" when eating gingerbread; or "Nice moon!" after sentimentally contemplating the moonlight, the necessity with which he was delivered of his exclamation was made apparent to everybody, and contained a world of concentration. We have nothing of this now. The sayings are old and reiterated, and the occasions gratuitous. Pantomime used formerly to be the representative of the Old Comedy, and gave us some good Aristophanic satire on the events of the day. It attempts this but sparely now, and but seldom does it well. The contrivers appear to be worn out, and the managers stingy of their money. Even the slaps on the face are not what they used to be, nor the boltings through flap-doors in the walls. Mr. Eller, we think, treated us with but one throughout the whole of Monday night.

In short, Pantomimes seem to have become partakers of the serious spirit of the age, and to be waiting for the settlement of certain great questions and heavy national accounts, to know when they are to laugh and be merry again.—*Tatler* (Dec. 28, 1831), III, 613.

ON PANTOMIME, CONTINUED FROM A LATE PAPER

1. *Examiner* (Jan. 26, 1817), p. 57. This continuation of the preceding article was appended to the "Theatrical Examiner," in which Hazlitt reviewed Kean in *Oroonoko*, and a performance of Beaumont and Fletcher's *Humourous Lieutenant*.

[DON GIOVANNI]

1. "Theatrical Examiner," No. 293, *Examiner* (Aug. 17, 1817), pp. 522–524. Hunt's romanticism is apparent in his conception of the supernatural. Edmund Blunden comments: "Hunt must have been one of the first Englishmen to write general appreciation of Mozart." —*Leigh Hunt and His Circle* (New York, London: Harper & Bros., 1930), p. 24.

2. Hunt reviewed *Don Giovanni* in the "Theatrical Examiner" for Aug. 3, 1817.

3. *Paradise Lost,* II, 672–673.

4. *Comus,* ll. 204–208.

5. Michael Kelly (1764?–1826).

6. Signor Carlo Angrisani, distinguished Italian bass, born c. 1760.

[DRURY-LANE REDECORATED]

1. "Theatrical Examiner," No. 296, *Examiner* (Sept. 7, 1817), pp. 570–571.

2. *Paradise Lost,* VI, 579–580.

3. Ovid, *Amorum,* Liber Primus, V, 7–8.

4. Samuel James Arnold (1774–1852).

5. Hunt described the decorations of Covent Garden in the "Theatrical Examiner," Oct. 5, 1817 (p. 632):

Covent-Garden

This theatre as much surpasses the other in its internal decorations, as in its architecture. The lobby upstairs we rejoice to see in its old state, with its poetical busts and statues, though the latter might have been kept cleaner. The entrance to the boxes below has been turned into another lobby, from which you ascend into the theatre by steps consisting of a kind of bridge of mahogany, placed sideways against the wall, and railed with brass. It is very elegant. There is also the most beautiful lustre of gas light we have ever seen, hanging over the first flight of steps between the porphyry pillars at the pay-entrance. It consists of a chandelier of seven parts, one of them in the middle; and is suspended from the ceiling by a straight pipe, and interspersed in a very light and tasteful manner with flowery workmanship in gilt. We say the most beautiful, for it so happens that we had yet seen only the *effect* of the great chandelier in the middle of the theatre; as we had been thrown by accident into parts of the boxes where it was not visible, and have not been able to get into our proper critical situation in the pit. The effect we speak of is certainly most lustrous and pervading, and does not appear to us to be too powerful, as some think; though, to be sure, we have not been in the full shine of it. It is found inconvenient, we dare say, both to over and under-dressers, to those who paint, and those who are inclined to be negligent; for it renders every one as visible as in daylight, and has had an evident effect on the boxes, in making the company take double pains with their dress. There is no other light besides this in the theatre, except at the lowest tier of boxes, which is hung also with a few gas-light chandeliers, not in so tasteful a style as the one above-mentioned. The chandeliers themselves are elegant; but the stem from which they hang is too thick, perhaps from necessity in conveying the gas. The look of it, however, might have been improved, we think, by throwing it a little up, as it issues from the boxes.

CIBBER'S COMEDY OF "THE REFUSAL"

1. "Theatrical Examiner," No. 301, *Examiner* (Oct. 12, 1817), pp. 648–650. This is Hunt's only extended review of one of the Colley Cibber revivals and the only review in which Hunt introduces some general comments on Cibber as a dramatist. On Sept. 1, 1811, Hunt criticized *The Provoked Husband* for the *Examiner*, but spent most of his article damning Mr. Holman as Lord Townley. On Nov. 15, 1818, Hunt gave two paragraphs in the *Examiner* to *Love Makes a Man*, which he said was performed spiritedly and successfully, although he believed that Cibber had neutralized his hero by making him "a commonplace declaimer and moral pedant."—*Examiner* (Nov. 15, 1818), p. 727. In the *Tatler* (Sept. 2, 1831), Hunt reviewed briefly *Belles Have At Ye All*, a play founded on Cibber's *Double Gallant*, but he concerned himself almost wholly with a summary of the plot. *The Refusal*, which Hunt reviews here, was first performed at Drury Lane, Feb. 14, 1721, and, according to Genest, was not produced between 1775 and 1817. Hunt's reaction to the play should be compared with Hazlitt's, published in the *Times* (Oct. 6, 1817). Cf. *The Complete Works of William Hazlitt*, ed. P. P. Howe (London, Toronto: J. M. Dent & Sons, 1930–1934), XVIII (1933), 254–255.

2. John Pritt Harley (1786–1858).

3. In the "Theatrical Examiner" for July 20, 1817 (p. 456), Hunt generalized about comedy:

. . . the two theatres we prefer are Drury-Lane and the Haymarket, probably because they both deal principally in comedy, and thus afford us the pleasantest associations. Of tragedies there are quite sufficient in the real world; and plenty of gravity is to be found or acquired, wherever there is care, or bad health, or resentment, or sulkiness, or affectation, or money-scraping, or any other sorrow, selfishness, or stupidity. But to put us at ease with ourselves and others is unfortunately neither the talent nor the inclination of many, as the world goes; and therefore a good social comedy or farce we hold to be a most refreshing and virtuous thing. Indeed, without the humane wisdom of Shakspeare, the humbler pleasantries and philosophies of the farce writers, and the fiddles and piano-fortes about town, we cannot tell what poor morality would do, now that some classes are so eaten up with the methodistical, and others with the mercenary and the money-getting; for the taste which the world has got of late years for the prudential, or what it conceives to be such, is founded in saving-knowledges of such meanness, and has turned cities into such mere overgrown heaps of selfishness, that if the inhabitants were not reminded now and then, and reminded pleasantly too, of the existence and the virtues of people differing with themselves, they would either stand a chance of forgetting every one out of the pale of their own houses and interests, or grow, as is usual with folly, more dull and obstinate at having their vanity mortified. We look upon the playhouses, in short, as the finest antidotes to sullen and selfish opinions of all sorts. They help virtue and vice both from degenerating into mere want of feeling. They scatter egotism and collect sociality. They assemble people together smilingly and in contact, not cut off from each other by hard pews and harder abstractions. They give scenes from nature, not vile hard walls from the bricklayer. They make people think how they shall best enjoy life and hope with each other, not how they shall be best off individually here and hereafter. They win, not frighten; are universal, not exclusive; in a word, one good-tempered little farce at the Haymarket is worth all the Methodist sermons preached the rest of the week—aye, and all the other grave mistakes of selfishness, not methodistical.

4. Note Hunt's progressiveness in his views about the education of women.

5. Probably Richard John Smith (1786-1855).

6. In Thomas Otway's *Venice Preserved,* first performed in the Duke's Theatre at Dorset Garden, February, 1682. In this and the following paragraph, Hunt is reviewing the performance given at Drury Lane, Oct. 9, 1817.

ACCUSATION OF SEVERITY MADE AGAINST THE "EXAMINER"

1. "Theatrical Examiner," No. 302, *Examiner* (Oct. 19, 1817), pp. 666-667.

2. See the "Theatrical Examiner" for Sept. 7, 1817, pp. 153-156 of our text.

3. Hunt apparently has in mind the following passage which accompanied his condemnation of Mr. Maywood and Mr. Stanley in the "Theatrical Examiner" for Oct. 5, 1817 (p. 633):

We need say little about the new actor here, Mr. Maywood. It may be thought by some—the Managers for instance—ill-natured not to say a great deal, and all of it very favourable; but whatever pain we may feel in doing otherwise (and in spite of our critical sincerity on these occasions, we are not using a mere phrase when we say so) we are persuaded that it is quite as hurtful to the interests of the theatre, as to those of the public, to give praise where it is not deserved. It does no good on any side, or rather harm on every. It renders the opinion of the critic of no value; fosters an erroneous opinion of himself in the actor, which will afterwards embitter the pain of disappointment; first deceives and then irritates the public; and with regard to the theatre itself, can only serve to muddle the Managers' heads with a succession of prolonged experiments, ending in mortification and waste of money.

4. Richard Cumberland (1732–1811).

5. George Bartley (1782?–1858).

6. James Cobb's opera, the *Haunted Tower*, was first given at Drury Lane, Nov. 24, 1789. This revival is not listed by Genest.

"CHARACTERS OF SHAKESPEAR'S PLAYS,"

BY WILLIAM HAZLITT

1. "Literary Notices," No. 34, published in three parts in the *Examiner* (Oct. 26, Nov. 2, and 23, 1817), pp. 683, 697–698, 746–748. Hunt and Hazlitt had been friends since the latter, then a little-known writer, had first visited Hunt in prison. Between 1814 and 1817, Hazlitt had contributed many articles to the *Examiner*, including much of the dramatic criticism. The two men had collaborated on a series of essays for the *Examiner* (1815–1817) entitled "The Round Table," the majority of which had been by Hazlitt. Hunt had published a tribute to him in the epistle "To William Hazlitt" in the *Examiner* (July 14, 1816), reprinted in the Oxford edition (1923) of Hunt's poems, pp. 228–230. By the time that Hunt wrote the present review, however, the friendship between the two men had begun to cool. Hazlitt had become the dramatic critic for the *Times* in June, 1817, and although he contributed a few articles to the *Examiner* in 1818 and 1819, and to the *Liberal* later, the old intimacy with Hunt was never restored. Professor Louis Landré, who gives a full account of the relationship between Hunt and Hazlitt, suggests several causes for the alienation:

Peut-être commençait-il [Hazlitt] à se fatiguer du style ou des manières de Hunt qu'il rencontrait assez souvent; peut-être souffrit-il de voir attaquer dans la *Quarterly Review* [April, 1817] les articles de la *Round Table* qu'il avait écrits en collaboration avec Hunt. Celui-ci de son côté n'avait pas sujet d'être très flatté de la critique de *Rimini* dans l'*Edinburgh Review* [June, 1816] dont Hazlitt était le principal auteur. La réputation de l'un grandissait, alors que l'autre était de plus en plus discuté. Hazlitt se détache de son ancien ami. . . . Les deux auteurs ne se rencontrent plus guère; ils sont tous deux très occupés, l'un à affermir son succes, l'autre à soutenir sa fortune chancelante.—Louis Landré, *Leigh Hunt (1784–1859)*; *Contribution à l'histoire du romantisme anglais* (Paris: Société d'Édition "Les Belles-Lettres," 1935), I, 119.

Hunt's admiration of Hazlitt is apparent, nevertheless, in the present review; and neither here nor in his subsequent articles on Hazlitt's *Lectures on the English Comic Poets* (*Examiner*, Apr. 18, 1819) and *Lectures on the Literature of the Age of Elizabeth* (*Examiner*, Mar. 19, 1820) does Hunt's criticism appear biased by any personal pain he may have felt at Hazlitt's indifference to him. Concerning the *Lectures on the English Comic Poets*, Hunt observed:

> The reader will find in this book the usual characteristics of Mr. Hazlitt's criticism,—the same knowledge of human nature, the same contempt of prudery and self-love in displaying it, the same readiness to be pleased with what is reconciling and kind, the same metaphysical nicety, the same apparent love of paradox in his zeal to see fair play, and the same abrupt and powerful style, which like an oak-tree throws out its branches in short and pithy divisions, often terminating however in a profusion of poetical verdure, and blossoming into floridity.
>
> We guess that this book will rank next in popularity to the Lectures on Shakspeare. Its subject, being artificial life, will find a more general reflection in people's experience, than that of mere poetry. . . . —*Examiner* (April 18, 1819), p. 250.

In reviewing the *Lectures on the Literature of the Age of Elizabeth* during the following year, Hunt commented:

> Mr. Hazlitt occasionally startles us with a criticism, which seems as if it would run counter to his own zeal for the improvement of the social condition; as where he values Shakspeare for not interfering with any of the received notions of his time. But he is sure to see fair play in some other part of his book, as he does on this very subject when he vindicates the applause given to such dramas as the *Stranger*. It is the same with his arguments for and against a devotion to classical learning. The whole work is sprinkled with his usual relish of pithy sentences, apposite similes, and sharp detections of poor sophisticated human nature, pleasantly relieved of their sourness by a sense of the sweetness of what is unsophisticate.—*Examiner* (March 19, 1820), p. 190.

Hunt, indeed, was one of the earliest and most eminent journalists to praise Hazlitt. For Hunt's most extended article on Hazlitt, see his review of the *Plain Speaker* in the *Companion* (March 12 and 19, 1828), pp. 113–136. See also "Mr. Hazlitt and the Utilitarians," *Tatler* (Sept. 28, 1830), I, 81–82. The year following Hazlitt's death, Hunt described him and Lamb as "the two best dramatic critics, by far, that England has produced."—*Tatler* (March 21, 1831), II, 677. When he had occasion to quote Hazlitt's opinions of Scott, Hunt praised them as "the masterly observations of a great writer."—*Tatler* (March 30, 1831), II, 711.

2. See the appendix, pp. 289–291 for an unreprinted passage by Hunt on Hazlitt's *Characters of Shakespear's Plays*, which appeared in

the "Theatrical Examiner" for July 20, 1817. Perhaps the most significant feature of Hunt's remarks in this earlier notice, and one to which attention has not been called, is his high estimate of Schlegel as a Shakespeare critic and his complete ignoring of Coleridge. With this estimate should be compared Hunt's assertion in the November 2 *Examiner:* "Indeed, it has been a singular stain on the national character hitherto, that as far as criticism is concerned, Mr. Hazlitt has been the first to do justice to Shakspeare's characters in general." Although Coleridge's criticism of Shakespeare was not published until after his death, Hunt had attended at least one of his 1811 lectures on Shakespeare, and undoubtedly had heard Lamb and other friends discuss Coleridge's opinions. Regarding these lectures, Hunt had called Coleridge an unworthy critic (*Examiner*, Feb. 9, 1812, p. 91), and had attacked him in shallow fashion in the *Feast of the Poets* (*Reflector*, March 23, 1812). Near the end of his life, Hunt tried to defend his earlier remarks:

The lectures alluded to, though not wanting in masterly passages, had been counted failures upon the whole; and the only one which I heard (the first, I think) had been singularly such, being little more than the promise of a better next time. The poet, with his usual dilatoriness, had either not properly prepared himself, or trusted too much to his admirable extemporaneous powers, which may have been daunted by his having to address an audience not entirely presenting familiar faces.—*Poetical Works of Leigh Hunt*, ed. Thornton Hunt (London, New York: Routledge, Warne, and Routledge, 1860), p. 442.

One should observe, however, that Hunt's admiration of Schlegel, whom he knew probably through John Black's 1815 translation, was not unqualified. In the preface to *Foliage* (1818), Hunt took issue with Schlegel for attempting to show that Shakespeare's tragic spirit owed its grandeur to the same use of destiny as in Greek tragedy. (Leigh Hunt, *Foliage* [Philadelphia: Littell and Henry; and Edward Earle, 1818], p. xxxv.) Hunt's opening generalization on Shylock in the "Theatrical Examiner" just quoted, recalls Schlegel's similar description of him as "one of the inimitable masterpieces of characterization which are to be found only in Shakspeare."—A. W. Schlegel, *op. cit.*, p. 388.

3. Hunt is answering Francis Jeffrey's charge that Hazlitt's book was "written more to show extraordinary love, than extraordinary knowledge" of Shakespeare's productions. Cf. *Edinburgh Review*, (August, 1817), XXVIII, 472.

4. One phase of Hunt's contribution to the romantic movement is evident here in his enthusiastic praise of a leading romantic Shakespeare critic. One notes that the second trait which Hunt finds strik-

ing in Hazlitt's book is his appreciation of Shakespeare's "most beautiful and impartial spirit of humanity"—a quality characteristically
admired by romantic critics.

5. Beginning of the second part of the review, "Literary Notices,"
No. 35, *Examiner* (Nov. 2, 1817).

6. "With purple grapes. . . ."—*Midsummer Night's Dream*, III,
i, 170.

7. *Romeo and Juliet*, I, v, 28.

8. ". . . the welkin dance indeed. . . . that will draw three
souls. . . ."—*Twelfth Night*, II, iii, 59–61.

9. "Round about the cauldron go."—*Macbeth*, IV, i, 4.

10. Beginning of the third part of the review, "Literary Notices,"
No. 36, *Examiner* (Nov. 23, 1817).

11. . . . I'll see no more:
And yet the eighth appears. . . .—*Macbeth*, IV, i, 118–119.

12. *Romeo and Juliet*, II, ii, 24.

13. The "thorough and never-failing nature of all that Shakspeare
does" is a recurrent theme among the romantic Shakespeare critics.
Hunt's defense of Romeo's language against the charge of artificiality
recalls Coleridge's reported opinion that "the conceits put into the
mouths of Romeo and Juliet were perfectly natural to their age and
inexperience." Eighth lecture (Dec. 12, 1811), *Coleridge's Shakespearean Criticism*, ed. T. M. Raysor, II, 207. Lamb and Henry
Crabb Robinson were among Hunt's friends who had attended Coleridge's 1811–1812 lectures (e.g., *ibid.*, II, 216–217). Hunt may
here be developing an idea derived from Coleridge through the
conversations of his friends.

14. *Romeo and Juliet*, II, ii, 133–134.

15. Hazlitt attacks the theme of Wordsworth's "Ode on the In-
timations of Immortality." Cf. *The Complete Works of William Hazlitt*, ed. P. P. Howe, IV (1930), 250–251.

16. The conception of Hamlet's character implied in this brief
comment suggests the famous and historically influential interpretation made by Coleridge. In his twelfth lecture, January 2, 1812, Coleridge had spoken of Hamlet's "endless reasoning and hesitating—
constant urging and solicitation of the mind to act, and as constant
an escape from action; ceaseless reproaches of himself for sloth and
negligence, while the whole energy of his resolution evaporates in
these reproaches. This, too, . . . merely from that aversion to
action. . . ."—*Coleridge's Shakespearean Criticism*, II, 192–193. Not
long before he gave this lecture (*ibid.*, II, 236), Coleridge had first
become acquainted with Schlegel's lectures on Shakespeare, in which
the German critic had advanced the idea that *Hamlet* "is intended

to show that a calculating consideration, which exhausts all the relations and possible consequences of a deed, must cripple the power of acting. . . ."—A. W. Schlegel, *op. cit.*, p. 404. His analysis of Hamlet's character follows.

17. The idea which Hunt touches upon in this sentence had been developed in detail in Coleridge's eighth lecture. Cf. *Coleridge's Shakespearean Criticism*, II, 156–157.

[RICHARD, DUKE OF YORK]

1. "Theatrical Examiner," No. 307, *Examiner* (Dec. 28, 1817), pp. 825–826.

2. Samuel Penley (d. 1832).

3. The compilation was made by J. H. Merivale. Cf. H. N. Hillebrand, *op. cit.*, p. 173. For a summary of *Richard, Duke of York*, with an indication of the borrowings from Chapman and Webster, see Genest, *op. cit.*, VIII, 636–641.

[FIGARO]

1. "Theatrical Examiner," No. 309, *Examiner* (Jan. 25, 1818), pp. 57–58. For another review of *Figaro*, see the *Examiner* (Dec. 26, 1819), pp. 827–828.

2. See Hunt's earlier review of *Don Giovanni*, pp. 146–152, above.

3. Madame Violante Camporese (1785–1839), Italian soprano who excelled in Mozart operas.

4. Probably Madame Joséphine Fodor-Mainvielle (1789–1870), French operatic soprano.

5. Madame Giuditta Pasta (1789–1865), Italian dramatic soprano. Although she was not very successful when she first sang in London, she later gained great repute.

6. Giuseppe Naldi (1770–1820), Italian baritone, particularly famed for his singing of *Figaro* and *Cosi fan tutte*.

7. Giuseppe Ambrogetti (b. 1780), Italian bass.

8. John Dillon's *Retribution* was first performed at Covent Garden, Jan. 1, 1818.

[THE BARBER OF SEVILLE]

1. "Theatrical Examiner," No. 315, *Examiner* (March 22, 1818), p. 188.

2. The popularity of Paisiello's *Barbiere di Siviglia* (1782) caused the opera of Rossini, who was then only twenty-four (1816), to be received at first with resentment.

3. Cf. Hunt's long discussion of the popularity of Rossini in Italy, in a letter to Vincent Novello, March, 1823, *Century Magazine*, XXIII (March, 1882), n.s. I, 708–709.

4. "The theme of the 'Zitti, zitti' trio in *Il barbiere* comes, of course, from the ploughman's song in Haydn's *Seasons*. The paramount influence on Rossini's music is that of Mozart."—Pitts Sanborn, "Gioacchino Antonio Rossini," *The International Cyclopedia of Music and Musicians* (New York: Dodd, Mead & Co., 1938), p. 1582.

["BELLAMIRA" AND "THE JEW OF MALTA"]

1. "Theatrical Examiner," No. 320, published in two parts in the *Examiner* (April 26 and May 3, 1818), pp. 267–269, 284–285.

2. Richard Lalor Sheil (1791–1851). Hunt misspells the name.

3. William Charles Macready (1793–1873).

4. First performed at Covent Garden, Nov. 23, 1778. According to Genest, this is an opera derived by Dr. Kenrick from the play *Country Lasses*.

5. Isaac Bickerstaffe (1735?–1812?); Mrs. Frances Brooke (1724–1789).

6. This was an alteration by Samuel Penley, who, says Genest, "inserted too much of his own, and omitted too much of the original. . . ."—Genest, *op. cit.*, VIII, 647.

7. An extravaganza by James Robinson Planché (1796–1880). After 1840, when Hunt's play *The Legend of Florence* was produced at Covent Garden, he and Planché became intimate friends. An account of their friendship appears in *The Recollections and Reflections of J. R. Planché* (London: Tinsley Bros., 1872), II, 36–40, 198–199. Through an oversight, Professor Landré has omitted from his bibliography some of Hunt's letters which are published in Planché's autobiography: *ibid.*, II, 39–40 (previously published in *The Correspondence of Leigh Hunt*, ed. by his eldest son [London: Smith, Elder and Co., 1862]) and pp. 198–199 (two letters from Hunt to Planché, c. 1856 and 1857, not in the *Correspondence*).

8. Beginning of the second part of the review, "Theatrical Examiner," No. 321 (May 3, 1818).

9. Hunt's extended attempt here to establish Marlowe's Jew as within "the pale of human nature" has no parallel in Lamb, Schlegel, Coleridge, or Hazlitt. Concerning Barabas, Lamb wrote to Southey in 1798, "The Jew is a famous character, quite out of nature; but, when we consider the terrible idea our simple ancestors had of a Jew, not more to be discommended for a certain discolouring (I think Addison calls it) than the witches and fairies of Marlow's

mighty successor."—*The Letters of Charles Lamb*, ed. E. V. Lucas (New Haven: Yale University Press, 1935), I, 132. Again, in the *Specimens of English Dramatic Poets* (1808), Lamb noted: "Shylock, in the midst of his savage purpose, is a man. . . . Barabas is a mere monster, brought in with a large painted nose, to please the rabble." —*The Works of Charles and Mary Lamb*, ed. E. V. Lucas (New York: G. P. Putnam's Sons; London: Methuen & Co., 1904), IV, 26. Hunt has a chapter on Marlowe as a poet in *Imagination and Fancy* (1844).

10. Hunt's concluding eulogy of Shakespeare is characteristically romantic.

[COSI FAN TUTTE]

1. "Theatrical Examiner," No. 330, *Examiner* (Aug. 2, 1818), p. 492.

2. Pierre Ignace Begrez (1787–1863?), a French tenor; Manuel del Popolo Vicente García (1775–1832), Spanish composer and tenor.

[OTHELLO]

1. "Theatrical Examiner," No. 338, *Examiner* (Oct. 4, 1818), p. 632. This article should be compared with Hazlitt's numerous reports on Kean as Othello.

2. This statement aroused one of Hunt's readers:

To the Editor of the "Examiner"

SIR,—At the following paragraph in the Theatrical Article of your last number I was much struck: "We have admired Mrs. Siddons, been infinitely amused with Lewis, been sore with laughing at Munden, been charmed with Mrs. Jordan; but we never saw anything that so completely held us suspended and heart-stricken as Mr. Kean's *Othello*."

That Mr. Kean's *Othello* is not to be excelled is very true; but in mentioning the above celebrated performers, why, Mr. Editor, was John Kemble omitted? It is true, I have heard, that while Mr. Kemble was Manager of Covent-Garden Theatre, you offered him a Play of your own writing, which he returned to you, it being so very like some other piece (the name I forgot) that he could not venture to bring it forward; but surely your private feelings cannot have dictated the present neglect, nor induced you to write so ungraciously of Mr. Kemble, as you have done for many years past?

Having been frequently informed, by those who have been in your company, that you are always willing to give publicity to criticisms on your conduct as a writer or an Editor, I can have no doubt of seeing this letter in your next number.—I am, Sir, your obedient servant, Z.
Oxford-street, Oct. 6, 1818

[We insert the above letter as containing one out of many specimens of the misrepresentations which a writer encounters who would be impartial, whatever pains he may take to draw the line between public difference of opinion and private malignity. We need not add that the alleged report about the play is a fabrication. The other day the Editor heard that somebody was very angry with him once for writing in the *Scourge!* a publication, which, we believe, used to lash the air at him, like the *Satirist* and the *Quarterly Review.—Exam.]—Examiner* (Oct. 12, 1818), p. 650.

3. *Othello,* IV, ii, 47–49.

4. Mrs. West (1790–1876).

5. Hunt was less pleased, later this season, with Kean's acting of Hotspur in *Henry IV,* Part I:

The disappointment in Mr. Kean's performance has, we believe, been pretty general. The character was naturally supposed to be one in which he would excel; but whether it was that he was hoarse with a bad cold, or whether something yet hidden in the mysteries of green rooms and management made him dislike the part, or whether actors prefer having a doubtful part which they can have the credit of giving ideas to and elevating, rather than one completely filled as well as marked out for them, certain it is that his *Hotspur* was comparatively tame and indifferent. If he was less vehement than usual, for fear of being too much so, this was a great mistake. *Hotspur* is a character of decided, intentional, and excessive vehemence, sometimes indeed working himself up into extravagance, as in that famous passage of which honest *Major Bath* was so fond—

> By heavens! I think it were an easy leap
> To pluck bright honour fron the pale-faced Moon, &c.

He is the Mars of the play, as contrasted with the serener and more Jove-like greatness of the young prince. Perhaps however, Mr. Kean was really unwell, for he was excessively hoarse. The play has been repeated, and he may since have acted differently. The fighting scene roused him up. He fought with his usual mixture of vehemence and grace—*amabile fierezza.* Some of our brother-critics seem inclined to object to what they call his "fondness for gladiatorial exhibitions." But gladiatorial exhibitions are fine things when managed in this way—with all their grace and nothing of their cruelty. The cruelty was a bad Roman taste enough: the grace is from the Greeks. The beauty of Mr. Kean's attitudes would have adorned the palestra, . . . —*Examiner* (March 14, 1819), p. 170.

[MR. FARREN]

1. "Theatrical Examiner," No. 339, *Examiner* (Oct. 12, 1818), pp. 649–650. William Farren (1786–1861). This was his first season in London. He had previously acted in Plymouth and Dublin.

2. Arthur Murphy's *The Way to Keep Him* was first performed at Drury Lane, Jan. 24, 1760, as a three-act play, and later expanded to five acts.

[THE RECRUITING OFFICER]

1. "Theatrical Examiner," No. 341, *Examiner* (Oct. 25, 1818), pp. 679–680. Farquhar's *Recruiting Officer* was first produced at Drury Lane, April 8, 1706.

2. Hunt reviewed Farquhar's *The Inconstant* in the *News* (Dec. 6, 1807), *The Constant Couple* in the *Examiner* (Oct. 30, 1808), and *The Beaux Stratagem* in the *Tatler* (Dec. 3, 1830). His fullest comment on Farquhar appeared in the biographical and critical notice prefaced to his edition of *The Dramatic Works of Wycherley, Congreve, Vanbrugh, and Farquhar* (London: Ed. Moxon, 1840). Professor Landré says of Hunt's observations in the 1840 edition: ". . . il utilise ce que ses prédécesseurs, notamment Charles Lamb et William Hazlitt, ont écrit sur ces auteurs. . . ."—*Op. cit.*, II, 124.

3. First performed at Drury Lane, March 17, 1712.

4. Hunt's attitude toward the French stage was not wholly one of condemnation. In reviewing an afterpiece, *The Youthful Days of Frederick the Great* in the "Theatrical Examiner" for Oct. 5, 1817, Hunt observes:

All the performers too are dressed in the exact costume of the times, which is one of the few good things borrowable from the French stage—and indeed an excellent one. Our own stage wants great amendment in that matter, for its unusual dresses are not only untrue to the times, but so miscellaneous and inconsistent as to defy all times. We often see, in these legitimate days, a coat of two hundred years standing, bowing to a fellow of yesterday; and a young lady behaving irreverently to an aunt, who by her stomacher and head-dress cannot be younger than her own grandfather.—*Examiner* (Oct. 5, 1817), p. 633.

[THE FAIR ITALIAN IN ALGIERS]

1. "Theatrical Examiner," No. 349, *Examiner* (Jan. 31, 1819), pp. 77–78.

2. See this text, pp. 188–189.

3. Teresa Giorgi Trombetta Belloc (1784–1855), French mezzo-soprano.

4. Gaetano Crivelli (1774–1836), Italian tenor.

[THE MAGIC FLUTE]

1. "Theatrical Examiner," No. 365, *Examiner* (May 30, 1819), pp. 346–347.

2. For the soundness of Hunt's prediction, see Allardyce Nicoll, *op. cit.*, I, 22–25.

[RICHARD III]

1. "Theatrical Examiner," No. 379, *Examiner* (Oct. 31, 1819), pp. 699–700.

2. Richard III was one of Kean's most celebrated parts. For Hunt's first opinion of Kean as Richard III, see pp. 112–115, above.

3. For Hunt's review of Kean as Othello, see pp. 201–202, above.

4. Dryden's *King Arthur* was first performed in 1691.

5. Ann Maria Tree, later Mrs. James Bradshaw (1801–1862); older sister of Ellen Tree.

[CORIOLANUS]

1. "Theatrical Examiner," No. 383, *Examiner* (Dec. 5, 1819), pp. 783–784.

2. See Hunt's review of Macready as Richard III in the "Theatrical Examiner" for Oct. 31, 1819, pp. 219–222 of this text.

3. Maria Foote, later Countess of Harrington (1797?–1867).

4. Morton's *A Roland for an Oliver* was first performed at Covent Garden, April 29, 1818. Miss Foote played Maria Darlington.

5. William Blanchard (1769–1835).

6. In Philip Massinger's *A New Way to Pay Old Debts* (c. 1625).

7. Elliston was manager of Drury Lane at this time.

8. John Tobin (1770–1804).

9. William Pearman (b. 1792; fl. 1810–1824). Hunt describes him, in 1817, as follows:

Lyceum

A Mr. Pearman from Bath made his appearance here on Monday in Mr. Braham's part of *Prince Orlando* in the *Cabinet*,. He is an acquisition to the Managers; and seems altogether suited to their establishment, being what is called, we believe, on the stage a miniature performer. In other words, he is not of a great order of singers, but has some taste, more execution, and a sweet voice of reasonable power. His falsetto will remind the public of Incledon's, which it surpasses in reach and sweetness. He plays upon it like a flute. His transition to it however from the natural voice is not happy. It is not indeed so violent as Incledon's, who in his leap from one to the other slammed the larynx in his throat, like a Harlequin jumping through a window shutter; but it is poor and unskilful; neither does he seem to care upon what sort of words or expression he does it, so as the note is such as he can jump up to. This will be sufficient to give the reader an idea of his general deficiency in expression. He seems to have little notion of any except those usual alternations of loudness and gentleness, common to the very best singers out of the pale of inspiration. One of the very few varieties which he displays consists in that swelling and subsiding, or opening and shutting of the voice, which in Mr. Braham's powerful instrument is like a French-horn, but which in Mr. Pearman's is like a drinking glass rubbed round the edge with a wet finger. He reminded us sometimes of Mr. Braham, both in singing and acting; but this is perhaps hardly avoidable by an inferior performer in such a part; and in acting he really seems capable of going beyond him—which, to be sure, is no arduous journey. Mr. Pearman has an ordinary person, and a face that looks rather care-worn; but he is more genteel than singers in general, and seems a most unassuming man. In short, he is a sweet singer worth hearing, and may become a formidable rival to another of the same class, Mr. Sinclair, who, we must confess, grows very tiresome (to use the phraseology of the ladies) with his miminy-piminy affectations, and his *weeths, waines,* and *diviones* (with, wine, and divine).—*Examiner* (July 13, 1817), p. 442.

10. Samuel Thomas Russell (1769?–1845).

11. By George Colman, the Younger; first performed at the Haymarket, Aug. 3, 1793.

TWELFTH NIGHT

1. "Theatrical Examiner," No. 412, *Examiner* (Nov. 12, 1820), pp. 733–734. See Hunt's review of *Twelfth Night,* pp. 41–44, above.

2. The second part of Hunt's "Theatrical Examiner" for Dec. 26, 1819, reviewed a musical version of this play:

Covent-Garden

The performance of the *Comedy of Errors* here is a curiosity. People think they are going to see a play of Shakspeare's; and so they are in one respect; for the words are chiefly his: but for the first time perhaps since the performance of one of Shakspeare's plays, the audience have little or no consciousness of the great dramatist, except occasionally perhaps a feeling of wonder at its being so little like him. The general impression is from the singing of Miss Stephens and Miss Tree, and the judicious grinning of Liston. These three things it must be allowed are excellent. It is only a pity that Liston has not still more to do, and that the ladies with their songs do a great deal more than the original gives warrant for. The original is not an opera, where everything, being to be sung, is made to be sung and the very discords become concordant. It is a play of endless puzzle and confusion, with characters anything but harmonious; a game at improbable cross-purposes, which are obscure to nobody but the parties concerned; and which have neither time, nor temper, nor anything else, to be dallying with duets and sostenutos.

We cannot conceive that Shakspeare wrote this play with any satisfaction. It has unquestionable marks of his hand; but the classical stories that it was his fortune to choose, or to have chosen for him, are the things in which he gives us the least pleasure, whether in comedy or tragedy. We allude in the latter to *Coriolanus*. They came from Rome; and there is something in the Roman genius that strikes as cold as the marble of their buildings. It is impossible for the spectators' imagination, however willing, to get over the utter improbability of two masters quite alike, and two servants quite alike, who cross and confound each other at every step, without coming to an explanation. And the thing is made worse by the parties being represented by different performers. It is otherwise with such a performance as that of the *Three and the Deuce*, where the three brothers are all represented by one actor. And it was otherwise with the original drama of Plautus, when actors performed in masks. It is the production, and most probably was the suggestion, of a stage that knew no other faces. But in an English *Comedy of Errors*, two men altogether as different as their chins, Jones and Duruset for instance, disenact the two masters; and we are to believe in the identity of their two servants, Liston and Farren, persons no more resembling each other than moisture and drought, or a bowl of cream and a tobacco pipe, or a plum-pudding and a pepper-box, or an easy chair and a tall counting-house stool, or a bill of fare and the payment, or a laughing face and the razor that cuts it. The actors might manage their faces however a little better than they do, with whiskers and other disguises; especially the servants, who may caricature their faces more. A pasteboard nose or so would go a good way. Perhaps they had some such contrivances in Shakspeare's time; but the spectators then were more used to make enormous allowances, having no such scenery and other helps as they have now.

We do not wonder however that people go to see a comedy which ought only to be read, now that we have heard Miss Stephens and Miss Tree sing together. It is certainly a treat, as delightful as it is new. It is seldom that two such singers come together; and seldomer that their voices so well unite, or that the undertones of the female who sings second are deep enough without being masculine. Miss Tree's however are so. If they have any fault, it is perhaps that they are occasionally too luscious, and contrasted with her upper. But they are exquisitely true. Her ear indeed throughout is one of the finest we ever witnessed. Miss Stephens's voice we think the finer of the two. It is even, clear, and sweet; and has an exquisite vein of gentle pathos throughout it, that perpetually seems to appeal to you. You wish to reassure it;—to "kiss it up, and ease its pain." In musical science the ladies are perhaps upon a par; and they almost appear to be so in popularity. It is pleasant to see them performing together with an appearance of cordiality. The public have been so used to expect jealousies between performers, and performers have been in such a hurry to answer their expectations, that we are persuaded any two eminent ones who should really make common cause with one another would each get more popularity individually than if he or she had flourished alone. It is a vulgar mistake among stage people to imagine that their interests and reputation are advanced by a contrary behaviour. The greater an age, and the greater the geniuses that have adorned it, it will always be found that the finest of them have had a regard for each other.

The songs are taken from Shakspeare's other plays, and from his miscellaneous poems. The music is chiefly from Arne, Sir John Stevenson, and Mr. Stevens, with supplies and arrangements by Mr. Bishop. We cannot say that it is altogether managed happily. Arne was a man of genius; Sir John Stevenson is a man of taste; Mr. Stevens is author of one of the happiest glees in the language, *Sigh no more, Ladies*—besides being a composer, we believe, of great science; and Mr. Bishop, we trust, would not be the most unequal writer living, if he were not the musician of all-work at a theatre. But fine English poetry, generally speaking, is a thing not to be reached by English music. The latter wants wing to overtake it; wants airiness, ardour, continuity of flight. It is too apt, in its liveliest moments, to take melancholy breath; to halt, and drag back, into psalmody. If we were made to excel in any music, it is church music; and we have excelled in it. But for one true flight of gaiety and inspiration, like Arne's *Where the Bee Sucks*, we have fifty happy pieces of poetry ludicrously contradicted by doleful and pompous music; especially in those solemn personages called Glees, who play into each other's hands as gravely as old ladies at whist.—*Examiner* (Dec. 26, 1819), pp. 828–829.

3. Sir Henry Rowley Bishop (1786–1855) composed music for several of Shakespeare's plays: *Midsummer Night's Dream*, 1816; *Comedy of Errors*, 1819; *Twelfth Night*, 1820; *Henry IV*, Part II, 1821; *Two Gentlemen of Verona*, 1821; *As You Like It*, 1824; *Hamlet*, 1830; *Love's Labour's Lost*, 1839.

4. Peter von Winter (1755–1825); Sir John Andrew Stevenson (1760?–1833).

5. Thomas Morley (1557–1604?); Thomas Ravenscroft (1592?–1635?).

6. *Venus and Adonis*, 145–148. Line 147: ". . . with long dishevell'd hair."

7. *Twelfth Night*, II, iii, 123–125.

8. *Ibid.*, II, iii, 194–197.

9. *Merry Wives of Windsor*, III, v, 118–119.

10. *Twelfth Night*, II, v, 72–74.

11. *Ibid.*, V, i, 398.

12. An erroneous dating of the play.

THE PLAY-BILLS

1. *Tatler* (Sept. 17, 1830), I, 45.

2. *Troilus and Cressida*, IV, iv, 132–133.

3. Tyrone Power (1797–1841), an Irish comedian. The following month, Hunt wrote of him:

He is very clever, off-hand, easy, and natural, with a certain want of richness. The galleries delight in him, and the boxes cannot help sympathizing with the galleries, for more reasons than they are aware of. He walks the stage as comfortably as if he was in his own house, and he is conscious of his humour too, and rarely fails to make some little comment upon it of look or tone; but after all, the comment is not enough. He is so natural, that he seems as if he could no more help what he does than a real Irishman could in his situation; but there is something too much of dry fac-simile in it, and not enough of garnish and ebullition. You think that an Irishman picked up on the quay at Dublin would do just as the actor does,—neither more nor less.—*Tatler* (Oct. 14, 1830), I, 139.

PERFORMANCES FOR THIS EVENING

1. *Tatler* (Jan. 10, 1831), II, 440. A typical *Tatler* play-bill. The content is verbatim, but no attempt has been made to follow the original typography.

[MISS PATON]

1. "The Play-Goer," *Tatler* (Sept. 22, 1830), I, 64. Mary Ann Paton, later Mrs. Wood (1802–1864), was a fine soprano, and, from 1826, was considered at the head of her profession.

[THE BALLET]

1. "The Play-Goer," *Tatler* (Oct. 30, 1830), I, 195–196.
2. The famous epic, 1572, of Luis vaz de Camoens (1524–1580).

[THE RIVALS]

1. "The Play-Goer," *Tatler* (Dec. 2, 1830), I, 307–308. For a general article on Sheridan by Hunt, see *Examiner* (July 14, 1816), pp. 433–436.
2. Two months previous, Hunt had written of the actors at Drury Lane:

There are a number of walking, frowning, and smiling gentlemen at this theatre whom we have not seen before, and whom we may as well see again before we particularize them. We fear there will be found a dearth of good comic gentry, and lovers. Oh Lewis! where art thou for the fops and flutterers, with thy person almost as light as thy voice, thy winking eyes, and little teeth-shewing laugh! And where art thou, Elliston, the best lover we ever saw in a comedy, for in the midst of vigorous gaiety thy voice could tremble with emotion, and no actor *approached* a woman as thou didst, fervid, and as if she really attracted thee? Thy raptures are not at arm's length, at the tip-end of a white glove.—*Tatler* (Oct. 6, 1830), I, 112.

3. Henry John Wallack (1790–1870).
4. John Cooper (fl. 1810–1870).

[ENJOYMENTS OF THE THEATRE]

1. "The Play-Goer," *Tatler* (Dec. 13, 1830), I, 343–344.
2. Benjamin Wrench (1778–1843).
3. George Farquhar's play, 1706.
4. A month earlier, Hunt had written:

To go to the play on Saturday night was like going through a dark stormy sea to an enchanted island. The wind roared, the rain came down in torrents; pattens clacked; the lamps were like beacons in the tempest; old gentlemen were seen, by their light, pulled along by their inverted umbrellas; the hackney coaches plunged about like Dutch luggers; the carriages were the skiffs; the "mudshine" was seen in all its horror, gleaming through the dark, in gutter and on pavement; in short, all the world was roar, clatter, and deluge. The coach lands at the step of a mansion inviting as an enchanted house in the Black Sea: we enter, and find hundreds of faces all bent upon the dry and comfortable platform called a stage, and laughing at the pleasant woman yclept Orger.—*Tatler* (Nov. 8, 1830), I, 223.

[CHRISTMAS AND THE THEATRE]

1. "The Play-Goer," *Tatler* (Dec. 25, 1830), I, 387.
2. No doubt the same as saloop-men, vendors of a "hot drink consisting of an infusion of powdered salep or (later) of sassafras, with milk and sugar, formerly sold in the streets of London in the night and early morning."—*N.E.D.*
3. See also Hunt's essay on Christmas Day in this issue of the *Tatler*, I, 385–386.

PATENT THEATRES AND MR. ARNOLD

1. *Tatler* (Jan. 27, 1831), II, 497–498. This is the third of a series of *Tatler* articles by Hunt, occasioned by the petition of Mr. Arnold, proprietor of the English Opera, "for a license to perform all the year round, in order to indemnify him for losses occasioned by the fire at the Lyceum."—*Tatler*, II, 489. At the time of the petition, his performances were restricted to the summer months, "stated to be the

most unfavourable season for theatrical performances."—*Ibid.* The patentees of Drury Lane and Covent Garden, however, were objecting on the grounds that an extension of Mr. Arnold's license would "be injurious to their own interests, which are of a larger nature than Mr. Arnold's, and have long been struggling with difficulties" (*ibid.*), and that they themselves had inherited the exclusive right of acting plays. Hunt's first article on the subject, in the *Tatler* for Jan. 25, 1831, was entitled "Twenty-Three Reasons Why the Managers of the Great Theatres Ought Not to Prevail against Mr. Arnold." The second article, published the next day, listed seven more arguments in favor of Mr. Arnold, and concluded:

An existing drama springs out of the nature of the times. Comedy is the flower of manners; tragedy of passion and thought. The greatest era of tragedy in England was when the minds of people had been set free, and their purposes invigorated, by the Reformation. The most flourishing period of comedy, was when artificial manners were predominant, and the greatest things in people's heads were the feathers in their caps. The mind of the age has been again shaken up by the revival of noble doctrines, by the diffusion of that knowledge of which his Lordship [Lord Brougham, the Lord Chancellor] has been so eminent a promoter, and by the glorious example of the second French revolution, which has exhibited the social virtues in a new and almost unhoped-for light, and given confidence to the noblest expectations. On all these accounts, and in common with every other improvement, the drama is likely to revive. At all events, a social feeling, including a love of the drama and . . . [a delight] to draw on the theatrical stock of our lively and illustrious neighbours, is rapidly on the increase, as may be seen by the increasing number of theatres and the pieces they produce.—*Tatler* (Jan. 26, 1831), II, 494.

2. *Venice Preserved.*

3. Sir Charles Wetherell (1770–1846), lawyer and politician.

4. Elizabeth Inverarity (1813–1846), later Mrs. Charles Martyn; actress and singer.

5. Douglas William Jerrold (1803–1857).

[THE MESSIAH]

1. "The Play-Goer," *Tatler* (Feb. 24, 1831), II, 595. Cf. Hunt's article on the oratorio, *Examiner* (Feb. 20, 1812), pp. 61–64 of this text. On March 17, 1831, Hunt wrote in the *Tatler* (II, 667): "The reader understands that we do not profess to witness the whole evening's performance of the Oratorios, or Musical Selections. We believe, as it is, that *The Tatler* is the only journal that takes notice of them; which appears somewhat extraordinary, considering the good houses they draw. Perhaps our brother-critics take them to be more sombre than they are."

2. Hunt began his review of this performance:

We have usually had an unpleasant, heavy impression of Oratorios, partly no doubt on account of their presenting a sombre mixture both of audience and music, and partly for their making a pretence to something devotional without the reality. Last night they appeared to us better, perhaps because they are no longer called Oratorios, but Selections of Music; the consequence of which was, that the sacred pieces really had a more sacred effect, while the earthlier ones did not seem to have crept in upon tolerance, but took their station at once as things reasonable and innocent.—*Tatler* (Feb. 19, 1831), II, 579.

3. By visual pomp, and by the tie
    Of sweet and threatening harmony
From "1815 Ode," ll. 70–71; in *Poetical Works of William Wordsworth*, ed. William Knight, VI (1884), 89.

4. Louis François Roubiliac or Roubillac (1695–1762), sculptor; his statue of Handel was erected at Vauxhall in 1738.

5. Henry Phillips (1801–1876), bass singer.

6. Charles Nicholson (1795–1837), flautist and composer.

7. Sir Thomas Urquhart or Urchard (1611–1660); his translation of Rabelais was published in 1653 and 1693.

[BONNETS AT THE THEATRE]

1. "The Play-Goer," *Tatler* (March 23, 1831), II, 687.

2. Ovid, *Artis Amatoriae*, I, 99.

[MADAME PASTA]

1. "The Play-Goer," *Tatler* (May 13, 1831), II, 863.

2. Giuditta Pasta (1798–1865), Italian soprano. Cf. Hunt's remarks about her, May 20, 1831, *Correspondence*, I, 261.

3. With store of ladies, whose bright eyes
    Rain influence. . . .

                         —*L'Allegro*, ll. 121–122.

4. *Medea*, 1813, was written by the popular opera composer Johann Simon Mayr (1763–1845).

5. Reviewing the *Grecian Daughter*, Hunt wrote:

Of all common-place dramas, none are so intolerable as those that are called classical, with a Greek or Roman story. They are like the old clipped gardens, with bad statues in them; or rather (for a garden must have something good in it) they resemble a cold modern apartment, of the would-be elegant order, with a fine marble paper, and not a painting in it. We revolt from the attempt to pass insipidity upon us for taste, and the absence of colour and warmth for the presence of perfection. We hate the attempt of the declaimer to avail himself of the sacred names of antiquity and patriotism, and make the heroes of Plutarch fight the battles of his feeble wit. He makes the very dresses of the "classical" times look ugly to us, the white robes cold, the helmets and swords bits of common metal, the whole affair a piece of grown boy's play, with the real enthusiasm of neither boy nor man.—*Tatler* (Oct. 26, 1830), I, 179.

6. Marie Sophie Taglioni (1804–1884), celebrated Swedish ballerina. Hunt expressed disappointment at her dancing:

Its chief character is a graceful repose. The extreme ease of it is indeed wonderful, especially when we consider the laborious and artificial exercises which dancers have to practice, and which generally produce an indelible stiffness in their manners. Mademoiselle Taglioni winds hither and thither with singular smoothness: she is perfect mistress of her actions, her deportment, her face: she does whatever she pleases. But we cannot help wishing that she would be pleased to do something more. Dancing, after all, in its greatest repose, is an extraordinary departure from our ordinary style of movement: it can only be supposed warranted by a certain enthusiasm; and in the repose of Mademoiselle Taglioni, there is too much repose.—*Tatler* (May 30, 1831), II, 919.

7. Luigi Lablache (1794–1858), Italian operatic bass.
8. Fanny Ayton (b. 1806), English opera singer.
9. Alberico Curioni (born c. 1790), Italian tenor.
10. Giovanni Battista Rubini (1795–1854), Italian tenor.

[PAGANINI]

1. "The Play-Goer," published in two parts in the *Tatler* (June 23 and 25, 1831), II, 1003–1004, 1011. Hunt's description of the famous violinist should be compared with that in his fine blank verse fragment, "Paganini," published in *Leigh Hunt's London Journal* (April 16, 1834), reprinted in the Oxford edition (1923) of Hunt's poems, pp. 255–257.

2. Probably Luigi Lablache (1794–1858), Italian operatic bass.
3. Probably Alberico Curioni (c. 1790–?), Italian tenor.
4. Paganini was forty-seven at the time of this performance.
5. Beginning of the second part of the review, *Tatler* (June 25, 1831).
6. Timotheus (B.C. 446–357), celebrated Greek musician and poet.
7. Terpander (fl. B.C. 700–650), founder of the first musical school or system in Greece; father of Greek music.

[FURTHER REMARKS ON PAGANINI]

1. "The Play-Goer," *Tatler* (June 27, 1831), II, 1015–1016. Hunt wrote still another article on Paganini for the *Tatler* (Aug. 6, 1831), III, 127–128.

[LATE HOURS AT THE THEATRE]

1. "The Play-Goer," *Tatler* (July 7, 1831), III, 23–24.
2. John Reeve (1799–1838).
3. *The Middle Temple; or, "Which Is My Son?"* (played at the Adelphi).
4. Lucia Elizabeth Bartolozzi, later Mrs. Charles Mathews, known as Madame Vestris (1797–1856), actress; opened the Olympic in 1831, with Maria Foote. Hunt described the theatre in the *Tatler:*

. . . though the Olympic be a gay and comfortable-looking place inside, it seems, outside, just such a box as Gulliver was carried away in by the Brobdingnagian bird. You seem as if you could lift it from the street. We do not remember what the interior was, when we last saw it; nor did it appear very probable, when we got in last night, that we should be able to refresh our memory; for we beheld nothing but a crowded lobby, with a multitude of men and hats filling up the spaces over the open backs of the boxes. The house was overflowing. When we afterwards got a view of it, we found one of the prettiest interiors we are acquainted with, a perfect circle all but the stage, with the fronts of the boxes painted in medallions, and the whole presenting an aspect warm and cheerful. The lobbies are not so well. The backs of the boxes are no higher than pews; and although this be convenient for increasing the number of spectators, and perhaps for ventilating the house, yet it is bad for the hearing of those who sit farthest from the stage, and presents obstacles in the way of such as like to have everything smooth and pleasant in the way to the seats they have taken. However, we cannot but think that Madame Vestris has made a good speculation.—*Tatler* (Jan. 4, 1831), II, 418.

5. On this subject, Hunt later wrote:

The complaints of the public are increasing with regard to the late hours at the Haymarket. Four pieces are in the habit of being performed there, and people who live at any distance often do not get home till half-past one, or near two, in the morning. It has been charged on this theatre that as there is no half-price there, the performances are protracted in this manner to accommodate a certain description of visitors, and attract a sort of company, which excludes others. Knowing what we do of the present state of society, and the cause of it, nothing shall ever induce us to degrade our pen with one word against the poor girls alluded to; but this we must say, that when the decline of a love of the drama among the fashionable circles is attributed, among other causes, to these visitations of the lobbies, nothing can shew a greater want of acquaintance with the thoughts and cares of the fashionable world, or with the theatres as they existed twenty years ago. The influx of the visitors in question was never greater in the most frequented theatres than at that time, nor was the stage ever more in favour with the circles. The late hours are a nuisance, and ought to be abated; but whatever may be the cause of those, it has nothing to do with keeping away the polite world. They can outface anything, when they have a mind to it, as well as the most ingenuous!

Difference of manners, in a hundred respects, has produced this difference in the popularity of the stage, and transferred it to the less educated part of the community. We will mention one among others, which has alone had a great effect; and that is, the cessation of tavern-habits, caused in great measure by the simple decline of *smoking*. When the gentry smoked their pipes, they were obliged to go to taverns for that purpose, and were ready for all the amusement connected with a town-life. When smoking went out, the gentry went home; and books, and music, newspapers, magazines, &c. have detained them there.—*Tatler* (Aug. 11, 1831), III, 144.

[ROMEO AND JULIET]

1. "The Play-Goer," *Tatler* (July 12, 1831), III, 39–40.
2. Harriette Deborah Taylor, later Mrs. Lacy (1807–1874).
3. The famous Fanny Kemble, later Mrs. Butler (1809–1893), daughter of Charles Kemble. She first played Juliet in 1829 with great success. Hunt, however, considered her performance of Juliet overrated. Cf. *Tatler* (Oct. 5, 1830) and (Oct. 12, 1830), reprinted in Archer and Lowe.
4. James Vining (1795–1870).
5. Probably Mrs. Gibbs (fl. 1783–1844), who, in her late years, appeared principally at the Haymarket.

[HENRY VIII]

1. "The Play-Goer," *Tatler* (Oct. 25, 1831), III, 394–395.
2. Henry Phillpotts (1778–1869), bishop of Exeter.
3. Ellen Tree, later Mrs. Charles Kean (1805–1880), younger sister of Ann Maria Tree.

INDEX